Wittgenstein's Critique of Russell's Multiple Relation Theory of Judgement

Anthem Studies in Wittgenstein publishes new and classic works on Wittgenstein and Wittgensteinian philosophy. This book series aims to bring Wittgenstein's thought into the mainstream by highlighting its relevance to 21st century concerns. Titles include original monographs, themed edited volumes, forgotten classics, biographical works and books intended to introduce Wittgenstein to the general public. The series is published in association with the British Wittgenstein Society.

Anthem Studies in Wittgenstein sets out to put in place whatever measures may emerge as necessary in order to carry out the editorial selection process purely on merit and to counter bias on the basis of gender, race, ethnicity, religion, sexual orientation and other characteristics protected by law. These measures include subscribing to the British Philosophical Association/Society for Women in Philosophy (UK) Good Practice Scheme.

Series Editor
Constantine Sandis – University of Hertfordshire, UK

Editorial Board
Hanne K. Appelqvist – University of Turku, Finland
Maria Balaska – University of Hertfordshire, UK
Adrian Brockless – British Wittgenstein Society, UK
Bill Child – University College, University of Oxford, UK
David Cockburn – Welsh Philosophical Society, UK
Juliet Floyd – Boston University, USA
Hans-Johann Glock – University of Zurich, Switzerland
Ian Ground – British Wittgenstein Society, UK
Garry Hagberg – Bard College, USA
Richard H. Harper – University of Lancaster, UK
Daniel Hutto – University of Wollongong, Australia
Edward Kanterian – Kent University, UK
James C. Klagge – Virginia Tech, USA
Martin Kusch – University of Vienna, Austria
Oskari Kuusela – University of East Anglia, UK
Sandra Laugier – University of Paris 1, Panthéon-Sorbonne, France
Mathieu Marion – University of Quebec, Canada
Ray Monk – University of Southampton, UK
Daniele Moyal-Sharrock – University of Hertfordshire, UK
Stephen Mulhall – New College, University of Oxford, UK
Alois Pichler – University of Bergen, Norway
John Preston – University of Reading, UK
Duncan Pritchard – University of California, Irvine, USA
Genia Schonbaumsfeld – University of Southampton, UK
Joachim Schulte – University of Zurich, Switzerland
Severin Schroeder – University of Reading, UK
Paul Standish – UCL Institute of Education, UK
Chon Tejedor – University of Valencia, Spain
Dawn Wilson – University of Hull, UK
Rachael Wiseman – University of Liverpool, UK

Forthcoming Titles in the Series
Wittgenstein, Scepticism and Naturalism: Essays on the Later Philosophy
Wittgenstein, Human Beings and Conversation

Wittgenstein's Critique of Russell's Multiple Relation Theory of Judgement

James R. Connelly

ANTHEM PRESS

Anthem Press
An imprint of Wimbledon Publishing Company
www.anthempress.com

This edition first published in UK and USA 2025
by ANTHEM PRESS
75–76 Blackfriars Road, London SE1 8HA, UK
or PO Box 9779, London SW19 7ZG, UK
and
244 Madison Ave #116, New York, NY 10016, USA

First published in the UK and USA by Anthem Press in 2021

Copyright © James R. Connelly 2025

The author asserts the moral right to be identified as the author of this work.
All rights reserved. Without limiting the rights under copyright reserved above,
no part of this publication may be reproduced, stored or introduced into
a retrieval system, or transmitted, in any form or by any means
(electronic, mechanical, photocopying, recording or otherwise),
without the prior written permission of both the copyright
owner and the above publisher of this book.

British Library Cataloguing-in-Publication Data
A catalogue record for this book is available from the British Library.

Library of Congress Control Number: 2025930164

ISBN-13: 978-1-83999-478-4 (Pbk)
ISBN-10: 1-83999-478-9 (Pbk)

This title is also available as an e-book.

For Russell Buckley

I'm very sorry to hear that my objection to your theory of judgement paralyses you. I think it can only be removed by a correct theory of propositions.

– Wittgenstein to Russell, 22 July 1913

CONTENTS

List of Figures   ix
Acknowledgements   xi
List of Common Abbreviations   xiii

    Introduction   1

1. Historical and Philosophical Background   7
   - 1.1 Neo-Hegelian Origins   7
   - 1.2 Russellian Propositions   9
   - 1.3 Why Did Russell Abandon Russellian Propositions?   13
   - 1.4 The Multiple Relation Theory   19
   - 1.5 Wittgenstein at Cambridge   26
   - 1.6 The *Theory of Knowledge* Manuscript   27

2. The Scholarly Controversy   33
   - 2.1 The Direction Problems   33
   - 2.2 The Standard Reading   39
   - 2.3 Stevens's First Critique of EI: Direct Inspection and the MRTJ   42
   - 2.4 Stevens's Second Critique of EI: The Logical Status of the Subordinate Relation   45
   - 2.5 The Ontological Interpretation   46
   - 2.6 Hanks's Critique of the Standard Reading   48
   - 2.7 Hanks on How Wittgenstein 'Defeated' the MRTJ   50
   - 2.8 Pincock on the Standard Reading   51
   - 2.9 Pincock on Hanks and the Unity of Judgement   54
   - 2.10 The Correspondence Problem   54
   - 2.11 Landini and Giaretta on Type* Distinctions   60
   - 2.12 Landini on Wittgenstein's Critique of the MRTJ   64
   - 2.13 Lebens on the 'Representation Concern' and the Stoutian Evolution of the MRTJ   69
   - 2.14 Lebens on the Demise of the MRTJ   72

CONTENTS

3. Russell's Paralysis — 75
   - 3.1 The Logical Interpretation — 75
   - 3.2 Revising the Standard Reading — 82
   - 3.3 Re-examining Stevens on EI and OI — 85
   - 3.4 Hanks on the Judging Relation and Wittgenstein's Critique of the MRTJ — 91
   - 3.5 Pincock on the Proposition Problem — 93
   - 3.6 Pincock on the Correspondence Problem — 102
   - 3.7 Russell's Diagram of Understanding — 109
   - 3.8 'Props' — 114
   - 3.9 Type* Distinctions Reappraised — 119
   - 3.10 Revisiting Landini on Wittgenstein's Critique of the MRTJ — 123
   - 3.11 Reconsidering the Representation Concern — 128
   - 3.12 The Demise of *TK* and of the MRTJ — 130

4. Wittgenstein on Truth, Logic and Representation — 135
   - 4.1 The Picture Theory of Propositions — 135
   - 4.2 Wittgenstein and Type-Theory — 141
   - 4.3 Logical Form — 144
   - 4.4 Bipolarity and Extensionalism — 147
   - 4.5 Saying and Showing — 154
   - 4.6 Inference — 156
   - 4.7 Sense-Truth Regress — 161
   - 4.8 The Fundamental Thought (*Grundgedanke*) — 165
   - 4.9 The General Propositional Form — 170
   - 4.10 Transition — 178
   - 4.11 The Later View: Continuities amidst Contrasts — 183
   - 4.12 Conclusion — 191

References — 195
Index — 201

FIGURES

3.1	Russell's diagram of understanding	98
3.2	Props #1 (Russell's neutral facts)	116
3.3	Props #2 (Russell's neutral facts)	116
3.4	Wittgenstein's diagram of 'A believes that p'	118
4.1	aRb :. aRb v ~aRb	157
4.2	*Modus ponens*	158
4.3	Corresponding material conditional (valid)	159
4.4	Corresponding material conditional (invalid)	160
4.5	Affirming the consequent	161
4.6	Conjunction	162
4.7	Sense-truth regress	163
4.8	Interdefinability	167
4.9	The *Grundgedanke*	168
4.10	Truth-functional truth	168
4.11	Extensionality	176
4.12	The limits of sense	176
4.13	The colour-exclusion problem	183

ACKNOWLEDGEMENTS

Since I began researching and writing on the topic of Wittgenstein's critique of Russell's MRTJ roughly 15 years ago, I have had the opportunity to meet, engage or otherwise interact with a number of exceptional scholars whose own work, and critical feedback on mine, has substantially influenced the ideas presented in this book. These scholars include Nicholas Griffin, Graham Stevens, Christopher Pincock, Peter Hanks, Samuel Lebens, Michael Potter, Rosalind Carey, Judy Pelham, Stuart Shanker, Kenneth Blackwell, Landon Elkind, Jolen Galaugher and Gregory Landini. I would also like to acknowledge several anonymous reviewers for their many helpful critical comments and suggestions and for their support in the book's publication.

Additionally, I would like to thank the Bertrand Russell Society and the organizers of their annual conference for the opportunity to present some of the material contained in this book at their conference.

I would also like to thank Megan Greiving and Constantine Sandis for the opportunity to publish a book with Anthem Studies in Wittgenstein and for their assistance in bringing this about.

I have enjoyed teaching this material in a number of undergraduate seminars and have benefitted from students' engagement and enthusiasm. Among these students are Taylor McDowell, Drake Sullivan, Katherine Bark, Tyler Martin, Jacob Quinlan and Jonathan Cruz.

Special credit is due to my student Jeremiah Cashore, who assisted in the production of notation and diagrams for the book and has also offered many stimulating suggestions.

Aside from these Trent philosophy students, I have also benefitted greatly from the ongoing support of the faculty at Trent University's Department of Philosophy, including Byron Stoyles, Kate Norlock, Moira Howes, Michael Hickson and Douglas McDermid.

On a number of occasions, I have had the chance to visit or interact with the staff of the Bertrand Russell Archives at McMaster University and would like to acknowledge their assistance and the important role played by the Archives in the production of this work. In particular, I would like to thank the Archives for their permission to use figures and diagrams associated with volume 7 of Russell's *Collected Papers*.

Finally, I would like to thank my family for their love and tireless support. I appreciate the support of my brother Andy, his wife Natashya and my niece Cedar. I would also like to acknowledge the encouragement and support of Russell Buckley. And, of course, none of this would have been possible without the unwavering love and support of my parents, John and Sue Connelly.

COMMON ABBREVIATIONS

Works by Russell

ABR *The Autobiography of Bertrand Russell*. With an introduction by Michael Foot. London: Routledge (1967/98)

CP *The Collected Papers of Bertrand Russell*
Vol. 2: *Philosophical Papers, 1896–99*. Ed. Nicholas Griffin and Albert C. Lewis. London: Unwin Hyman (1990)
Vol. 3: *Toward the 'Principles of Mathematics', 1900–02*. Ed. Gregory H. Moore. London: Routledge (1993)
Vol. 4: *Foundations of Logic 1903–5*. Ed. Alasdair Urquhart and Albert C. Lewis. London: Routledge (1994)
Vol. 8: *The Philosophy of Logical Atomism and Other Essays, 1914–19*. Ed. John G. Slater. London: George Allen & Unwin (1986)
An Essay on the Foundations of Geometry (1st paperback ed.). Cambridge, UK: Cambridge University Press (1897/2011)

MPD *My Philosophical Development*. London: George Allen & Unwin (1959)

OD 'On Denoting'. *Mind* 14(56): 479–93 (1905)

OKEW *Our Knowledge of the External World as a Field for Scientific Method in Philosophy*. Chicago, IL: Open Court (1914)

PLA 'The Philosophy of Logical Atomism'. In *Logic and Knowledge: Essays 1901–1950*. Ed. R. C. Marsh. London: George Allen & Unwin (1918/56)

PM *Principia Mathematica to *56*. Co-authored with Alfred North Whitehead. Cambridge, UK: Cambridge University Press (1910–13/97)

PoM *The Principles of Mathematics*. New York: W. W. Norton (1903/37)

PP *The Problems of Philosophy*. Scotts Valley, CA: Create Space International (1912/2017)

TK *Theory of Knowledge: The 1913 Manuscript*. London: Routledge (1992)

Works by Wittgenstein

BT	*The Big Typescript: TS 213, German-English Scholar's Edition.* Ed. and trans. C. Grant Luckhardt and Maximilian A. E. Aue. Malden, MA: Blackwell (2005)
CL	*Cambridge Letters: Correspondence with Russell, Keynes, Moore, Ramsey, and Sraffa.* Ed. Brian McGuiness and G. H. von Wright. Oxford, UK: Basil Blackwell (1995)
NB	*Notebooks 1914–1916*, 2nd ed. Ed. G. H. von Wright and G. E. M. Anscombe. Oxford, UK: Basil Blackwell (1961)
NL	'Notes on Logic'. In *NB* (Appendix I, pp. 94–108)
PI	*Philosophical Investigations*, 3rd ed. Trans. Elizabeth Anscombe. Englewood Cliffs, NJ: Prentice Hall (1953/2001)
PT	*Prototractatus.* Ed. B. F. McGuiness, T. Nyberg and G. H. von Wright. London: Routledge (1997)
TLP	*Tractatus Logico-Philosophicus.* Trans. D. F. Pears and B. F. McGuiness, with an introduction by Bertrand Russell. London: Routledge (1967)
TLP 1922	*Tractatus Logico-Philosophicus.* Trans. C. K. Odgen. London: Routledge & Keegan Paul (1922)

Other Abbreviations

CI	correspondence interpretation
CP	correspondence problem
EI	epistemological interpretation
IRI	irrelevance interpretation
LI	logical interpretation
MRTJ	multiple relation theory of judgement
ND	narrow direction problem
NFI	neutral facts interpretation
OI	ontological interpretation
SI	showing interpretation
SR	standard reading
UI	unity interpretation
UP	unity problem
WD	wide direction problem

INTRODUCTION

Wittgenstein's May–June 1913 critique of Russell's multiple relation theory of judgement (or MRTJ) marked a crucial turning point in the lives of each of two great twentieth-century thinkers. But it was also a watershed moment within the history of analytic philosophy itself. The critique led Russell to abandon his 1913 *Theory of Knowledge* manuscript and left a significant breach within his epistemology. It represented an important milestone within Wittgenstein's philosophical career and marked the point at which he emerged on the scene as an independent philosophical force. It inaugurated a linguistic turn in twentieth-century philosophy which would dominate the course of analytic philosophy throughout the early and middle part of that century.[1] The critique directly concerns and engages with the weightiest and most fundamental topics and concepts of philosophical semantics, including those of sense, truth, meaning, inference, logical form and information content, as well as the nature, structure and unity of propositions.

For these and other reasons it is worthy of careful study and deep understanding. Yet scholarly consensus around a satisfactory interpretation of the nature of the critique, the extent of and reasons for its impact on Russell and the role it played within Wittgenstein's philosophical development has remained elusive. This partly reflects the fact that a correct interpretation of Wittgenstein's critique depends upon the satisfactory resolution of several other related exegetical controversies within the interpretation of Russell's and Wittgenstein's respective philosophies. Such controversies include, for instance, those surrounding the nature and import of type distinctions introduced in Russell and Whitehead's *Principia Mathematica*. They also include those concerning the timeline on which important ideas emerged within Wittgenstein's early philosophy, such as bipolarity, extensionalism and

---

[1] Specifically, I have in mind *the* linguistic turn as characterized by Glock and Kalhat (2018), as well as Hacker (2013). I discuss this characterization of the linguistic turn and the reasons to prefer it in more detail in Section 4.11. In that section I also identify and briefly address other alternative characterizations of the linguistic turn, including those of Dummett (1981, 1991) and Bergmann (1953/67, 1960).

the saying/showing distinction. The relationship between exegesis which aims to resolve these broader sorts of controversies and that which more specifically concerns Wittgenstein's May–June 1913 critique of Russell's MRTJ is thus a symbiotic one. Sound interpretation of the latter stands to illuminate the former and vice versa. This perhaps partly explains why, as Michael Potter has noted, 'offering an exegesis of Wittgenstein's objection seems to have become a sort of rite of passage for scholars of early analytic philosophy' (2009, 119).

With these facts in mind, this book aims to accomplish four interrelated goals. The first is to develop a compelling reading of Wittgenstein's May–June 1913 critique of Russell's MRTJ. For reasons which will become clear over the course of the book, I call my reading the 'logical interpretation' (or LI). The second main objective of the book is to defend LI against its most prominent competitors in the scholarly literature. These include interpretations of Wittgenstein's objection offered by Nicholas Griffin and Steven Sommerville, Gregory Landini, Graham Stevens, Peter Hanks, Christopher Pincock, Rosalind Carey, Fraser MacBride and Samuel Lebens. Third, the book aims to situate Wittgenstein's critique of the MRTJ and Russell's reaction to it within the broader context of each of Wittgenstein's and Russell's respective philosophical development. While much scholarship has focused on probing the role played by the objection within the evolution of Russell's thought, much less has been done to explore the impact on Wittgenstein's developmental trajectory. Still less, if any, scholarship has been devoted to highlighting the significant traces of Wittgenstein's critique which can be found latent within his later philosophical outlook. This book seeks to fill these lacunae in the scholarship on Wittgenstein while also adding to the high-quality work on Russell which has already been done in this area. Fourth and finally, the book aims to introduce students and scholars of early analytic philosophy to, and familiarize them with, the historical events, textual evidence, scholarly controversies, letters, notes and diagrams, the consideration of which is integral to constructing a plausible reading of Wittgenstein's objection. To that end, it brings together a broad selection of relevant materials and information in a clear, accessible and organized way into one, relatively concise source. The author's sincere hope is that someone who is starting more or less from scratch, with little if any knowledge concerning Wittgenstein's May–June critique of Russell's MRTJ, could pick up this book and upon reading it have enough familiarity with the issues to proceed to attempt to adjudicate the central debates and perhaps write something fruitful on the topic themselves.

Chapter 1 introduces the reader to the relevant historical and philosophical background crucial to a proper appreciation of Wittgenstein's critique of the MRTJ and of Russell's reaction to it. The chapter begins, in Section 1.1, by probing the neo-Hegelian origins of Russell's early semantic, logical and metaphysical outlook. Relying greatly on work done on this topic by Nicholas Griffin, I show how Russell's views about relations emerge out of his reflections on the 'contradiction of relativity'. According to LI, these views about relations and Russell's unwillingness to compromise on them play an important role in Wittgenstein's later critique of the MRTJ as well as the 'paralysis' Russell experienced in response to that critique. In Section 1.2 I then focus on the 'Russellian propositions' which Russell defended as a theory of propositional content in *Principles of Mathematics* (or *PoM*), before abandoning them in favour of the MRTJ. In Section 1.3 I explore the question of why Russell ultimately abandoned Russellian propositions in favour of the MRTJ and critically adjudicate some of the possible explanations proposed in the scholarly literature, including those by Bernard Linsky, Jolen Galaugher and Graham Stevens. In Section 1.4 I introduce the MRTJ and trace its evolution through three somewhat distinct versions over the period of 1910–13, namely the 1910 version defended in Russell's paper 'On the Nature of Truth and Falsehood', the 1912 version defended in *Problems of Philosophy* (or *PP*) and the 1913 version defended in *Theory of Knowledge* (*TK*). In Section 1.5 I introduce Wittgenstein into the narrative and share the philosophical as well as biographical details concerning how it is he came to study with Russell at Cambridge in 1911. In Section 1.6 I home in on the *TK* manuscript and summarize the uncontroversial philosophical and biographical details concerning how it is that Russell came to embark upon and then ultimately abandon it. In this section I also highlight the uncontroversial historical details concerning Wittgenstein's May–June 1913 critique of Russell's MRTJ, so they can be presupposed in later chapters when we adjudicate the more controversial issues surrounding it.

In Chapter 2 I then explicate the scholarly controversy surrounding Wittgenstein's critique of the MRTJ. The details of each of LI's competitors are laid out, while no attempt is made, at this stage, to adjudicate between them and either LI or one another. In Section 2.1 I introduce two related but distinct 'direction problems', known as the 'wide direction problem' (WD) and the 'narrow direction problem' (ND). These problems figure prominently within several readings of Wittgenstein's objection, including LI, and thus it is crucial that the reader be familiar with them so as to appreciate integral aspects of the scholarly controversy. In Section 2.2 I then move on to explicate the Griffin/Sommerville interpretation of Wittgenstein's objection, which enjoyed wide acceptance for nearly two decades (1985–2003) and is thus often referred to in the literature as the standard reading (SR). In Section 2.3 I then introduce and explore the first of two alleged problems for the Griffin/Sommerville interpretation identified by Graham Stevens (2003a, 2004, 2018). Stevens calls the Griffin/Sommerville interpretation the 'epistemological interpretation' (EI) and claims, first, that EI misconstrues the nature of the relationship between Russell's MRTJ and *PM*'s theory of types. In Section 2.4 I then elucidate Stevens's second critique of EI, which concerns its failure to address the logical status of the subordinate relation (i.e. the relation referred to by 'loves' in 'Othello believes that Desdemona loves Cassio'). In Section 2.5 I introduce Stevens's alternative interpretation, which he calls the 'ontological interpretation' (OI). In Section 2.6 I cover Peter Hanks's critique of SR before exploring his alternative reading of how Wittgenstein 'defeated' the MRTJ, in Section 2.7. In Section 2.8 I consider what Christopher Pincock has to say about SR before looking at his critique of Hanks's unity interpretation (UI) in Section 2.9. In Section 2.10 I introduce Pincock's correspondence interpretation (CI) of Wittgenstein's critique of Russell's MRTJ, according to which it is meant to highlight what Pincock calls the 'correspondence problem' (CP). In Section 2.11 I then introduce type* distinctions and examine what Landini and Giaretta, respectively, have to say about them. As we shall see, type* distinctions are significant from the perspective of a defender of LI, since it is precisely these sorts of distinctions which, according to a defender of LI, Russell cannot make without introducing illicit supplemental premises highlighted in a mid-June 1913 letter in which Wittgenstein claims to express his objection to Russell's MRTJ 'exactly'. In Section 2.12 I then home in on and explicate Landini's reading of Wittgenstein's critique of the MRTJ. Finally, in Sections 2.13 and 2.14, I explore what Samuel Lebens has to say about, first, the Stoutian evolution of the MRTJ and then the demise of the MRTJ.

In Chapter 3 I then adjudicate the scholarly controversy surrounding Wittgenstein's critique of Russell's MRTJ and defend LI against each of its competitors in the scholarly literature. Section 3.1 is devoted to explicating LI as well as describing each of the three distinctive waves or phases of criticism which, according to LI, are characteristic of what Russell called Wittgenstein's 'onslaught' (*ABR*, 282). In Section 3.2 I revise Griffin and Sommerville's standard reading (SR) of Wittgenstein's objection and provide the reasons to think that LI is preferable to that interpretation, although it bears a significant family resemblance to it. In Section 3.3 I re-examine what Stevens had to say about EI and OI. In so doing, I highlight some important errors with respect to Stevens's reading of the Griffin/Sommerville interpretation as EI and also explain why LI is to be preferred over OI. In Section 3.4 I revisit Hanks's unity interpretation (UI) of Wittgenstein's critique, highlighting some of its problems and in turn explaining the reasons why LI is to be preferred over it. In Sections 3.5 and 3.6 I revisit Pincock's CI of Wittgenstein's objection, highlight several problems for it and explain why LI is preferable to it. Notably, this involves reflecting in some detail on Pincock's reading of the diagram of understanding Russell provides at the end of chapter 1 of part II of *TK*. In

Section 3.7 I delve deeper into Russell's diagram of understanding by examining what Katarina Perovic has to say about it in her 2017 paper. I highlight the ways in which what she has to say in that paper either align or conflict with LI, and in the cases in which her interpretation conflicts with LI, I explain the reasons to prefer LI over her interpretation. In Section 3.8 I then examine an alternative reading of Wittgenstein's mid-June 1913 letter, due to Rosalind Carey, according to which the 'exactly' expressed objection contained therein refers to a set of working notes called 'Props' which Russell composed on or about 26 May 1913. I explain mistakes Carey has made in the interpretation of diagrams contained with 'Props' and show how a proper appreciation of what Russell is doing in 'Props' actually supports LI as opposed to her alternative, neutral facts interpretation (NFI). In Section 3.9 I reappraise Landini and Giaretta on type* distinctions, with a view to explaining, in Section 3.10, the reasons why LI should be preferred over Landini's showing interpretation (SI) of Wittgenstein's critique of the MRTJ. In Sections 3.11 and 3.12, I then reconsider Lebens on the evolution and demise of the MRTJ, explaining why LI is to be preferred over his irrelevancy interpretation (IRI) of Wittgenstein's objection. Notably, like Landini, MacBride and others, Lebens struggles to explain the seriousness and severity with which Russell reacted to Wittgenstein's objection. This is because they each take Wittgenstein's objection to be more or less innocuous or unmotivated. By contrast, since LI construes Wittgenstein's critique as a well-motivated objection based in commitments and concerns shared by both men, it can easily explain Russell's self-described 'paralysis'. Here and elsewhere in the chapter, notably in my discussion of Pincock's reading, I build on LI in order to highlight the impact of Wittgenstein's critique on Russell's subsequent philosophical development over the remainder of the decade.

In Chapter 4 I then move on to examine the legacy of the May–June critique of Russell's MRTJ within Wittgenstein's philosophical development. To that end, I explore several themes within Wittgenstein's early philosophy, and to the extent that they originate within that critique, I trace their thematic, historical and developmental connections to it. In Section 4.1 I focus on the picture theory of propositions and show how it emerged out of considerations highlighted by Wittgenstein's critique of Russell's MRTJ. Building on Wittgenstein's concept of an 'expression', in Section 4.2, I then examine what Wittgenstein has to say about type-theory and Russell's paradox in *TLP*, showing how the ideas contained in these remarks grow out of concerns operative within Wittgenstein's critique of the MRTJ. I go on to show how similar concerns are at work in Wittgenstein's evolving conception of logical form in Section 4.3 before examining how the themes of bipolarity and extensionalism emerge out of Wittgenstein's critique of the MRTJ in Section

4.4. In particular, I look at how an interest in bipolarity as such, in abstraction from truth-functionality, emerged out of Wittgenstein's critique of the MRTJ and at how Wittgenstein deployed his ab-notation to study bipolarity and reach some interesting conclusions thereby concerning molecular logical form. (I will explain what Wittgenstein's ab-notation is in more detail in Section 4.4.) In Section 4.5 I focus on the distinction between saying and showing and consider how it emerged while Wittgenstein was in Norway, out of attempts to give an account of molecular and especially atomic logical form which was impervious to his own objections to the account Russell had given of logical form in the context of the *TK* version of the MRTJ. In Section 4.6 I then show how Wittgenstein's account of inference builds upon his critique of Russell's MRTJ along with other themes, such as bipolarity, logical form, saying and showing and so on, whose provenance can also be traced to that critique. In Section 4.7 Wittgenstein's account of inference is tied to another key theme manifest within his critique of the MRTJ, namely the 'sense-truth regress'. As I show in Section 4.7, the 'sense-truth regress' is closely associated with yet another core commitment of Wittgenstein's early logical and semantic viewpoint, namely that of the logical independence of elementary propositions. In Section 4.8 I then consider Wittgenstein's 'fundamental thought' (or *Grundgedanke*) and show that, while the basic idea predates Wittgenstein's critique of the MRTJ, its final manifestation in *TLP* is influenced by interaction with other ideas which emerge more directly from Wittgenstein's critique of the MRTJ. In Section 4.9 I then show how Wittgenstein's conception of the general propositional form is also influenced by such interaction, though in contrast to the 'fundamental thought', the concept of a general propositional form is something which post-dates Wittgenstein's critique of the MRTJ and emerges from his reflections on molecular truth-functions via the ab-notation. In Section 4.10 I look at some of the problems inherent in the Tractarian system and at how reflection on these problems motivated the transition from Wittgenstein's earlier to his later mode of thought. In Section 4.11 I examine some of the continuities between the early and later philosophical perspectives with an emphasis on those continuities whose provenance can be traced to Wittgenstein's May–June 1913 critique of Russell's MRTJ. Notably, I highlight how the 'linguistic turn' which characterized much of early and mid-twentieth-century analytic philosophy, and which involves and implicates several important points of continuity between the early and later views, originates in Wittgenstein's critique of the MRTJ and in particular the rejection therein of what Glock and Kalhat (2018) call 'ideal language philosophy'. Finally, in Section 4.12, I provide a brief concluding summary.

Chapter 1

HISTORICAL AND PHILOSOPHICAL BACKGROUND

1.1 Neo-Hegelian Origins

In his *Autobiography*, Russell recalls a 'cold, bright day' early in the spring of 1895 when, while walking through the Tiergarten in Berlin and making plans for future work, he was struck by a philosophical vision. His vision is as remarkable, perhaps, for its prescience as for its sheer scope, profundity and ambition:

> I thought that I would write one series of books on the philosophy of the sciences from pure mathematics to physiology, and another series of books on social questions. I hoped that the two series might ultimately meet in a synthesis at once both scientific and practical. My scheme was largely inspired by Hegelian ideas. Nevertheless, I have to some extent followed it in later years, as much at any rate as could have been expected. (*ABR* vol. i, 125)

Russell would go on to pursue the first (scientific) strain of this 'Tiergarten programme' (Griffin 1991, 80) in the context of an 'idealist apprenticeship' (Griffin 1991) undertaken over the next several years. As a budding neo-Hegelian, more specifically, Russell set out to construct what he called a 'dialectic of the sciences' (80; *MPD*, 42–44). He initially developed this 'dialectic of the sciences' in his first book, *An Essay on the Foundations of Geometry*, before then pursuing it in the realm of physics (*MPD*, 41) and, ultimately, pure mathematics (Griffin 1991, 191). In the realm of pure mathematics, Russell would eventually come to defend the view, associated with his *Principles of Mathematics* (1903) and (co-authored with A. N. Whitehead) *Principia Mathematica* (1910–13), that the fundamental principles and concepts of mathematics are logical in nature (Griffin 2003, 105; cf. *PoM*, 1; *MPD*, 74). Though it eventually emerged out of these earlier, neo-Hegelian researches into pure mathematics, he appears not to have arrived at this view, known as 'logicism', until the second half of the year 1900 (Griffin 2003, 105).

By this time, Russell had already abandoned neo-Hegelianism in favour of an extreme brand of pluralist and Platonist realism. Appreciating how precisely this transition came about by late 1898 is important for understanding why, in 1913, Russell found Wittgenstein's criticisms of his MRTJ so devastating. As Russell pursued his 'dialectic of the sciences', first in the realm of geometry and then physics and pure mathematics, he encountered several interrelated 'antinomies' (Griffin 1991, 315–23). Over time, he began to see these various antinomies each as symptomatic of a deeper problem which he called 'the contradiction of relativity' (Griffin 2003, 98). When he ultimately came to diagnose this deeper problem as being caused by the neo-Hegelian doctrine of internal relations (100–101), and found a more congenial, alternative metaphysical perspective in the work of G. E. Moore (1899) (cf. *MPD*, 54; *PoM*, v), he abandoned neo-Hegelianism. As Elkind and Landini explain: 'At the turn of the twentieth century, Russell and Moore had broken with Bradley's Idealism and were exploring a new philosophical frontier grounded in the realist metaphysics of external relations' (2018, xvii).

Russell had followed Bradley in denying the independent reality of external relations, thinking that ostensibly relational propositions should instead be understood as asserting intrinsic properties of the terms contained in the original proposition and, ultimately, of the whole composed of the terms (*MPD*, 54; Griffin 2003, 88; *CP*, 2: 224). Yet, following McTaggart, among others, Russell viewed thought as inherently discursive and thus as involving complexity essentially. This entailed pluralism, 'since the complexity required for thought implies a plurality of parts in the object of thought' (Griffin 2003, 88). Russell's identification of the contradiction of relativity showed this 'relationless pluralism' (ibid.) to be untenable, however, with respect to the case of asymmetrical, transitive relations of the sort crucial to the analysis of mathematical and geometrical order (98–101; *MPD*, 55). As Griffin explains: 'Russell's general difficulty is not hard to appreciate. In case after case, he found that each of the special sciences was committed to a plurality of items of some kind, but that it lacked the resources to individuate these items by means of their intrinsic qualities' (2003, 98). Since geometrical points do not differ from one another intrinsically, for instance, the asymmetrical, transitive relationships between them characteristic of their being ordered in a series on a line cannot be reducible to their intrinsic properties. If point **a** is to the right of point **b** on a line, then point **b** is *not* to the right of point **a** (asymmetry). If point **b** is to the right of point **a**, moreover, and point **c** is to the right of point **b**, then point **c** must be to the right of point **a** (transitivity). If these asymmetrical, transitive relationships do not hold between them, then points **a**, **b** and **c** cannot be ordered on a line. But these crucial relationships cannot be reducible to the intrinsic properties of points **a**, **b** and **c** themselves since geometrical points do not differ in any of their intrinsic properties. This, in essence, is the contradiction of relativity as it applies to geometrical order, though, as was noted by Griffin earlier, Russell saw this contradiction as a more general problem affecting a variety of special sciences and ultimately came to think of it as generated by the neo-Hegelian doctrine of internal relations. The concept of an 'internal relation' is simply that of one which is unreal, since it is reducible to the intrinsic properties of its terms and, ultimately, of the whole composed of them (*MPD*, 54).

In this and other cases, according to Russell, making sense of the geometrically, and mathematically, crucial phenomenon of order requires the admission of external and fully real relations, since only then can we make sense of the idea, for example, that points **a** and **b** can *differ* in their order, despite the fact that they do not differ *intrinsically*. The 'contradiction of relativity' is, essentially, simply the inability to make out this 'conception of difference', without a 'difference of conception' (Griffin 2003, 98; *CP*, 2: 24, 81). Once we abandon the neo-Hegelian doctrine of internal relations, however, we no longer have this problem. In that case, the relevant difference between **a** and **b** concerns not their *intrinsic properties* but instead their *external relationships* (of order) relative to the other points on the line. In order to resolve the contradiction of relativity for this and other cases, relations must therefore be conceived to be both external to, and independent of, their *relata* and thus fully, and independently, real in their own right.

1.2 Russellian Propositions

As mentioned, a significant factor motivating the transition away from neo-Hegelianism had to do with the availability of a new, alternative metaphysical outlook, derived from G. E. Moore, which appeared more congenial to Russell's scientific, logical and mathematical ambitions. As he explains in the preface to *PoM*: 'On fundamental questions of philosophy my position, in all its chief features, is derived from G.E. Moore' (*PoM*, viii). Among these fundamental features Russell includes the non-mental character of propositions, pluralism of existents and entities and the irreducible reality of relations (ibid.; cf. *MPD*, 62). Before adopting these views from Moore, Russell insists:

> I found myself completely unable to construct any philosophy of arithmetic, whereas their acceptance brought about an immediate liberation from a large number of difficulties which I believe to be otherwise insuperable. (*PoM*, viii)

While it therefore seems indisputable that several integral features of Russell's *PoM* theory of propositions were derived from Moore, it has nevertheless become common to refer to the propositions posited by Russell in *PoM* as 'Russellian' and to regard anyone defending a theory of propositions sufficiently similar to that developed in *PoM* as a defender of 'Russellian propositions' (Linsky 1993).

For our purposes, Russellian propositions are significant because Russell ultimately abandoned them in favour of his MRTJ. So understanding the nature of Russell's motivations for adopting and then abandoning Russellian propositions can help us to appreciate his motivations for adopting and then subsequently revising the MRTJ. Russellian propositions are associated with a set of logical and semantic problems that the multiple relation theory is, in part, designed to solve. Better understanding these logical and semantic problems, as well as Russell's evolving attempts to solve them, will thus ultimately help us to more thoroughly appreciate the nature and force of Wittgenstein's objections to the MRTJ.

For Russell, however, at the time of authoring *PoM*, Russellian propositions are seen as integral to his logicist programme and to his associated characterization of what pure mathematics, that is, logic, is: 'Pure mathematics is the class of all propositions of the form "p implies q", where p and q are propositions containing one or more variables, the same in the two propositions, and neither p nor q contains any constants except logical constants' (*PoM*, 3). Propositions are the non-mental, non-linguistic bearers of truth and falsity (ix), which figure in logical deductions as either axioms or theorems. Pure mathematics, that is, logic, is the class of all propositions specifying which propositions follow from what other propositions in virtue of purely general, logical relationships alone.

Being extra-mental, and non-linguistic, Russellian propositions are not to be identified with declarative sentences so much as with the mind and language-independent meanings of those sentences. Thus, propositions do not contain words but are instead composed of 'the entities indicated by words' (*PoM*, 47). Philosophical analysis of propositions yields their constituents and mode of combination, and the correctness of such analyses can be 'checked by the exercise of assigning the meaning of each word in the sentence expressing the proposition' (42). Words thus have meaning, according to Russell, 'in the simple sense that they are symbols which stand for something other than themselves' (42; cf. *MPD*, 63), specifically, the propositional constituent indicated by them. What Russell calls 'philosophical grammar' is thus a helpful guide to understanding the underlying structure and composition of propositions, although he is careful to note that 'a grammatical distinction cannot be uncritically assumed to correspond to a genuine philosophical difference' (ibid.).

Russell uses the word 'term' to refer to the constituents of propositions, conceived in the widest possible sense:

Whatever may be an object of thought, or may occur in a true or false proposition, or can be counted as *one*, I call a *term*. This, then, is the widest word in the philosophical vocabulary [...] I shall speak of the *terms* of a proposition as those terms, however numerous, which occur in a proposition and may be regarded as subjects about which the proposition is. (*PoM*, 43, 45; emphases in the original)

A term is anything a proposition can be about, whether it be a man, a moment, a number, a class, a relation or a chimaera (43). Thus, if any term of a proposition be replaced by any other entity whatsoever, one will still have a proposition, albeit a different proposition (45). Yet, important limitations upon substitutivity emerge, integral to understanding Russell's later MRTJ, and Wittgenstein's criticisms thereof, when we reflect further on the differences between two distinct kinds of terms, specifically, 'things' and 'concepts' (44). While both things and concepts *are* terms and can thus be the subject of a proposition, 'things' correspond to proper names (like 'Caesar') while 'concepts' correspond to verbs and adjectives (like 'died' or 'is powerful') (ibid.). This means that, while any 'thing' may be replaced in a proposition by a concept, without the result thereby ceasing to be a proposition, a 'concept' may not be so replaceable within a proposition by a thing, depending upon the concept's position and role in the proposition. For instance, while it makes sense to say 'Caesar died', it makes no sense to say 'Caesar Caesared'. The former expresses a proposition, while the latter is garbled and so expresses nothing. Likewise, to say that 'Caesar is Caesar' expresses a proposition of a different form than 'Caesar is powerful' and thus cannot result from substituting 'Caesar' for 'is powerful' in the proposition expressed by 'Caesar is powerful' (cf. *TLP* 3.323–3.325).

According to Russell, this is because the terms corresponding to verbs and adjectives often, though not always, play distinct roles in a proposition than do those corresponding to proper names. Most interesting for our purposes, the terms corresponding to verbs often though not always play an integral role within propositions, one which cannot be performed by the 'things' corresponding to proper names. For instance, when a verb occurs in a sentence, then it indicates a special type of concept known as a 'relation'. However, depending upon whether the verb is used *as a verb* or as what Russell calls a 'verbal noun', the role played by the relation within that proposition is different. When the verb is used *as a verb* (e.g. 'died' in 'Caesar died'), it corresponds to a relation which relates, or unites the other constituents, or terms of the proposition into a structured unity. On the other hand, when a verb occurs in what Russell calls a 'verbal noun' (e.g. 'The death of Caesar' in 'The death of Caesar was brutal'), the relation it indicates does not serve to unify the other constituents or terms of the proposition so much as it *is* simply one among the terms so related (in this second case, the 'copula' of the proposition corresponds to the word 'was', not 'death') (cf. *MPD*, 63). Thus, while every proposition must contain a relation which relates, not every relation contained in a proposition need be a 'relating relation'. (A 'relating relation' is simply a relation which actually relates the other constituents of the proposition, e.g., 'loves' in 'Romeo loves Juliet'.)

When a relation does occur within a proposition as a 'relating relation' rather than merely as the term *of* a relation, it bears a special connection to truth, as well as to what Russell calls 'assertion' in the logical sense:

> There appears to be an ultimate notion of assertion, given by the verb, which is lost as soon as we substitute a verbal noun, and is lost when the proposition in question is made the subject of some other proposition [...] There is [...] [a] sense of assertion, very difficult to bring clearly before the mind, and yet quite undeniable, in which only true propositions are asserted. True and false propositions alike are in some sense entities, and are in some sense capable of being logical subjects; but when a proposition happens to be true, it has a further quality, over and above that which it shares with false propositions, and it is this further quality which is what I mean by assertion in a logical [...] sense. (*PoM*, 48–49)

One way of framing Russell's analysis of the relationships between relations, assertion and truth here would be to say that Russell has conflated truth with sense. While this is not, perhaps, especially charitable to Russell, thinking of the problem this way is helpful, for our purposes, because it anticipates both Russell's later concerns about the possibility of false propositions as well as Wittgenstein's later concerns about sense-truth regresses (e.g. *TLP* 2.0211–2.0212). I will have more to say about sense-truth regresses, along with the role they play both in Wittgenstein's critique of the MRTJ in particular, as well as his early philosophical viewpoint more generally, in Section 4.7. For now the important point is that in order to have sense, a sentence must contain a verb used *as a verb*, and correspondingly, on the view of propositions we are considering, a proposition must contain a relation which relates in order to constitute the sort of structured unity which provides the meaning of a sentence. Yet, not all sentences which contain verbs used as verbs, and thus have sense, are true. As we shall see, once Russell eventually adopted the MRTJ, he was apt to characterize what he then called a 'corresponding complex', much as he here characterizes a true proposition. However, before moving on to explicate the key features, and evolution, of Russell's MRTJ, it will be helpful to consider the question of why Russell came to abandon these Russellian propositions in favour of the MRTJ.

1.3 Why Did Russell Abandon Russellian Propositions?

In *PoM*, as we have seen, Russell defended the view that propositions are structured, mind- and language-independent unities. However, by the time he publishes his paper 'On the Nature of Truth and Falsehood' in 1910, he has abandoned Russellian propositions in favour of the MRTJ. In the next section (1.4), we will look in more detail at the version of the MRTJ defended in that paper, along with revised versions thereof developed in his 1912 *Problems of Philosophy* (or *PP*) and, subsequently, the 1913 *Theory of Knowledge* manuscript (or *TK*). In this section, however, we will first examine the question of why Russell abandoned Russellian propositions to better understand and appreciate Russell's motivations for adopting the MRTJ.

Three distinct but interrelated and ultimately consistent explanations have been offered in the scholarly literature. First, it has been maintained by Linsky (1993, 200), for example, that Russell abandoned Russellian propositions due to what can be called the 'problem of false propositions' (see also Griffin 1985–86, 134; 1985, 214; Hanks 2007, 124–25; Stevens 2018, 94–95). This problem is related to the one discussed at the end of Section 1.2 concerning the conflation of truth and sense. More specifically, Russell came to have misgivings about how propositions could be adequately distinguished from facts, given that propositions were characterized as being (1) composed of the very things indicated by the words in the sentence expressing the propositions and (2) united by the relating relation indicated by the verb used as a verb within the sentence. But then, given that a proposition has sense, it would seem to be hard to distinguish from the fact which, intuitively, makes belief in the proposition true.

While this is counter-intuitive enough in the case of true propositions, since it makes it difficult to see how one might distinguish true propositions from facts (Linsky 1993, 200–201), it becomes especially problematic with respect to false propositions, since it is hard to see how belief in a proposition, so characterized, *could* be false. If the object of one's belief is a structured unity very much like the fact that would, intuitively, *make* the belief true, then the belief, it would seem, must *be* true (see Russell 1910, 155). Alternatively, one might propose that, over and above true propositions, which may simply be identified with facts, there are also false propositions which may then be identified with 'objective falsehoods' or 'false facts' (Linsky 1993, 200). As Russell put it, perhaps 'some propositions are true and some are false, just as some roses are red and some white' (*CP*, 4: 473; cf. 1901, 75–76). The former would be the content of true beliefs, while the latter would be the content of false beliefs.

As Russell later came to realize, however, such an approach is bound to offend our ontological sensibilities. While we might be prepared to admit the existence of *negative* facts, what could a *false* fact possibly be? Note that the problem here is not the more general one of being committed to dubious, abstract or Platonic objects, which Russell was readily prepared to be in the case of universals, for instance (Linsky 1993, 200). Instead, the problem is to conceive just what sort of abstract object a false fact, or false proposition, could possibly be (*TK*, 110). In other words, it is not that abstract or Platonic objects as such are dubious; it is rather that false facts would have to be abstract objects of a very dubious sort.

If someone falsely believes that Charles I died in his bed, for instance, then on the view of propositions under consideration, this would seem to involve them bearing a cognitive relation to a structured unity consisting of Charles I, and his bed, somehow united by the relation corresponding to the prepositional verb 'died in'. But intuitively, if the belief is false, there is no such structured unity. Moreover, even if we were prepared to grant that there is one, it would be hard to conceive of what such a unity would have to be like in order to embody the content of a false belief. Interestingly, Russell deploys this very same example of Charles I dying is bed (versus dying on the scaffold) in order to motivate acceptance of his MRTJ in each of 'On the Nature of Truth and Falsehood' (1910/67, 149–54, 157), *Problems of Philosophy* (*PP*, 106) and the 1913 *Theory of Knowledge* manuscript (*TK*, 109).

This fact highlights one crucial merit of this account of why Russell abandoned Russellian propositions, which is that Russell himself can consistently be found invoking the sorts of concerns characteristic of it in order to motivate his new theory that judgement, or belief, is a multiple as opposed to a dual relation. In 'On the Nature of Truth and Falsehood', for instance, he claims that 'the possibility of false judgements compels us to adopt' (1910, 150) the view that judgement is a multiple, as opposed to a dual, relation. In chapter XII of the *Problems of Philosophy*, where he also defends the MRTJ, he argues that 'the necessity of allowing for falsehood makes it impossible to regard belief as a relation of the mind to a single object, which could be said to be what is believed' (*PP*, 109; cf. 106). Finally, in the 1913 *Theory of Knowledge* manuscript, Russell writes:

> We might be induced to admit that *true* propositions are entities, but it is very difficult, except under the lash of a tyrannous theory, to admit that *false* propositions are entities. 'Charles I dying in his bed' or 'that Charles I died in his bed' does not seem to stand for any entity. (*TK*, 109; emphases in the original)

In Section 1.4, we will explore how Russell's characterization of the MRTJ evolved over the course of writing first 'The Nature of Truth and Falsehood', then *Problems of Philosophy* and the *Theory of Knowledge* manuscript. Yet one thing remains consistent throughout the three works, which is that in each of them Russell can be found invoking this 'problem of false propositions' in order to motivate the idea that belief, or judgement, is in fact a multiple relation of a certain level of sophistication. Though the situation is more complicated, as we shall see momentarily, this would tend to lend credence to the idea that this 'problem of false propositions' provided at least some motivation for Russell to abandon Russellian propositions.

That said, a second sort of possible explanation as to why Russell abandoned Russellian propositions, explored by Galaugher (2013), among others (e.g. Landini 1998; Stevens 2003b, 166–68; 2018, 94–95; Bostock 2012, Chapter 5), is that Russell was motivated to do so in light of paradoxes of propositions, including the liar paradox, the Epimenides paradox and a more technical version of the Epimenides, known as the 'p_0/a_0' paradox (Galaugher 2013, 8; cf. Landini 1998). While the Epimenides paradox is the classic one concerning Epimenides the Cretan, whose only statement was that 'all Cretans are liars', the p_0/a_0 paradox emerges in association with a theory known as the 'substitutional theory' of classes and relations, defended by Russell between roughly 1905 and 1907 (Landini 1998; Stevens 2003b, 162). Indeed, Russell goes so far as to claim, in a 1907 letter to Hawtrey, that the p_0/a_0 paradox 'pilled' the substitution theory (Galaugher 2013, 7). So what was the substitution theory?

The substitution theory[1] was an attempt to circumvent logical paradoxes, including 'Russell's paradox' concerning the class of all classes that are not members of themselves (which is a member of itself if it is not, and is not a member of itself if it is), by eliminating classes in favour of what are called 'matrices of substitution'. The use of such matrices allowed Russell to *emulate* classes without requiring him to make problematical ontological commitments to them (Galaugher 2013, 6; Stevens 2003a, 12; 2003b, 164). In other words, it would prevent paradoxes associated with classes by eliminating them, while nevertheless allowing Russell to emulate classes to a degree sufficient to derive mathematics from logic.

Matrices are simply what result when one substitutes a variable entity, for example, x, for an argument, for example, a, within a prototype p/a, where p is a proposition (Stevens 2003b, 164). Crucially, while this theory does away with ontological commitment to classes, it retains ontological commitment to propositions, along with logical commitment to unrestricted, universal entity

---

[1] See Landini (1998) for a more detailed scholarly account of Russell's substitution theory.

variables (ibid.). Taken together, these two features entail that it is licit within this theory for propositional matrices to take propositions themselves as substitution instances and thus for propositions to refer to themselves. These features of the substitutional theory thus allow for the generation of self-referential, propositional paradoxes, the simplest and least technical of which is the so-called liar paradox, that is, 'This sentence is false'. Like Epimenides' statement that 'all Cretans are liars', the statement that 'this sentence is false' is, paradoxically, true if false but false if true (cf. *MPD*, 77). Just as the substitution theory was devised to evade Russell's paradox by eliminating ontological commitment to classes, the MRTJ is designed, according to this second possible explanation, to evade propositional paradoxes associated with the substitutional theory by eliminating ontological commitment to propositions.

Why is it so important for Russell to evade paradoxes associated with classes and propositions? Recall that Russell's main philosophical project during this period is logicism, the attempt to show that pure mathematics is part of general logic (*PoM*, 124) and thus that 'pure mathematics follows from purely logical premises and uses only concepts definable in logical terms' (*MPD*, 74). However, if a system consisting of such concepts and premises leads to paradoxes, then it cannot be a sound, logical system. So, if we want to discover and articulate a sound, logical system capable of generating mathematics, we have to eliminate any elements responsible for producing paradoxes, while retaining elements necessary for generating mathematics.

Initially, like Frege, Russell construed numbers as logical objects, specifically, as classes of 'equinumerous' classes.[2] Classes are said to be 'equinumerous' if each of the members of one can be paired off one-to-one with a member of the other, and vice versa, with no exceptions or remainder. 'Equinumerosity' and class membership may thus be defined purely logically, in terms of one-to-one and many-to-one relations (cf. *MPD*, 88). Relying on the fact that higher mathematics had already been 'arithmetized' (i.e. defined arithmetically) in the work of Cantor and Dedekind, arithmetic could then in turn be derived from a set of axioms, known as the Peano postulates, which both involved fundamental notions characteristic of, and captured integral, logical relationships between, these classes of classes (i.e. the natural numbers) (cf. *MPD*, 72). Among these postulates are included axioms such as that '0 is a number', 'every number has a successor' and 'no two numbers have the same successor'. In addition to involving fundamental arithmetical notions such as 'number'

---

[2] This is somewhat of an oversimplification, but for our purposes it is not worth getting into the associated complications. See Landini (1998, chapter 1) for a more thorough and detailed discussion of the historical complexities within Russell's logicist programme, along with its similarities with and differences from Frege's.

and 'successor' that could be defined in terms of logical concepts alone, such axioms also capture the transitive, asymmetrical relationships which characterize 'progression' along the natural number line, or series (*PoM*, 125). Arithmetic could thus be derived from logic *via* axioms formulated with, and applying to, nothing other than logical concepts and constants. Since it had been shown that higher mathematics could be defined arithmetically, Russell initially had reason for optimism in the validity of his logicist thesis.

In 1901, however, Russell discovered that this naïve viewpoint led to contradictions (*MPD*, 75–76). Most notably, there was Russell's paradox, which in *PoM* he called simply 'the contradiction' (*PoM*, 101–5). The ramified type theory developed and defended nearly a decade later in *PM* represents Russell's mature attempt to salvage logicism by devising and deploying a more sophisticated and paradox-free logical system. To Russell, the various paradoxes of propositions identified here seemed to indicate the need to develop, over and above a class-free logical system such as the substitutional theory, a proposition-free logical system. The multiple relation theory thus figured prominently within Russell's subsequent, ramified type theory as a means of emulating propositions without requiring ontological commitment to them.

Third, and relatedly, Stevens (2003a, 2004) has argued, under Landini's (1993, 1998) influence, that Russell abandoned Russellian propositions in favour of the MRTJ so as to reconcile the technical advantages of ramification with the unrestricted variable of quantification. Due to concerns about paradoxes of classes and propositions of precisely the sort outlined earlier, in *PM* Russell defends a 'ramified' type theory characterized by two interrelated hierarchies, specifically, a 'hierarchy of functions' and a 'hierarchy of orders'. The hierarchy of functions 'ensures that any function [...] can only be predicated of functions or individuals of the type immediately below its own' (Stevens 2004, 33). Overlaid upon this hierarchy of functions, Russell then imposes a hierarchy of orders which 'limits the admissible values of a bound variable in any quantified statement to ensure that no proposition or function can be a value of a bound variable contained in itself or in any other proposition of the same or lower order' (ibid.). While the hierarchy of functions emulates a simple theory of types, the hierarchy of orders overlaid upon this hierarchy of functions results in the 'ramified' theory of types. Taken together, the two hierarchies are designed to prevent what Russell calls 'vicious circle fallacies', which result from failure to adhere to the principle that 'whatever involves all of a collection must not be one of the collection' (*PM*, 37). The hierarchy of functions blocks vicious circle fallacies of a set-theoretical nature (such as Russell's paradox) by preventing propositional functions from taking themselves as arguments. The hierarchy of orders blocks vicious circle fallacies of a propositional nature (such as the liar paradox or the Epimenides) by preventing bound variables contained within quantified propositions from ranging over themselves or anything defined in terms of them. Under Landini's (1998) influence, Stevens sees both hierarchies as nominal rather than ontological. That is, while each involves a hierarchy of types (or orders) of *symbols*, neither involves ontological commitment to a hierarchy of different types of *entities*. This allows Russell to maintain his philosophical commitment to the unrestricted variable of quantification, and in the case of the hierarchy of orders in particular, this is facilitated by the MRTJ, which allows Russell to eliminate propositions as entities while retaining them as symbols or 'logical fictions'. As we will see in more detail in Section 1.4, while introducing judgements as proxies for propositions, the MRTJ involves no ontological commitment to anything over and above the individuals or relations which are constituents, or terms, of those judgements.

Before moving on it is worth pausing to reflect on the overall consistency and relative merit of these three distinct accounts of why Russell abandoned Russellian propositions. It is important to note at the outset that each of these explanations is mutually consistent with the others, and together they are mutually reinforcing. It is likely that each of the three sorts of considerations provided Russell with some degree of motivation to abandon his *PoM* theory of propositions. That said, it is probable that Russell placed more weight on the second and third of these factors than he did on the first. After all, he was willing to defend his earlier theory of propositions until it became clear that they were associated inevitably with insoluble paradoxes. Only then did he abandon them in favour of a theory more congenial to his logicist ambitions, specifically the MRTJ. As Stevens explains:

> Although it is undoubtedly true that one benefit of the multiple-relation theory is its ability to avoid the problem of false beliefs [...] it is a grave error to think that this is the full story, or even the most significant element in the story, of why Russell abandoned propositions in favour of judgement complexes. From his discovery of the famous Russell paradox in 1901 until the completion of the formal system of *Principia* almost a decade later, Russell was single mindedly devoted to the resolution of the paradoxes of mathematical logic [...] Virtually every logical and philosophical innovation he produced during this remarkably fruitful period is primarily directed towards this end. The multiple-relation theory is no different. (2004, 31)

Ultimately, then, Russell appears to have abandoned Russellian propositions in favour of the MRTJ, not principally or primarily as the result of scruples regarding the ontological status of objective falsehoods or false propositions but instead as part of an endeavour to reconcile his logicist ambitions, with key logical and philosophical commitments, including, and especially, the doctrine of the unrestricted entity variable. Russell's commitment to the unrestricted entity variable reflects an overall philosophical commitment to the universality of logic and to a conception of logical truth as essentially categorical or perfectly general (Landini 1993, 363; cf. Hacker 1996, 15).

1.4 The Multiple Relation Theory

As we saw earlier, there are significant continuities between the three distinct versions of the MRTJ defended in 'On the Nature of Truth and Falsehood' (1910), the *Problems of Philosophy* (1912) and the 1913 *Theory of Knowledge* manuscript. Nevertheless, there are crucial differences reflecting revisions Russell undertook in order to improve the theory and respond to criticisms. In this section, we will start by laying out the basic features of the theory as articulated in the 1910 version, before moving on to look at the crucial adjustments Russell made over the course of its development. At this point, we will be focusing more on the broad strokes of the theory and on the textual justifications that Russell himself provides for various revisions to it, saving more detailed analysis and discussion of external criticism for later sections and chapters.

We saw that, in the context of *PoM*, Russell was apt to talk of propositions being 'asserted' rather than 'judged'. Nevertheless, once he abandons Russellian propositions by 1910, he tends to characterize his earlier view in terms of judgement and as involving the idea that judgement is a 'dual' relation. He now frames his earlier view this way in order to highlight the contrast with, and motivate, his new theory of judgement according to which it is to be conceived as a 'multiple' as opposed to a 'dual' relation:

> We will give the name '*multiple* relations' to such as require more than two terms. Thus a relation is 'multiple' if the simplest propositions in which it occurs are propositions involving more than two terms (not counting the relation) [...] Relations which have only two terms we shall call 'dual relations'. The theory of judgement which I am advocating is, that judgement is not a dual relation of the mind to a single objective, but a multiple relation of the mind to the various other terms with which the judgement is concerned. (Russell 1910/67, 155; cf. *PP*, 109–10; emphasis in the original)

Aside from being a theory of judgement, the MRTJ is also a theory of truth. It is, in particular, a canonical correspondence theory of truth. As Marian David (2016) explains:

> Narrowly speaking, the correspondence theory of truth is the view that truth is correspondence to, or with, a fact – a view that was advocated by Russell [...] early in the 20th century. But the label is usually applied much more broadly to any view explicitly embracing the idea that truth consists in a relation to reality [...] The correspondence theory of truth is often associated with metaphysical realism.

In the previous section (1.3), we saw that when developing each of the 1910, 1912 and 1913 versions of the theory, Russell was apt to invoke the problem of falsehood in order to motivate rejection of a dual in favour of a MRTJ. Here is how he articulates the problem in 1910:

> If I judge that A loves B, that is not a relation of me to 'A's love for B', but a relation between me and A and love and B. If it were a relation of me to 'A's love for B', it would be impossible unless there were such a thing as 'A's love for B', i.e., unless A loved B, i.e., unless the judgement were true; but in fact false judgements are possible. (Russell 1910/67, 155)

So again, the theory according to which judgement is a dual relation cannot account for the distinction between true and false judgements. But then how, on this new view according to which judgement is a multiple relation, can we account for this distinction? According to the MRTJ:

> Every judgement is a relation of a mind to several objects, one of which is a relation; the judgement is *true* when the relation which is one of the objects relates the other objects, otherwise it is false. (156; emphasis in the original)

While in 1910 Russell characterized truth in terms of a relationship between judgements, and what he calls 'corresponding complexes' (158) by the time we get to the 1912 version of the theory, Russell tends to characterize this relationship in terms of a correspondence between two distinct complexes: the belief (or judgement) complex, and the fact complex – 'the belief is true when there is a corresponding fact, and is false when there is no corresponding fact' (*PP*, 114). In the context of each of both the 1912 and 1913 versions of the theory, moreover, Russell is wont to characterize the fact complex corresponding to a true judgement as the 'corresponding complex' (113; *TK*, 144, 148) or 'corresponding fact' (*TK*, 144).

Before moving on from the 1910 version of the theory to discuss the unique features of the 1912 and 1913 versions in more detail, it is especially important to highlight one unique feature of the 1910 version, which has to do with how it construes the unity and ordering of the constituents within the judgement.

In particular, what Russell will later characterize as the 'subordinate relation', that is, the relation of 'love' in the judgement that 'A loves B', plays an integral role, in this regard, within the 1910 version of the MRTJ. As Russell explains:

> We may now give an exact account of the 'correspondence' which constitutes truth. Let us take the judgement 'A loves B'. This consists of a relation of the person judging to A and love and B, i.e., to the two terms A and B and the relation 'love'. But the judgement is not the same as the judgement 'B loves A'; thus the relation must not be abstractly before the mind, but must be before it as proceeding from A to B rather than from B to A. The 'corresponding' complex object which is required to make our judgement true consists of A related to B by the relation which was before us in our judgement. We may distinguish two 'senses' of a relation according as it goes from A to B or from B to A. Then the relation as it enters into the judgement must have a 'sense', and in the corresponding complex it must have the same 'sense' [...] Thus, the corresponding complex consists of the two terms related by the relation R with the same sense. (1910/67, 158)

Here Russell can be seen as anticipating and attempting to resolve what following Griffin (1985, 224; 1985–86, 135) has come to be known in the scholarly literature as the 'narrow direction problem' (ND) (Stevens 2018, 96). (We will explicate ND in significantly greater detail in Section 2.1.) He does this by appealing to the 'sense' of the subordinate relation to distinguish between the judgement that 'A loves B' and the judgement that 'B loves A'. In general terms, the 'direction problem' is just that both of these two judgements share the same constituents and form. So how can they be distinguished? Within the context of his earlier *PoM* theory of propositions, the solution is more straightforward. 'A loves B' expresses a distinct, structured unity from that expressed by 'B loves A'. In particular the two propositions differ with regards to the respective positions of A and B within the complex, structured unity that each of the two distinct propositions are (cf. Griffin 1985, 214; 1985–86, 134). By 1910, by contrast, Russell no longer adheres to the perspective according to which there are propositions in which A and B may be united by, and differently ordered with respect to, the relation 'loves'. Instead, Russell thinks that the *judgement* that 'A loves B' can be distinguished from the *judgement* that 'B loves A' by the fact that the subordinate relation, in this case 'loves', has a different 'sense' in the two distinct judgements. In the first judgement, that 'A loves B', it is before the mind as proceeding from A to B, whereas in the second judgement, that 'B loves A', it is before the mind as proceeding from B to A. The judgement is true if there is a corresponding complex in which 'loves' has the same sense or direction as it does in the judgement.

By 1912 when Russell goes on to defend the MRTJ in chapter XII of *Problems of Philosophy*, he has become dissatisfied with this analysis and so revises the theory accordingly. In particular, Russell has come to realize that it is problematic to rely on the sense of the subordinate relation to unite and order the constituents of the judgement so as to distinguish, for example, Othello's belief that Desdemona loves Cassio from Othello's belief that Cassio loves Desdemona. If the subordinate relation 'loves' did unite and order Cassio and Desdemona, distinctly in the case of the two distinct judgements, the result would be hard to distinguish from a dual relation theory in which the subject, in this case Othello, stands to a structured, complex object, that is, either 'Desdemona loves Cassio' or 'Cassio loves Desdemona' as the case may be. According to Russell, it must therefore be the judging or believing relation which unites and orders the constituents of the judgement, not the subordinate relation. Russell puts the point this way:

> When the act of believing occurs, there is a complex, in which 'believing' is the uniting relation, and subject and objects are arranged in a certain order by the 'sense' of the relation of believing. Among the objects, as we saw in considering 'Othello believes that Desdemona loves Cassio', one must be a relation – in this instance, the relation of 'loving'. But this relation, as it occurs in the act of believing, is not the relation which created the unity of the complex whole consisting of the subject and the objects. The relation 'loving', as it occurs in the act of believing, is one of the objects – it is a brick in the structure, not the cement. The cement is the relation of believing. (*PP*, 112)

Like any other relation, judging or believing is capable of uniting and ordering its *relata* into a complex, structured unity. However, not all occurrences of relations do relate *relata* into complex unities. As was noted also in the context of Russell's earlier theory of propositions, in some cases relations occur as the terms or *relata* of other relations, as opposed to occurring as 'relating relations'. In a judgement or belief complex, only the judging relation occurs as a 'relating relation' according to Russell. The subordinate relation, for example, 'loves', occurs as one term or *relata* of the relation of judgement or belief among others. It is, as Russell puts it, 'a brick in the structure, not the cement' (ibid.).

On the 1910 version of the MRTJ as we saw, the judgement that 'A loves B' was true if there existed a correspondence in 'sense' between the relation 'loves' as it occurs in the belief and in the complex corresponding to the judgement. In the 1912 version of the MRTJ, for reasons identified earlier, Russell no longer wishes to put so much weight on the sense of the subordinate relation in his account of how judgements may have both sense and truth-value. So he revises his account of truth in accordance with the aforementioned changes to his account of judgement. He writes:

> When the belief is *true*, there is another complex unity, in which the relation which was one of the objects of the belief relates the other objects. Thus, e.g., if Othello believes truly that Desdemona loves Cassio, then there is a complex unity, 'Desdemona's love for Cassio', which is composed exclusively of the *objects* of the belief, in the same order as they had in the belief, with the relation which was one of the objects occurring now as the cement that binds together the other objects of the belief. On the other hand, when a belief is *false*, there is no such complex unity composed only of the objects of the belief. If Othello believes *falsely* that Desdemona loves Cassio, then there is no such complex unity as 'Desdemona's love for Cassio'. (*PP*, 112–13; emphases in the original)

As on the 1910 version of the MRTJ, on the 1912 version truth involves a relation of correspondence between a judgement complex and a corresponding complex, or fact (114). The nature of this correspondence, however, is subtly but importantly different. On the 1910 version of the theory, the correspondence was a correspondence of sense between two occurrences of the subordinate relation of the judgement, that is, 'loves' in the case of the judgement that 'A loves B'. The judgement that 'A loves B', for example, is true if the relation 'loves' has the same sense or direction in the judgement complex as it does in another, corresponding, complex. If there is no such corresponding complex, then the judgement is false. In the context of the 1912 theory, by contrast, the judgement or belief is true if the relation of judging unites and orders the constituents of the judgement in the same way as they are united and ordered in a corresponding fact complex. If there is no corresponding complex, or fact complex in which the constituents of the judgement are so ordered, then the judgement is false. In 1912 Russell thus relies on the sense or direction of the judging relation, as opposed to that of the subordinate relation, in order to provide the requisite unity and ordering of the judgement's constituent objects.

According to Russell, the 1912 version of the MRTJ satisfies three significant requirements which he thinks any adequate theory of the nature of truth and falsehood must fulfil (*PP*, 106). First, the MRTJ admits the possibility of falsehood. We have seen that Russell came to think that his earlier theory of propositions did not fulfil this requirement. Second, truth and falsehood must be properties of beliefs and statements, not facts. In a world of mere matter, he insists, devoid of any beliefs or language or thoughts, there would be facts but there would not be any truths (cf. 1910/67, 158). Facts cannot be false in the way that beliefs or judgements can be, and thus given requirement number one, facts cannot be true either. Finally, according to Russell, while truth and falsehood are properties of beliefs, whether a belief is true or false depends not on any intrinsic features, or internal qualities of the belief, but on facts which exist outside of and obtain independently of the belief (cf. *TK*, 109). If, Russell argues, I erroneously believe that Charles I died in his bed, this belief is false not due to any internal or intrinsic quality of the belief but rather because of an event which happened long ago (*PP*, 106–7).

Many of the features of the MRTJ we have explicated to this point are retained within the 1913 version defended in *TK*. One key revision characteristic of the 1913 version has to do with the status and function of the judging relation. We saw that in the 1912 version of the MRTJ Russell had leaned on the judging relation, and in particular on the idea that it could have 'sense' or direction, in order to explain how the constituents of a judgement could be united and ordered. More specifically, the sense of the judging relation was supposed to explain how the constituents could be differently ordered in the case, for example, of Othello's belief that Desdemona loves Cassio versus Othello's belief that Cassio loves Desdemona. By May 1913 when Russell articulates the version of the MRTJ which appears in chapter I of part II of the *Theory of Knowledge* manuscript, he has become dissatisfied with this solution and convinced that the judging relation can no longer be relied upon to unite and order the constituents of the judgement. For this reason, we find him introducing 'logical forms' as a new innovation within the MRTJ and as an additional constituent of what he now calls the 'relation of understanding' (*TK*, 116). 'Understanding' is conceived by Russell as a sort of general purpose, cognitive multiple relation, presupposed in other propositional attitudes such as believing, judging, asserting or doubting (107–8, 110). Russell elaborates as follows upon his reasons for incorporating logical forms into his latest version of the MRTJ:

> What is the proof that we must understand the 'form' before we can understand the proposition? I held formerly that the objects alone sufficed, and that the 'sense' of the relation of understanding would put them in the right order; this, however, no longer seems to me to be the case. Suppose we wish to understand 'A and B are similar'. It is essential that our thought should [...] 'unite' or 'synthesize' the two terms and the relation; but we cannot *actually* 'unite' them, since either A and B are similar, in which case they are already united, or they are dissimilar, in which case no amount of thinking can force them to become united. The process of 'uniting' which we *can* effect in thought is the process of bringing them into relation with the general form of dual complexes. The form being 'something and something have a certain relation', our understanding of the proposition might be expressed in the words, 'something, namely A, and

something, namely B, have a certain relation, namely similarity'. (116; emphases in the original)

Here we find Russell grappling with an important and controversial problem associated with the MRTJ: the unity of the proposition. Whatever has propositional content, whether it be a judgement or a sentence or a Platonic abstraction, cannot simply be an arbitrary list, collection or jumble of symbols and/or their meanings (cf. Stevens 2018, 95; Hanks 2007, 123–4; *PoM*, 49). It must instead unite and order its constituents into an articulate structure which expresses something intelligible. On Russell's earlier theory of propositions, as we saw, the requisite unity of a proposition was provided by the relating relation corresponding to the verb qua verb. On the MRTJ, by contrast, and as we have seen, the verb contained within the content clause of a judgement, for example, 'loves', no longer denotes a 'relating relation' which unifies the other constituents of the judgement. Instead this 'subordinate relation' is itself a constituent of the judgement which must be unified in some other way. Here Russell appears to be arguing that relying on the cognitive relation of understanding to unite and order the constituents will be equally as problematic as was the attempt to rely on the subordinate relation. Russell's argument takes the form of a dilemma: either A is similar to B or it is not. If the judgement that A is similar to B is true, then A and B are already united together in a structured complex, and the cognitive relation of understanding is not needed to unite them. On this horn of the dilemma, the cognitive relation of understanding is superfluous to the unity of the proposition. However, if the judgement is false and A is not similar to B, then the cognitive relation of understanding is incapable of bringing that unification about. On this horn of the dilemma, in other words, the cognitive relation of understanding is impotent to effect the unity of the proposition.

The analysis of belief or judgement is 'precisely analogous to the analysis of understanding a proposition' (*TK*, 142). Applying these conclusions to judgement, then, Russell is arguing that the judging relation is too psychological a mechanism to account for the unity of the constituents of a judgement into a complex, structured whole (Griffin 1985, 221; 1985–86, 136). Short of mastering the art of Jedi, in other words, mental conduct of the type corresponding to propositional attitude verbs is not the sort of thing which can move constituents of judgements around, put them in the right order and bring them together into a complex, fact-like unity. For Russell, remember, the constituents of judgements (as of propositions on his earlier view) are mind- and language-independent objects; the things referred to by the words contained in the sentence expressing the judgement or proposition. Except in the special cases in which they *are*, judgements *are not* ordinarily about ideas, thoughts or words. They are about mind- and language-independent objects and, if true, true of facts made up of them. On the assumption that its objects are mind and language independent, thought cannot move its constituents around and unite them into complex, fact-like wholes. If the thought is false, then its constituents will simply not be united in the way they are thought to be. If, moreover, those thoughts are true, then thought is simply not needed to so unite them. But what can thought do?

According to Russell in this passage, what thought can do is bring objects into relation with the logical form of a complex. Understanding the proposition that A is similar to B, for instance, does not involve thought uniting A and B and similarity within a structured, fact-like complex. Instead it involves thinking each constituent severally in relation to the general, logical form of a dual complex and, in thought, assigning that constituent to a position within that form. As we shall see in more detail in Chapters 2 and 3, according to the reading of Wittgenstein's critique of the MRTJ defended in this book, this passage was likely contained within the 'crucial part' of the manuscript which Russell discussed with Wittgenstein at their tense meeting on or around 26 May 1913. Moreover, the view developed in it was likely the target of Wittgenstein's objection, expressed first inarticulately during this tense discussion and then 'exactly' in a mid-June 1913 letter to Russell.

1.5 Wittgenstein at Cambridge

The 1913 version of the MRTJ defended in *TK* is, in any case, the version in association with which, at least in large part, Wittgenstein developed the enigmatic and controversial criticisms which are the main focus of this book. Before we move on to explicate these criticisms and adjudicate the scholarly controversy surrounding them, it will be helpful to first introduce some uncontroversial historical, biographical and philosophical background details. Such details include those concerning how it is that Wittgenstein came to be associated with Russell at Cambridge, in a collaborative logical and philosophical enterprise which served as the common ground upon which they engaged with one another both in productive discussion and sometimes contentious debate over the nature and status of judgements and propositions.

On his father's advice, Wittgenstein enrolled as an aeronautical engineering student at Manchester University in 1908 (Schroeder 2006, 15). While pursuing experimental work first with kites and, subsequently, on the design and construction of an engine suitable for aeroplanes (ibid.), he developed an interest in pure mathematics (Monk 1991, 30). Consequently, he met regularly with fellow research students to discuss problems concerning the logical foundations of mathematics (ibid.). One of these students recommended that he read Russell's *The Principles of Mathematics* (ibid.). This would prove to be 'a decisive event in Wittgenstein's life' (ibid.). Over the next three years, Wittgenstein struggled with and vacillated regarding the question of whether to continue with his studies in aeronautical engineering or pursue philosophy instead (Schroeder 2006, 14–16). He became obsessed with Russell's work on the foundations of mathematics and especially with attempting to devise a solution to Russell's paradox (Monk 1991, 30–33). In April 1909, he submitted an attempted solution of the paradox to Philip E. B. Jourdain, who apparently discussed it with Russell (33). Discouraged by the fact that neither seemed inclined to accept it, Wittgenstein persevered in his aeronautical studies, at least for the time being (ibid.).

By late summer 1911, however, Wittgenstein's growing engrossment in philosophy overcame his resolve to persist in aeronautics (Monk 1991, 35). Having drawn up plans for a proposed book on philosophy, he 'travelled to Jena to discuss it with Frege' (36). Frege advised him to go study with Russell in Cambridge (ibid.), and thus on 18 October 1911 Wittgenstein showed up unannounced at Trinity College, Cambridge, and introduced himself to Russell (38). At that time, he also began to regularly attend Russell's lectures on mathematical logic (39). While initially Russell's attitude towards Wittgenstein and his philosophical abilities was ambivalent, over the subsequent months he began to view Wittgenstein as a friend, a protégé and, ultimately, a successor (Blackwell and Eames 1992, xi–xii). As he explained in a letter to Ottoline Morrell:

> I love him & feel he will solve the problems I am too old to solve – all kinds of problems that are raised by my work, but want a fresh mind and the vigour of youth. He is the young man one hopes for. (Quoted in Monk 1991, 41)

Wittgenstein's arrival at Cambridge in October 1911 proved to be fortuitous. While in Russell, Wittgenstein would find the encouragement and mentorship desperately needed at this key juncture in his life, Russell, too, was at a personal and philosophical crossroads. After many years of mentally exhausting labour on the foundations of mathematics, Russell was ready to pass the torch to a gifted and passionate apprentice such as Wittgenstein (Monk 1991, 36).

1.6 The *Theory of Knowledge* Manuscript

Following the completion of his work on *Principia Mathematica*, Russell vacillated with regards to the continued pursuit of what he called 'technical philosophy' (Blackwell and Eames 1992, x). By technical philosophy, Russell meant both mathematical logic of the sort developed in *PM* as well as the application thereof 'to problems in philosophy, in science, and in common sense' (ibid.). While he continued to work on these topics, at times he expressed a revulsion towards this sort of philosophy (xi) and a desire to relinquish the problems associated with it to Wittgenstein (xii).

By spring of 1913 his work and plans had begun to crystallize around the theory of knowledge (Blackwell and Eames 1992, xiv). In an important sense, this development was merely a continuation of the 'Tiergarten programme' described in Section 1.1 (cf. Blackwell and Eames 1992, xiv). Having completed his 'big book' on pure mathematics, he would move on to write another 'big book', this time concerning the epistemology of science. As Monk explains: 'The idea for the "big book" that gradually took shape in his mind was that of using the techniques of mathematical logic to provide a clear and precise philosophical foundation for physical science' (1997, 283). While Russell began writing this 'big book' on epistemology in earnest in early May 1913, as fate would have it, the project would never be completed. What Russell did complete of this project has come down to us in the form of the 1913 *Theory of Knowledge* manuscript.

Originally, Russell thought the book would consist of two large parts: one analytic and the other synthetic or constructive (Griffin 1985, 86, 132; Blackwell and Eames 1992, xiv). As the project evolved, Russell began to think of these two large 'parts' as two distinct books and of the *Theory of Knowledge* manuscript as the first of the two, dealing with the analytic part of the project (Blackwell and Eames 1992, xv–xvi). He later took up the constructive part of the original project in *Our Knowledge of the External World* (1914) and 'The Relation of Sense Data to Physics' (1914), among other publications (Griffin 1985, 86, 132). As Blackwell and Eames explain:

> The whole project would include an analytic section in which all of the components of knowledge would be separated out and formulated, and a constructive section in which on this basis points in space, moments in time, and units of matter would be logically constructed. (1992, xiv)

The first six chapters of the *Theory of Knowledge* manuscript were eventually published in the *Monist* in 1914–15 (Blackwell and Eames 1975, 5; Griffin 1985, 86, 133). The remainder of the manuscript remained unpublished and publically unknown until it was discovered and catalogued by Kenneth Blackwell in 1967, in preparation for the eventual sale of the Russell Archives ultimately to McMaster University in Hamilton, Ontario, Canada (Blackwell and Eames 1975, 4). This state of affairs reflects Russell's own subsequent assessment of the work, in light of Wittgenstein's critique. As reported in a letter to Ottoline Morrell in October 1913 (Russell to Morrell #900), he thought that the first six chapters, dealing with acquaintance with particulars, were quite good. But the manuscript, he laments, then 'goes to pieces' where Wittgenstein said it did (Blackwell and Eames 1992, xxi–xxii). While evidently, Russell also assessed his work on the constructive side of the project as fit to publish, Wittgenstein's critique of his MRTJ left a 'large breach' (xxxv) within the analytic side.

The (analytic) book was to have three parts: the first on acquaintance, the second on judgement and the third on inference (Blackwell and Eames 1992, xv). As things happened, Russell wrote only the first two parts, and the extant manuscript ends with chapter VII of part II. In total, Russell wrote 350 manuscript pages between 7 May and 7 June 1913. He stopped working on the project on 8 June and never resumed it (xvii). Substantial documentary evidence exists to suggest that Wittgenstein's criticisms of the MRTJ defended in *TK* played a major role in Russell's decision to abandon work on the manuscript. Referring back to these events in a 1916 letter to Ottoline Morell published in his *Autobiography*, for instance, Russell writes:

> Do you remember that at the time when you were seeing Vittoz [a Swiss physician who treated her] I wrote a lot of stuff about Theory of Knowledge, which Wittgenstein criticized with the greatest severity? His criticism, tho' I don't think you realised it at the time, was an event of first-rate importance in my life, and affected everything I have done since. I saw he was right, and I saw that I could not hope ever again to do fundamental work in philosophy. My impulse was shattered, like a wave dashed to pieces against a breakwater. I became filled with utter despair, and tried to turn to you for consolation [...] I *had* to produce lectures for America, but I took a metaphysical subject although I was and am convinced that all fundamental work in philosophy is logical. My reason was that Wittgenstein persuaded me that what wanted doing in logic was too difficult for me. So there was no really vital satisfaction of my philosophical impulse in that work, and philosophy lost its hold on me. That was due to Wittgenstein more than the war. (*ABR*, 282; emphasis in the original)

The lectures referred to in this letter are the Lowell Lectures, which Russell gave at Harvard in spring term of 1914. Preparing for these lectures appears to have been a precipitating factor in Russell's decision to write a book on *Theory of Knowledge* (Blackwell and Eames 1992, xiv; Monk 1991, 81). Consistent with Russell's ambition to deploy advances in mathematical logic to the epistemology of science, his goal in these lectures was to convert 'the American realists to a proper appreciation and mastery of the new logical techniques by which along their right-minded but inept attempts to answer epistemological problems could be made effective' (Blackwell and Eames 1992, xiv).

Additional documentary evidence that Wittgenstein's criticisms had a significant impact on Russell's decision to abandon the book comes in the form of a letter written by Wittgenstein to Russell on 22 July 1913, referring back to the events of May–June and presumably responding to a letter (not extant) in which Russell had claimed to be 'paralyzed' by Wittgenstein's objection: 'I'm very sorry to hear that my objection to your theory of judgement paralyses you. I think it can only be removed by a correct theory of propositions' (*CL*, 33). Much of the rest of this book will be taken up by the attempt to adjudicate the scholarly controversy surrounding the nature of Wittgenstein's objection as well as its effect on Russell, but for now it will suffice to highlight some of the uncontroversial details concerning the events Wittgenstein and Russell are referring to in their respective letters. In this regard, three additional pieces of correspondence are worth considering.

The first is a letter Russell wrote to Ottoline Morrell on 21 May, which refers back to a meeting between Russell and Wittgenstein the previous day. Russell writes:

> Wittgenstein came to see me last night with a refutation of the theory I used to hold. He was right, but I think the correction required is not very serious. I shall have to make up my mind within a week as I shall soon reach judgement. (Russell to Morell #782, quoted in Connelly 2014, 236)

What precisely the theory being referred to here as that which Russell 'used to hold' is is a matter of scholarly controversy, which will be dealt with in subsequent chapters. What is not controversial is that when this meeting with Wittgenstein took place on 20 May, Russell had taken that day off, after completing chapters I–VI of part I of the manuscript, 'On the Nature of Acquaintance' (Blackwell and Eames 1992, xvii). These six chapters would eventually become the *Monist* articles. On 21 May he then reports writing chapter VII of part I, dealing with acquaintance with universals (ibid.; Russell to Morell #782). When he speaks of 'reaching judgement' within a week, he is anticipating the commencement of work on part II of the manuscript, 'Atomic Propositional Thought'. As we shall see in more detail in the coming chapters, the MRTJ features prominently in part II of the manuscript, while the 'logical forms' Russell incorporated therein are an integral topic of discussion in the final chapter of part I, chapter IX on 'Logical Data'.

Russell completed part I on 23 May and began part II on 24 May (Griffin 1985, 282). In a second key piece of correspondence, a letter to Ottoline Morrell written on 27 May, Russell describes a tense meeting during which Wittgenstein posed an objection to a crucial part of what Russell had been writing:

Wittgenstein came to see me – we were both cross from the heat – I showed him a crucial part of what I had been writing. He said it was all wrong, not realizing the difficulties – that he had tried my view and knew it wouldn't work. I couldn't understand his objection – in fact he was very inarticulate – but I feel in my bones that he must be right, and that he has seen something that I have missed. If I could see it too I shouldn't mind, but as it is, it is worrying, and has rather destroyed the pleasure in my writing – I can only go on with what I see, and yet I feel it is probably all wrong, and that Wittgenstein will think me a dishonest scoundrel for going on with it. Well, well – it is the younger generation knocking at the door – I must make room for him when I can, or I shall become an incubus. But at the moment I was rather cross. (Quoted in Griffin 1992, 446)

We can be fairly certain that the crucial part of the manuscript which Russell showed Wittgenstein during this tense meeting consisted of, or was contained in, chapter I of part II and, perhaps, chapter IX of part I. Not only were these among the most recent chapters composed by Russell by this date, but of the material he had written up to this point *only* these two chapters deal directly with the MRTJ. Chapter I of part II deals directly with judgement, and chapter IX of part I addresses acquaintance with an important constituent of judgement on the 1913 version of the MRTJ, namely logical forms. On the assumption that Wittgenstein had criticized an earlier version of the MRTJ on 20 May, Russell would now presumably be showing Wittgenstein a revised version of the MRTJ intended to account for his criticisms. The personal and philosophical significance of these revisions is foreshadowed in Russell's correspondence with Morrell in the period leading up to the meeting with Wittgenstein on or around 26 May, with Russell going so far as to refer to 24 May, the day on which chapter I of part II was to be composed, as 'the Day of Judgement' (Russell to Morell #784A).

Elsewhere (Connelly 2014) I have argued that the view referred to here as that which Wittgenstein had 'tried but wouldn't work' can be found in a January 1913 letter from Wittgenstein to Russell (*CL*, 24–25). This claim will be developed and defended in greater detail in Section 3.1. For now I wish to highlight one last integral piece of correspondence associated with Wittgenstein's objection to the version of the MRTJ defended in the 1913 *TK* manuscript. In this mid-June letter, which is otherwise concerned with arranging a lunch meeting between Wittgenstein, his mother and Russell at the Savoy hotel on Wednesday, 18 June 1913, Wittgenstein claims to express his objection to Russell's theory of judgement 'exactly'. He writes:

I can now express my objection to your theory of judgment exactly: I believe it is obvious that, from the prop[osition] 'A judges that (say) a is in the Rel[ation] R to b', if correctly analysed, the prop[osition] 'aRb.v.~aRb' must follow directly *without the use of any other premiss.* This condition is not fulfilled by your theory. (*CL*, 29; emphasis in the original)

Since Wittgenstein refers to the forthcoming lunch date as being scheduled for 'Wednesday' at 1:15 p.m., presumably this letter was written within the week prior to 18 June, no earlier than 12 June. We know Russell permanently ceased work on the manuscript on 8 June. We saw from the letter to Morell on 27 May that Russell was already having misgivings about continued work on the manuscript but that he did not fully appreciate the significance of the objection in part because Wittgenstein had been very inarticulate in expressing it. In this mid-June letter, Wittgenstein seems to allude to this initial vagueness in the original expression of his objection before moving on to clarify it (cf. Griffin 1985, 238; 1985–86, 142). This helps us to be confident that the three pieces of correspondence we have looked at reflect the development of a continuous thread of less to more focused criticisms of Russell's MRTJ, culminating in the precise expression thereof in the mid-June letter. This also explains why, when Russell refers to these events in the 1916 letter to Morrell quoted earlier, he goes on to describe them as 'Wittgenstein's onslaught' (*ABR*, 282) suggesting that the critique came in several successive and increasingly devastating waves or phases.

As we move forward, we will see how this mid-June letter features prominently both in the Griffin/Sommerville interpretation (or 'standard reading' (SR)) of Wittgenstein's objection, as well as in the interpretation defended in this book, which I call the 'logical interpretation' (LI). Although problematic, as we shall see, for reasons outlined by Stevens (2003, 2004), perhaps the chief merit of SR, according to LI, is its identification of the 'premiss' referred to in this letter as a significant constraint on judgement, designed to circumvent the wide and narrow form of the direction problem. To better appreciate the merits of SR, however, as well as some of its drawbacks, we should now move on to survey and explicate several of the most noteworthy and influential contributions to the long-standing scholarly controversy concerning the nature and import of Wittgenstein's objection to the MRTJ. This is the task which will be undertaken in Chapter 2.

Chapter 2

THE SCHOLARLY CONTROVERSY

2.1 The Direction Problems

When explicating the basic features of the MRTJ in Section 1.4, we identified and gave a rudimentary exposition of the so-called narrow direction problem (ND). Alongside the 'wide direction problem' (WD), ND is one of two distinct but interrelated problems for Russell's MRTJ, an appreciation of which is integral to understanding the scholarly controversy surrounding Wittgenstein's critique of the MRTJ. WD and ND are sometimes referred to in the scholarly literature as two distinct versions of the 'direction problem' and at other times, alternatively, as two distinct 'direction problems'. Nothing of particular philosophical importance hinges on whether we refer to them one way or the other, and thus, in the interest of clarity, I will henceforth follow Stevens (2018) in referring to them as two distinct direction problems, ND and WD, respectively.

In broad strokes, and as we saw in Section 1.4, ND is simply the problem of distinguishing, for example, Othello's belief that Desdemona loves Cassio from Othello's belief that Cassio loves Desdemona. While Russell deploys this particular pair of beliefs for illustrative purposes in chapter XII of *Problems of Philosophy*, it is, in general, a problem which can emerge for any two beliefs, such as these, which have all and only the same constituents. Recall that in the MRTJ, judgement is a multiple relation between a judging subject and the various constituents of this judgement taken severally. But then, since each of these two judgements has the same subject and constituents, how can they express different beliefs and possess distinct truth-conditions? Following Stevens (2018), we can represent the first of Othello's candidate beliefs semi-formally as follows:

J(o, d, L, c).

Here 'J' is the relation of judgement (or belief), 'o' stands for Othello, 'd' for Desdemona, 'L' for the relation 'loves' and 'c' for Cassio. Within this judgement, each of 'o', 'd' and 'c' stands for particulars, whereas 'L' stands for a universal. The judging relation is, in this case, a four-place 'relating relation' which unites the other constituents of the judgement. 'Loves' is called the 'subordinate relation'. We might then try to represent the second, distinct candidate belief of Othello semi-formally as follows:

J(o, c, L, d).

The problem is that although superficially we have a distinction of order corresponding to the differing order of the letters in the symbolic expression of the judgement, it is more challenging to understand how precisely this reflects and is manifest as an ordering of constituents within the judgement being expressed. Indeed, this problem already shows up to an extent within these two distinct, symbolic representations themselves given that each, after all, essentially simply lists the constituents in an order without explaining how it is that they have that order or what it consists in. Recall that within the MRTJ, the constituents of judgements are not symbols on a page so much as they are the objects those symbols stand for. It is one thing to list symbols on a page in a particular order and quite another to explain how the constituents referred to by those symbols are ordered, and united within a cognitive complex in the way the symbols ostensibly represent them as being (cf. Stevens 2005, 92–93; Landini 1991, 49).

This highlights an important, associated problem for the MRTJ which is that of the unity of the proposition. Whatever is expressed by an intelligible declarative utterance or belief cannot simply be an unconnected list or collection of constituents. It must put those constituents together in an intelligible structure, and it must be clear what position the constituents occupy in the structure. In Russell's *PoM* theory of propositions, these functions had been performed by the relating relation corresponding to the main verb of the sentence expressing the proposition. Once Russell abandoned the idea that judgement involves a dual relation between a judging subject and a structured proposition of this sort, he needed some other account of the unity and ordering of the propositional content which is judged.

While Russell initially proposed, in 1910, to rely on the subordinate relation to provide the unity and ordering of the constituents, he subsequently came to reject this idea for reasons discussed in Section 1.4. Within the MRTJ, in a nutshell, the subordinate relation must merely be a *term* of the judging relation, not a relating relation. Indeed, the subordinate relation cannot be a relating relation; otherwise the judgement would relate the subject to a structured proposition. Such an approach would simply reproduce the various difficulties discussed in Section 1.3, which the MRTJ was designed to obviate. Absent further clarification and development, the MRTJ might thus seem to leave us with a list or collection of judgement constituents and no sense of how those constituents are supposed to be united and ordered. This situation gives rise, inter alia, to the narrow direction problem, which is fundamentally a problem about order. Othello's two distinct candidate beliefs each have two very different contents and, if true, are true by virtue of correspondence with two very different facts. The first candidate belief is true only if Desdemona loves Cassio, whereas the second candidate belief is true only if Cassio loves Desdemona. Yet both judgements have precisely the same subject and constituents. How can the MRTJ distinguish them?

After considering and rejecting the notion that the judging relation itself might unite and order its constituents (see Section 1.4) in *TK*, Russell hit upon the idea of deploying logical forms as constituents of judgements in order to address ND amongst other problems. Following Stevens (2018), we might then give the following semi-formal rendering of Othello's belief (or judgement) that Desdemona loves Cassio:

$J(o, d, L, c, xRy)$.

Along with the original constituents of our judgement, we now have a new constituent, which is the general, logical form of dual complexes, namely xRy (cf. *TK*, 117). Again, however, resolving ND is not as simple as listing the constituents of the judgement, now including the form. An account must be given of precisely how the logical form works to provide unity and ordering to the constituents of the judgement.

Before we look at the details of how Russell's proposed solution to ND was supposed to work, we should first explicate WD. Essentially, WD is the problem of ensuring that a judgement contains at least one predicate or relation, that the relation occurs in the correct position and thus that the judgement has sense. Following Stevens (2018, 96–97) we can represent WD as the problem of distinguishing genuine judgement complexes, such as that ostensibly represented by

$J(s, a, R, b)$,

from nonsensical pseudo-judgements, such as

$J(s, a, b, c)$.

Given that in the MRTJ the subordinate relation is merely the term of the judging relation, and not in itself a relating relation, the question naturally arises as to why it cannot be replaced by another term, which is not a relation.

Since the subordinate relation 'R' in this case has no unique role and performs no special function, but is instead simply another term of the judging relation alongside the others, why can we then not replace 'R' with 'b'? After all, is not 'b' also a possible judgement constituent (in, e.g., the judgement that aRb)?

That WD was a significant focus of Wittgenstein's critique of the MRTJ is strongly suggested by his remark in the 1913 *Notes on Logic* that 'every right theory of judgement must make it impossible for me to judge that this table penholders the book. Russell's theory does not satisfy this requirement' (*NL*, 103). Subsequently, more work will need to be done to unpack the full significance of this remark. For now it is important to note that Wittgenstein appears to be highlighting WD as a problem for Russell's MRTJ, since he is suggesting that Russell's theory does not rule out as impossible a 'judgement' such as 'this table penholders the book' in which a substantive referring to a particular, that is, 'penholders', occupies the position where a verb (referring to a relation) should go. Ultimately, we will see that Wittgenstein intends to deploy this example to highlight both ND and WD. He means us to see 'this table penholders the book' as resulting from two problematic substitutions performed upon the original, and perfectly intelligible, judgement that 'the book is on this table'.

For now, we can finish up our introduction to ND and WD by looking at how Russell purported to utilize logical forms to resolve them in *TK*. As part of an overall strategy to defuse the problems, Russell deploys logical forms in the service of what he calls 'position in a complex' analysis (*TK*, 88, 100, 111, 114, 122, 145–48). According to Russell, judgement (or belief) presupposes an understanding of the propositional content being judged. Understanding this propositional content involves being acquainted with the logical form of the complex which exists if the judgement is true. This logical form figures within the understanding complex presupposed by the judgement. Some understanding complexes are unambiguously determined once their constituents and form are given, while others are not. The latter, for reasons which shall become clear momentarily, Russell refers to as 'permutative', while the former he refers to as 'non-permutative'. In the case of a non-permutative judgement such as that 'A is similar to B', understanding the propositional content of the judgement simply means bringing the constituents of the judgement into relation with the logical form of the corresponding complex or fact. Here, we would bring the constituents of the judgement into relation with the general form of dual complexes, which Russell characterizes as being that 'something is somehow related to something':

> The form being 'something and something have a certain relation', our understanding of the proposition might be expressed in the words 'something,

namely A, and something, namely B, have a certain relation, namely similarity'. (*TK*, 116)

Once we assign the position of the relation (in this case, similarity) relative to the logical form, according to Russell, this places constraints on the sorts of positions that are available for other constituents to occupy in both the understanding complex and the corresponding complex. These positions are, as Russell insists, 'functions' of the relation (*TK*, 122). (The relation in question is the 'subordinate relation' within the understanding complex but the 'relating relation' of the corresponding complex in the event that there is one.) For instance, since 'similarity' is a symmetrical relation, once it is assigned to a position in the logical form of dual complexes, the other positions become qualitatively identical in the sense that they have no order:

> In general, in a complex of n terms, there are various 'positions' in the complex, corresponding to different relations (generally each of them functions of the relating relation) which the constituents have to the complex. A complex may be called 'symmetrical' with respect to two of its constituents if they occupy the same position in the complex. Thus, in 'A and B are similar', A and B occupy the same position. (*TK*, 122)

Because the positions within the complex 'A is similar to B' have no order, the complex is said to be 'non-permutative'. In the case of symmetrical relations such as 'similarity', no change of sense arises from interchanging the positions of A and B.

Things get more complicated once we turn to analyse judgements involving 'unsymmetrical' complexes. 'Unsymmetrical' complexes are those in which, once the position of the relation is assigned to the form, there are (at least) two distinct positions which the other constituents may occupy (*TK*, 122–23). Such complexes will be 'homogenous' if a logical possible complex results from interchanging the positions of its other constituents, while they will be 'heterogeneous' if no logically possible complex results from interchanging the positions of their constituents (*TK*, 123). So, for instance, 'A precedes B' is an unsymmetrical homogenous complex since a distinct, logically possible complex results from interchanging the positions of A and B. However, 'A precedes in the complex α' is heterogeneous and unsymmetrical because, although it has two distinct positions, no logically possible complex results from interchanging the positions of its constituents. Unsymmetrical and heterogeneous complexes are also non-permutative because the positions of their constituents cannot be interchanged so as to produce a logically possible complex, and thus the complex is unambiguously determined once its constituents and form are given: 'it is only in cases of unsymmetrical homogeneity that a complex is not determined by its form and its constituents' (*TK*, 123).

The problematic cases are thus those dealing with what Russell calls 'permutative' judgements, that is, those such as that 'A precedes B' or 'Desdemona loves Cassio', which assert belief in corresponding complexes that are unsymmetrical and homogeneous. In such cases a change of position entails a change of sense, and thus neither judgement complex nor corresponding complex is unambiguously determined by constituents and form. Notably, this problem of sense persists despite the fact that, according to Russell's analysis (*TK*, 85–87), the relation indicated by 'precedes' is neutral, in the sense that it is the very same relation between A and B, namely 'sequence', which obtains regardless of whether we describe the complex verbally or in writing as being that 'A precedes B' or that 'B succeeds A'. In other words, complexes may be unsymmetrical regardless of whether their relations are neutral, and such complexes give rise to problems of sense or direction which exist independently of any problems associated with ontological commitment to converse relations that Russell may be attempting to tackle by appealing to neutral relations.[1]

Even if Russell succeeds in eliminating commitment to converse relations by appealing to neutral relations, he will still face a direction problem concerning unsymmetrical complexes, since they will have different senses depending on which positions in the complex each constituent occupies. To deal with this problem, Russell proposes to analyse judgements allegedly asserting belief in unsymmetrical and homogenous complexes as instead asserting belief in 'associated complexes' (*TK*, 145) which are heterogeneous and so non-permutative. For example, the judgement allegedly asserting the existence of the atomic complex 'A precedes B' can, upon analysis, instead be seen to assert the existence of the molecular complex 'A is earlier in γ and B is later in γ' (ibid.). Such molecular complexes contain atomic complexes which are non-permutative, since no logically possible complex results from interchanging their constituents, for example, 'γ is later in B' is not a logically possible complex.

In sum, by assigning the constituents of a judgement to positions within the logical form of the fact complex which corresponds to it if it is true, Russell claims to be able to unambiguously determine the propositional content of any judgement, even those distinct judgements which share their constituents and form in common. Russell even goes so far as to insist

---

[1] For a more thorough discussion of neutral relations, and the role they may be proposed to play in eliminating problematic ontological commitment to converse relations, see MacBride (2007) and Fine (2000).

(*TK*, 147) that once our analysis reaches a certain level of depth and sophistication, we need not even mention the relation R in order to unambiguously describe the corresponding (or fact) complex, which exists in case our judgement is true. (Again, 'R' will be the 'relating relation' of the corresponding complex but the 'subordinate relation' within the judgement complex.) ND will thus no longer be a problem, since for any apparently permutative judgement asserting the existence of an unsymmetrical homogeneous complex, we can provide upon analysis an equivalent, non-permutative judgement asserting the existence of an associated heterogeneous complex. And WD will no longer be a problem since (1) complexes do not even have determinate positions for other constituents to illegitimately occupy until the position of the relation has been assigned, and once it has been assigned the other constituents have to go elsewhere; and (2) once our analysis reaches a certain level of sophistication, we need not even mention R. Apparently permutative judgements are analysable, without remainder, into non-permutative judgements which assert the existence of associated molecular complexes that are fully determined by the positions of the constituents within the heterogeneous, atomic complexes which make the associated complex up.

2.2 The Standard Reading

On the basis of the forgoing, Russell's MRTJ as articulated in *TK* would appear to be in rather good stead. Yet, following the meeting with Wittgenstein on 18 June at which they in all likelihood discussed the MRTJ and Wittgenstein's criticisms thereof, Russell wrote to Ottoline Morrell on the evening of 19 June that 'yesterday' he had felt 'ready for suicide' (Blackwell and Eames 1992, xix; Griffin 1985, 239):

> All that has gone wrong with me lately comes from Wittgenstein's attack on my work – I have only just realized this. It was very difficult to be honest about it, as it makes a large part of the book I meant to write impossible for years to come, probably. I tried to believe it wasn't as bad as that – then I felt I hadn't made enough effort over my work & must concentrate more severely […] I must be much sunk – it is the first time in my life that I have failed in honesty over my work. (Russell to Morrell #811)

Given the careful and detailed analysis and account outlined earlier in Section 2.1, how could things have gone so drastically and horribly wrong for Russell and for the MRTJ? What was the nature of 'Wittgenstein's attack', and why did it have such a profound effect on Russell?

According to an influential reading proffered by Nicholas Griffin (1985, 1985–86) and Stephen Sommerville (1979), Wittgenstein's objection focused on an alleged incompatibility between the MRTJ and the theory of types. Because it has been so influential, the Griffin/Sommerville reading has sometimes been referred to as the 'standard reading' (SR), and I will follow this convention where appropriate. SR places great weight on the manner in which Wittgenstein expressed his objection 'exactly' in the mid-June letter quoted in Section 1.6 earlier. According to SR, when Wittgenstein mentions a 'premiss' in the June letter, he is referring to a type-theoretic significance constraint on judgements, designed to preclude the sorts of problematic and illicit substitutions which characterize WD as outlined earlier in Section 2.2. Griffin and Sommerville see the significance constraint as modelled after *13.3 of *Principia Mathematica*:[2]

$$\vdash :: \varphi a \text{ v} \sim \varphi a. \rightarrow :. \varphi x \text{ v} \sim \varphi x. \leftrightarrow : x=a. \text{ v} . x \neq a.$$

For the illustrative case of a dyadic, first-order judgement, the relevant constraint will be the dyadic analogue of *13.3, which Griffin and Sommerville designate as *13.3a:

$$aRb \text{ v} \sim aRb \rightarrow . (xRy \text{ v} \sim xRy) \leftrightarrow [(x=a \text{ \& } y=b) \text{ v} (x \neq a \text{ \& } y=b) \text{ v} (x=a \text{ \& } y \neq b) \text{ v} (x \neq a \text{ \& } y \neq b)].$$

As Griffin notes (1985, 242; 1985–86, 144) *13.3 is used in *PM* (*20.81) to prove that any two types with a common member are identical. In *PM*, Russell himself provides the following gloss on *13.3:

> The following proposition is useful in the theory of types. Its purpose is to show that, if a is any argument for which 'φa' is significant, i.e., for which we have φa v $\sim \varphi a$, then 'φa' is significant when, and only when, x is either identical with a or not identical with a. It follows [...] that, if 'φa' and 'ψa' are both significant, the class of values of x for which 'φa' is significant is the same as the class of those for which 'ψa' is significant, i.e., two types which have a common member are identical. (*PM*, 171–72)

According to SR, Russell had hoped to deploy a related strategy in *TK* to defuse the wide direction problem by introducing a type-theoretic significance constraint upon the admissible constituents of judgements or beliefs. Applying

---

[2] For each of *13.3 and *13.3a, some source notation has been replaced with equivalent notation for the sake of consistency with the remainder of this book.

THE SCHOLARLY CONTROVERSY   41

the constraint would ensure that, given a judgement or belief is significant, its constituents would be of the right types.

This is reflected in the 'p only if q' conditional structure of the significance constraint (cf. Hanks 2007, 129). The antecedent specifies the hypothesis that aRb is significant, which, as Russell points out in the quotation from *PM* given earlier, is equivalent to saying that either aRb or its negation is true. The consequent then specifies the conditions which must hold in case the antecedent is true, that is, if the judgement, or belief, is significant. In particular it is specified that each of a and b must either be identical or not identical to x or y. This in turn ensures that a and b must be individuals and thus acceptable arguments to a dyadic, first-order function. The consequent of the conditional therefore specifies the necessary, type-theoretical conditions that any first-order judgement must satisfy in order to have sense. Nonsensical pseudo-judgements such as Wittgenstein's 'this table penholders the book' would thus be ruled out by this constraint as violations of type-theory. If the 'R' in aRb does not denote a dyadic, first-order relation, then $aRb \vee \sim aRb$ does not follow from aRb.

This, according to SR, explains why Wittgenstein words his objection in the way he does in the mid-June 1913 letter. Recall that, according to Wittgenstein, Russell's theory fails to meet the requirement that $aRb \vee \sim aRb$ follow from the judgement that aRb 'directly', that is, without the help of any other premises. Proponents of SR maintain that the 'premise' Wittgenstein targets in his objection is the type-theoretic significance constraint specified in *13.3a. Wittgenstein will not allow Russell to make the stipulations embodied in this significance constraint, according to SR, because

> to make them would require further judgements. We are trying to analyze what is supposed to be the simplest kind of elementary judgment. But to do so would seem to involve us in yet further judgments. Moreover, the further judgments required are of an extremely problematic character. For to judge that a and b are suitable arguments for a first-order relation is to make a judgment of higher than first-order. Yet, as Russell makes quite clear in *Principia* (pp. 44–6), higher-order judgments are to be defined cumulatively on lower-order ones. Thus we cannot presuppose second-order judgments in order to analyze elementary judgments. (Griffin 1985, 144)

Given that within ramified type-theory as developed and defended in *PM*, higher-order judgements are defined cumulatively upon lower-order judgements, a vicious regress will be generated by relying on supplemental, higher-order judgements in order to stipulate significance constraints on lower-order judgements. In this case, *13.3 is a higher-order judgement deployed to stipulate significance constraints on the dyadic, first-order judgement that aRb. According to SR, the MRTJ contained in *TK* is thus incompatible with the theory of types of *PM*.

Aside from linking up well with the wording contained in Wittgenstein's 'exactly expressed' objection to the MRTJ contained in the mid-June letter, an important merit of SR is that it explains the 'paralyzing' effect the objection had on Russell (cf. Stevens 2003a, 7). As we have seen, the MRTJ figures prominently not only within Russell's epistemology as developed in *TK* and *PP*, it also plays a highly significant role within Russell's logicist programme as developed and defended in *PM*. In that context, it serves to eliminate ontological commitment to propositions while providing a proxy of propositional content. Eliminating ontological commitment to propositions is crucial, for Russell, because they are associated with propositional paradoxes such as the liar paradox, the Epimenides and the 'p_0/a_0' paradox, discussed earlier in Section 1.3. Yet retaining some proxy of propositional content in the form of the MRTJ is equally essential, for Russell, since some such proxy is integral to the functioning and success of his logicist deductions. Nevertheless, SR has been thought to have significant drawbacks, two of which in particular have been identified by Stevens (2003a, 2004, 2018) and which we shall now move on to explore in Sections 2.3–2.4

2.3 Stevens's First Critique of EI: Direct Inspection and the MRTJ

Griffin and Sommerville's ingenious and highly influential interpretation of Wittgenstein's objection served as the definitive or standard reading in the scholarly literature for nearly two decades (1985–2003). Nevertheless, beginning in 2003, Graham Stevens published a series of papers (2003a, 2004, 2018) which have called its veracity into question. He has identified two main problems for the Griffin/Sommerville reading, which he refers to as the epistemological interpretation (EI) and describes as follows:

> [EI] is the view that Wittgenstein's criticisms exposed an incompatibility between Russell's epistemology and his theory of types in the sense that the theory of types is justified by Russell's epistemology (in particular, the epistemic relation of judgement as analyzed by the MRTJ), yet the MRTJ relies on a theory of types. Thus, the theory of types and the MRTJ cannot be rendered compatible with one another without circularity. (Stevens 2018, 99)

The first problem for EI, according to Stevens, is that it misconstrues the nature of the relationship between the MRTJ and the theory of types. In

Section 1.3, it was noted that the 'ramified' theory of types as developed and defended in *PM* involves two distinct, but interrelated, hierarchies: the hierarchy of types and the hierarchy of orders. As Stevens explains, 'In ramified type-theory, every level of the type hierarchy further divides into a hierarchy of orders (thus every level of types branches, or *ramifies*, into orders' (101; cf. *PM*, 48; emphasis in the original). As we saw in Section 1.3, Stevens follows Landini in viewing both hierarchies as nominal rather than ontological. In other words, each hierarchy is a hierarchy of types of symbols, not a hierarchy of types of objects. While the 'type' hierarchy addresses Russell's paradox by prohibiting propositional functions from taking themselves, or anything defined in terms of them, as arguments, the 'order' hierarchy addresses propositional paradoxes, such as the liar paradox, the Epimenides and the 'p_0/a_0' paradox, by restricting the range of bound variables within quantified propositions so as to prevent those variables from ranging over the proposition containing them or anything defined in terms of it. Stevens's first objection to EI, essentially, is that the MRTJ is only responsible for generating the hierarchy of orders, while the hierarchy of types is fixed independently of the MRTJ (2003, 24; 2018, 101). As Stevens himself explains:

> Without going too far into the formal details of this baroque edifice, we can note that the two hierarchies have quite independent justifications, and that only the hierarchy of orders is justified by appeal to the vicious circle principle. This in turn is unquestionably linked to the MRTJ as Russell and Whitehead explicitly argue that the hierarchy of orders has its origins in the recognition that the MRTJ leads to a hierarchy of orders of truth (*PM*, p. 42). Justification for the hierarchy of *types* (as opposed to *orders*), must come from elsewhere. Russell and Whitehead offer the 'direct inspection' argument as justification for the imposition of this hierarchy. (2018, 101; emphases in the original)

Because only the order and not the type hierarchy is generated by the MRTJ, the type hierarchy cannot come into conflict with the MRTJ in the way envisaged by Griffin and Sommerville. Recall that according to EI, type-theory requires that higher-order judgements such as *13.3a be defined cumulatively upon lower-order judgements, thus leading to a hierarchy of senses of truth and falsehood (*PM*, 42). This was supposed to be problematic for Russell because on the version of the MRTJ defended in *TK*, elementary judgements, including dyadic, first-order judgements, depend upon higher-order judgements such as *13.3a to guarantee their significance or sense, thus generating a regress. But according to Stevens, the hierarchy of judgements and of senses of truth and falsehood described by Russell (ibid.) represents the order hierarchy not the type hierarchy. The order hierarchy, Stevens explains, is derived from the 'vicious circle principle', 'according to which no statement made about a given totality can itself be a member of that totality' (2018, 101). The type hierarchy, by contrast, is derived not from the vicious circle principle but instead on the basis of 'direct inspection' (*PM*, 48; Stevens 2018, 101). As evidence that Russell and Whitehead provide a 'direct inspection' argument to justify the type hierarchy, Stevens quotes from the following passage of *PM*:

> A direct consideration of the kinds of functions which have functions as arguments and the kinds of functions which have arguments other than functions will show, if we are not mistaken, that not only is it impossible for a function $\phi\hat{z}$ to have itself or anything derived from it as argument, but that, if $\psi\hat{z}$ is another function such that there are arguments *a* with which both 'ϕa' and 'ψa' are significant, then $\psi\hat{z}$ and anything derived from it cannot significantly be an argument to $\phi\hat{z}$. (47)

In the remainder of the section of *PM* entitled 'Why a Given Function Requires Arguments of a Certain Type' in which this passage occurs, Russell and Whitehead go on to provide several examples of cases in which, intuitively, functions can and cannot take certain arguments. For instance, $(x).\varphi x$ can be a function of φx, in the sense that it can take φx as an argument. But '*x* is a man' cannot be a function of φx, since φx is a 'mere ambiguity' and not a determinate argument. As Russell explains, 'A function, in fact, is not a definite object, which could or could not be a man; it is a mere ambiguity awaiting determination' (48).

According to Stevens, then, the type hierarchy was intended to be justified by the sort of 'direct consideration' undertaken in this section of *PM* and is thus not supposed to be generated by the MRTJ or derived from the vicious circle principle in the way that the hierarchy of orders is. As he goes on to explain,

> The direct inspection argument, puzzling to interpret though it is, clearly has nothing whatsoever to do with acts of judgement. It is an argument to the effect that direct inspection of a propositional function will reveal it to have a logical type. (2018, 101)

Since it has nothing to do with acts of judgement, however, it can have nothing to do with the MRTJ and thus cannot be incompatible with it. In Chapter 3, we will critically revisit Stevens's reading of *PM* chapter II, part IV. For now, however, we will move on to elucidate the second of Stevens's two criticisms of EI.

2.4 Stevens's Second Critique of EI: The Logical Status of the Subordinate Relation

In essence, Stevens's second critique of EI is that by focusing too heavily on the epistemological aspects of the situation, EI misses the main target of Wittgenstein's objection, which is the logical, and so ontological, status of the subordinate relation. Simply stipulating that the object terms and subordinate relation are to occupy distinct positions within the judgement will not fundamentally alter or differentiate their logical status. Essentially, the thought that Russell might circumvent WD by availing himself of such stipulations, and that it was these stipulations that Wittgenstein objected to, overlooks a deeper problem for the MRTJ having to do with its inability to differentiate between the object terms and the subordinate relation of the judgement, without invoking ontological distinctions of type.

Following Landini, Stevens sees the point and purpose of the nominalist semantics for propositional functions which Russell develops in *PM* as being precisely to facilitate distinctions of type between propositional functions, and legitimate arguments to those functions, without having to posit type distinctions of an ontological nature. By construing type-theory nominalistically as opposed to ontologically, Russell was enabled to elude the paradoxes while retaining his fundamental, philosophical commitment to the unrestricted variable of quantification. But then, examining again the case of a dyadic, first-order judgement such as Othello's belief that Desdemona loves Cassio,

$B(o, d, L, c)$,

it would seem we have a four-place relation in which each variable position has been assigned a unique argument. According to Stevens, EI fails to take seriously the following question: 'If B is simply a 4-place relation, what gives L any special status?' (2018, 102). In other words, within the MRTJ the position occupied by L, in this case, is no different than any other position. If we were to replace it with a variable, we would replace it with the same, unrestricted entity variable with which we would replace any other position. So simply stipulating that L goes in that spot does not resolve this deeper logical and ontological worry. If L and c are on the same logical and ontological level, why can we not interchange them and assign them to one another's places, like so?

$B(o, d, c, L)$.

Moreover, why does our belief complex even need to contain L or any relation for that matter? Why can we not assign constituents to positions in the logical form as we please and so believe the following?

B(o, a, b, c).

Finally, and most importantly according to Stevens, these concerns have 'nothing whatsoever to do with epistemology' (ibid.). Therefore, if we want to properly understand Wittgenstein's objection and its paralyzing effect on Russell, we need an ontological as opposed to an epistemological interpretation.

2.5 The Ontological Interpretation

Stevens thus proceeds to develop and defend an ontological interpretation (OI) of Wittgenstein's objection, which, he claims, readily avoids the two concerns for EI developed in Sections 2.3–2.4. According to Stevens, Griffin and Sommerville were 'partly correct' (2003, 26) to characterize Wittgenstein's objection as concerning a clash between Russell's MRTJ and his theory of types. But it was a serious mistake to think the clash 'occurred at the level of epistemology' (Stevens 2018, 103). A more plausible and probable explanation (Stevens 2003a, 24) of the clash arises out of Wittgenstein's and Russell's differing conceptions of logic and in particular from the implications of Russell's conception of logic for his ontology:

> The central and defining feature of Russell's attitude towards logic is his insistence on the universality of logic; the view that logic applies equally and equivalently to all things. This, we saw earlier, is a constant theme throughout his struggle with set-theoretic and semantic antinomies and is a governing principle behind the multiple-relation theory. The purpose of the multiple-relation theory, reflecting this principle, is to generate orders of judgement without positing corresponding *ontological* divisions. Every logical subject is to be treated as an ontological equal. Wittgenstein's objection to the multiple-relation theory, however, exposes this enterprise as a failure. (25; emphasis in the original)

As we saw in Section 1.3 earlier, Russell abandoned Russellian propositions in large part because ontological commitment to them was apt to produce paradoxes, given the unrestricted variable of quantification. For example, the 'p_0/a_0' paradox which 'pilled' the substitution theory resulted from propositional matrices containing unrestricted entity variables which could thus take propositions themselves as arguments. Epimenides the Cretan's statement that 'all Cretans are liars' is paradoxical because the range of the quantifier it contains includes Epimenides' statement within its scope. The MRTJ allowed Russell to avoid these 'semantic' paradoxes by breaking propositions up into separate terms or judgement constituents. But then, because these terms would be arguments to the unrestricted entity variable, they would have to be on a logical and ontological par.

As we saw in Sections 1.1–1.2, however, upon his abandonment of neo-Hegelianism Russell had become a 'staunch realist' (Stevens 2003a, 25). The radical, pluralist realism Russell adopted from Moore applied not only to particulars but also, and even especially, to relations, which Russell construed as universals. Relations, it will be recalled, were crucial to Russell's analysis of geometrical and mathematical order. Indeed, in *PoM*, as we saw, Russell had lamented his inability to construct any adequate philosophy of mathematics in the absence of an ontological commitment to fully real, independent and external relations. As Stevens explains, throughout the 'entire period in Russell's thought' from 1898 up until the events in question (May–June 1913), universals

> were just as welcome in his ontology as particulars and, indeed, were necessary constituents of judgement complexes. The price of being admitted into Russell's ontology, however, is that all members of that ontology should, ideally, be of the same logical type. This ambition [...] places on the multiple-relation theory the requirement that all constituents of judgements stand on an equal ontological footing. Wittgenstein shows, however, that is analysis is inadequate for the treatment of universals. (2003, 25)

Because of its inability to distinguish ontologically between universals and particulars, the MRTJ cannot adequately account for the unique logical status of the subordinate relation. This leaves it impotent to distinguish intelligible judgements such as that 'the book is on the table' from garbled nonsense such as 'this table penholders the book'. If there is no fundamental, logical or ontological difference between particulars and universals, and if, correspondingly, any variable contained within the cognitive relation of understanding, believing or judging is simply the unrestricted entity variable, then Russell's MRTJ cannot rule out illicit substitutions into the position which should, intuitively, be occupied by the subordinate relation. It thus cannot effectively address WD, regardless of any supplemental, type-theoretic stipulations of the sort envisioned by Griffin and Sommerville. Russellian type-theory divides *symbols* into a hierarchy of types of propositional functions, and of orders of judgements, *without* positing corresponding ontological divisions. According to Stevens, 'the type distinctions that Wittgenstein shows to be required for the adequate regimentation of judgements', by contrast, 'will be ontological distinctions' (26). Since Russellian type-theory does not involve such ontological distinctions, it simply lacks the resources required to block the offending substitutions.

2.6 Hanks's Critique of the Standard Reading

Until it was destabilized by a series of articles written by Graham Stevens, beginning with his 're-examination' of Russell's paralysis in 2003, a consensus had built around SR. For this reason, and as mentioned, it is sometimes referred to as the 'standard reading'. Before moving on to identify several problems with it, Hanks describes this 'standard reading' as follows:

> Once Russell had traded in propositions for the multiple relation theory, whether or not an expression or entity belongs to a certain type becomes a matter of the kinds of expressions or entities it can be combined with in judgment. Thus, facts about type distinctions depend upon facts about which judgments are possible and which are not. But adding [...] additional premises to the analysis of judgement makes facts about judgment depend on facts about which expressions or entities belong to which types. (2007, 129)

The first problem Hanks identifies with this reading is that it cannot account for the seriousness and severity with which Russell reacted to it. If Wittgenstein's objection to Russell's MRTJ concerned its lacking any mechanism to impose required type restrictions on the constituents of judgements, then Russell would have had an 'obvious reply' (ibid.). Specifically, Russell could simply have identified the role that the judging relation itself plays in imposing the necessary type restrictions on its *relata*, thereby resolving WD without the need to appeal to any supplemental premises or significance constraints such as *13.3a or its ilk. In other words, like any other monadic or polyadic predicate within *PM*'s formal syntax, the judging relation would yield only a significant expression for certain types of arguments. For example, while 'φa' is a significant expression, and thus either true or false depending upon whether a is or is not φ, '$\varphi(\psi x)$' is not a significant expression since both 'φa' and 'ψx' are propositional functions of individuals and thus can only take individuals not propositional functions as arguments (ibid.). Following Church (1974), Hanks provides a rudimentary exposition of *PM*'s type-theory to illustrate how this would apply in the case of judgement. For the purposes of this exposition, i represents the type belonging to individual constants and variables, while (i) represents the type of a monadic predicate whose arguments are individuals and (i,i) represents the type of a dyadic predicate whose arguments are individuals. Othello's judgement that Desdemona loves Cassio would then be a four-place predicate with the following form:

Judges(i, i, i, (i,i)).

Here the first 'i' corresponds to the position occupied by Othello, the second 'i' to that occupied by Desdemona, the third 'i' to that occupied by Cassio and (i,i), finally, represents the position occupied by 'loves'. This fourth position, crucially, cannot be occupied by an individual, but only by a dyadic predicate whose arguments are of type i, that is, individual constants or variables. For simplicity, we can then abbreviate a series of 'i's' by replacing it with a corresponding numeral so that the type-theoretical form of Othello's judgement may then be represented as being of type (3,(2)). This, however,

> means that 'Judges (Othello, Desdemona, Iago, Cassio)' is not well formed because 'Judges' is of type (3,2) and 'Cassio' is type (1). And if 'Judges(A, a, b, R)' is well-formed, since 'Judges' is type (3,(2)), then 'a' and 'b' must be type (1) and 'R' type (2). This secures the implication to 'aRb v ~ aRb' without the need for any other premises. (Hanks 2007, 131)

Within *PM*'s type-theory, propositional functions contain the conditions of their significance within their own logical syntax. In this regard, 'Judges' will be just like any other such propositional function. It will be significant for certain combinations of types of arguments and meaningless for others. In particular, 'Judges' will be meaningless for the case in which it takes four individuals as arguments. Using the above convention, we might try to represent the Judging relation as:

J(i, i, i, i).

Abbreviating, we could then represent the logical form of judgement as:

J(4).

But 'Judges', as we have seen, is of type (3,2). Thus, 'Judges(Othello, Desdemona, Iago, Cassio)' is ill formed and so ruled out as meaningless. By contrast, 'Judges(A, a, b, R)' is well formed and thus significant, and so 'aRb v ~ aRb' follows from it without further ado. According to Hanks, 'The ease and obviousness of this reply casts doubt on the standard reading of the objection – it is inconceivable that Russell would not have thought of it' (130). In other words, SR cannot be correct since it cannot account for Russell's 'paralysis' in the face of Wittgenstein's objection. Had Wittgenstein come to him with this objection, Russell could simply have responded by telling Wittgenstein to 'brush up' on *PM*'s rules of formal syntax.

2.7 Hanks on How Wittgenstein 'Defeated' the MRTJ

According to Hanks, the considerations adduced in Section 2.6 suggest that the objection Wittgenstein raised to the MRTJ likely had little if anything to do with type-theory or with an incompatibility between the MRTJ and type-theory. This suggestion is reinforced by the observation that when Wittgenstein states his objection to Russell's MRTJ first in the *Notes on Logic* and then again in *TLP*, he says nothing about types or type-theory.

> Every right theory of judgement must make it impossible for me to judge that 'this table penholders the book'. (Russell's theory does not satisfy this requirement.) (*NL*, 103)

> The correct explanation of the form of the proposition, 'A makes the judgement p', must show that it is impossible for a judgement to be a piece of nonsense. (Russell's theory does not satisfy this requirement.) (*TLP* 5.5422)

As each of these passages indicate, Wittgenstein's objection focused not on any external concerns having to do with type-theory but instead, Hanks insists, on concerns internal to the MRTJ and more specifically its inability to provide a satisfactory account of how the MRTJ can yield a serviceable propositional content as opposed to a dis-unified nonsensical jumble.

According to Hanks, this same concern with nonsense as opposed to types shows up in the mid-June letter in the form of Wittgenstein's claim that the MRTJ cannot account for how aRb v ~ aRb follows from the judgement that aRb. This is just another way of saying that the MRTJ cannot guarantee that a judgement is significant in the sense that it yields a propositional content capable of being either true or false (Hanks 2007, 139). Wittgenstein's objection thus has nothing fundamentally to do with type-theory, which is a separate, external issue, dealt with in *TLP*, for instance, in the 3.3's not the 5.54's (134). Instead, Wittgenstein's concern has to do with the unity of judgement and in particular with the inability of the MRTJ to yield a unified propositional content. Call this interpretation of Wittgenstein's objection the unity interpretation (UI).

According to Hanks's UI, just as only a unified propositional content can be negated, only a unified propositional content can be judged (*NL*, 94). While it makes sense for Othello to judge that 'Desdemona loves Cassio', it is nonsense to suppose that Othello judges 'Desdemona, loves, Cassio'. This is because in the former case what is judged is a unified propositional content, whereas in the latter case what is allegedly 'judged' is simply a collection or list. As Hanks explains:

> This shows why Wittgenstein's objection is not really about types or type restrictions. Even if the terms of a judgement meet all the requirements necessary for making up a possible fact, as long as those terms are disunified and separate they are not something that can be judged. When Wittgenstein says that any correct theory of judgement must show that it is impossible to judge nonsense, by 'nonsense' he does not mean something that violates type restrictions. Rather, he means something that is not capable of being true or false. And the collection of a, b, and R, considered as a disunified collection, is not something that can be true or false. (2007, 138)

Wittgenstein 'defeated' the MRTJ, Hanks insists, not by demonstrating a subtle inconsistency between it and *PM*'s type-theory but by showing that it was impotent to recover the unity of propositions central to his earlier *PoM* theory of propositions. In a valiant effort to elude the problems and paradoxes of propositions, Russell had bartered away the unity of propositions and so failed to ensure that judgement relates to a unified, propositional content. Henceforth, we will often refer to this problem for Russell's MRTJ as UP, for short. In essence, Hanks's UI says that Wittgenstein's objection to Russell's MRTJ was UP. Once Russell split propositions up into several constituents, to which the subject then stood in multiple relations as opposed to a dual relation of propositional understanding, neither the King's horses nor the King's men, nor even Russell himself, try as he might, could put them back together again.

2.8 Pincock on the Standard Reading

Following Hanks, Pincock (2008) refers to the Griffin/Sommerville interpretation outlined in Section 2.2 as the 'standard reading'. Pincock insists that the version of the MRTJ defended in *TK* was immune to the sorts of concerns raised by SR. Moreover, Pincock claims, the MRTJ defended in *TK* itself contained the resources necessary to respond effectively to all of the other standard objections identified in the scholarly literature, including those of Hanks (UI) and Stevens (OI). Russell thus could not have been stymied by any of these objections, since none of them 'are problems that Russell had reason to take seriously' (120). Instead, Pincock sees the MRTJ as foundering on, and Wittgenstein as raising, a new and distinct problem, which he calls the 'correspondence problem' (or CP). This CP is supposed to contrast with various versions of what Pincock calls the 'proposition problem', which serves as an umbrella term that covers each of both ND and WD, as well as Hanks's worries about the unity of the proposition (UP) outlined in Section 2.7. In this section, we will look at Pincock's critique of SR, before examining his critique of Hanks's account of the objection in Section 2.9. In Section 2.10, we will then move on to explicate CP and examine Pincock's reasons for holding that it was this objection (allegedly raised by Wittgenstein) which left Russell 'paralysed'. Throughout, we will often refer to Pincock's interpretation, according to which Wittgenstein's objections targeted CP as opposed to ND, WD or UP, the correspondence interpretation (CI).

With regards to the SR, Pincock argues that this must be mistaken both because it misunderstands the nature of types within Russell's philosophy of logic and also because it fails to appreciate an integral distinction between 'types' and 'kinds' within Russell's theory of complexes. Following Landini (1991, 63), Pincock argues that type-theory is a theory which stratifies propositional functions[3] not entities into types. Even though it therefore divides *symbols* into a hierarchy, Russellian type-theory countenances only one metaphysical category of *entity* (Pincock 2008, 121). There are thus no distinct 'types' of entity for Russell to invoke to resolve WD by precluding illicit substitutions such as that characteristic of 'this table penholders the book'. The problem with the MRTJ thus cannot be, as supposed by SR, that it problematically depends on the imposition of type restrictions in order to preclude nonsensical judgements.

On the other hand, within his theory of complexes as developed in *TK*, according to Pincock, we find Russell distinguishing between different *kinds* of entities within the one broader metaphysical *category*. In order to resolve WD, Russell can thus simply 'make distinctions within a single metaphysical category based on the combinatorial properties of entities' (Pincock 2008, 112). Such distinctions of kind are, for instance, embodied in Russell's diagram of 'understanding a proposition' which occurs at the conclusion of chapter 1 of part II (118). As Pincock explains:

> What about the wide direction problem – why can S not understand that similarity A B? Such understandings are ruled out because there is no logically possible complex with the form of Russell's diagram and similarity substituted for A. A description of these constituents in these positions fails to describe

---

[3] Landini sometimes prefers to speak of indexed predicate variables as opposed to propositional functions as having a nominalistic semantics in *PM*. See, e.g., Landini (1998, 8).

a logically possible complex. Russell can solve this kind of direction problem, then, by resting on his general theory of complexes. (119)

We saw earlier in Section 2.1 that Russell described a complex as 'heterogeneous' if it was unsymmetrical in the sense that it had, for instance, two distinct positions, but no logically possible complex could result from interchanging the positions of the constituents occurring within them. As Pincock himself notes, a 'key assumption' (116) of Russell's is that if A is earlier in α, for instance, then there is no logically possible complex in which α is earlier in A. This, Pincock claims, implies that A and α are heterogeneous, meaning they are of distinct *kinds* and so cannot be substituted in one another's places. Although it is not made explicit here, Pincock appears to think that a similar sort of distinction of kind, or heterogeneity, explains why we cannot interchange the positions of A and 'similarity' within the complex represented by Russell's diagram of 'understanding a proposition'. Just as A could not occur as the relating relation within a logically possible corresponding complex or fact complex, it cannot occur within a logically possible cognitive complex in the position where a relation corresponding to a subordinate verb should go. We will examine this assumption critically and in greater detail, along with Russell's diagram of understanding, in Chapter 3.

For now, this still leaves Russell with ND, but according to Pincock this is also easily resolved by appealing to his theory of complexes. As opposed to the heterogeneous complexes at issue in the case of WD, ND arises for complexes which Russell calls 'homogenous' and 'unsymmetrical'. In other words, ND results in case there are two logically possible complexes with the same constituents and form, as in the case of the pair 'A is before B' and 'B is before A'. In this case, Russell can invoke his 'position in complex analysis' to disambiguate judgements dealing with these two, distinct, logically possible complexes. As Pincock observes,

> Wherever there is a complex in which sequence relates two terms, exactly one term will stand in the earlier than relation to this complex and exactly one will stand in the later than relation to this complex. So, by metaphysical fiat, we distinguish A's being before B from B's being before A by saying that even though both complexes involve the same constituents [...] in the former case A is earlier, while in the latter B is earlier [...] Russell's strategy is to adapt his general solution for all such relational complexes to the particular case where the complexes are instances of understanding. (2008, 116, 119)

In other words, when S judges that A is before B, this judgement has the same constituents and form as the judgement that B is before A. However, A and B bear distinct relations to the judgement complex in the case of S's judgement that A is before B than they would in case S judged that B is before A. The strategy in question is evident, for instance, when Russell writes that 'the proposition "*a* is before *b*" must be interpreted as meaning "there is a complex in which *a* is earlier and *b* is later"' (*TK*, 135).

2.9 Pincock on Hanks and the Unity of Judgement

Having thus disposed with WD and ND, only one of the various 'proposition problems' for Russell's MRTJ identified in the scholarly literature remains, according to Pincock. Specifically, it is UP, which was alleged by Hanks to be the target of Wittgenstein's 'paralysing' criticisms. Recall that according to Hanks's UI, in an attempt to circumvent problems and paradoxes of propositions, Russell's MRTJ bartered away the unity of the proposition and so failed to ensure that what is judged is a unified propositional content capable of being true or false. While Hanks's concern with truth and falsity is 'a marked step in the right direction' (Pincock 2008, 123) according to Pincock, UI falters in making a mistaken assumption about what, on Russell's account, are supposed to be the bearers of truth and falsity. As Pincock explains:

> Where I part from Hanks is his assumption that it is the collection involved in the understanding or belief complex that is the bearer of truth and falsity. Instead, on my development of the theory, it is the belief complex itself that is true or false. Assuming that the complex is unified by the believing relation, I see no problem with it having properties, including the properties of being true or false. (ibid.)

In other words, while Russell has certainly sacrificed the idea that propositions are the bearers of truth and falsity by adopting the MRTJ, he has not abandoned the idea that truth bearers must consist of a unified propositional content rather than a mere collection of terms. What is different now is simply that the truth bearers are judgements and their truth makers are corresponding facts. While Russell has traded in propositions for belief complexes, according to Pincock such complexes 'are just as unified as his earlier propositions were' (ibid.).

2.10 The Correspondence Problem

Since Russell could resolve each of these various 'proposition problems' by appealing to his theory of complexes in general and judgement complexes in particular, his 'paralysis' cannot have been initiated by any of the various objections concerning them identified in the scholarly literature. According to Pincock, then, Russell's 'last and best' version of the MRTJ, the one defended in *TK*, must have instead met its demise in the face of a distinct problem called the 'correspondence problem' (CP). Moreover, he insists, the textual evidence and extant correspondence are also consistent with the idea that Wittgenstein's objections targeted CP. So what is CP?

In a nutshell, CP has to do with the fact that although the MRTJ can clearly disambiguate distinct cognitive complexes which share constituents and form in common, it nevertheless cannot provide judgement complexes with the right truth-conditions (Pincock 2008, 126). According to Pincock's CI, Wittgenstein's objection thus targeted CP: 'Russell had no good way to sort his belief complexes into those that were true and those that were false. So no definition of truth in terms of correspondence is forthcoming' (ibid.). While specifying corresponding complexes is not a problem in the case that a belief is atomic and non-permutative, problems emerge when Russell attempts to specify complexes corresponding to permutative judgements such as S's belief that A is before B (ibid.). Such a judgement, as we saw in the context of examining ND, should be true in case there is a corresponding complex in which A is earlier and B is later. The problem, however, 'is that the ultimate constituents of the belief complex cannot be univocally mapped to a logically possible complex' (127). There are two logically possible complexes composed of the same constituents and form as our judgement, namely 'A is earlier in γ and B is later in γ' and 'B is earlier in γ and A is later in γ'. So how can we specify which of these two complexes is the correct corresponding complex? As Pincock laments:

> We cannot give a specific enough description using the ultimate constituents of the belief complex. What else could we use? It might seem like we could appeal to the atomic constituents of the belief complex: *A*'s being earlier in γ and *B*'s being later in γ. But for Russell this threatens to reintroduce false propositions as freestanding entities. For suppose that *A* is not before *B*. Then there will not be a complex in which *A* is earlier, even when *S* believes that *A* is before *B*. This tells Russell that he cannot appeal to such atomic constituents, but he is left with no other options. (127)

In other words, in order to clearly specify the truth-conditions of S's judgement that A is before B and to disambiguate the complex which corresponds to this judgement (in the event it is true) from the other logically possible complex composed of the same ultimate constituents and form, we must appeal to the atomic constituents of the associated molecular belief complex. But such atomic constituents will not exist in case the belief is false. Russell's MRTJ was thus ultimately felled, according to Pincock's CI, by an especially involved version of the problem of false propositions or beliefs which (in part) motivated his adoption of it in the first place.

So what is the evidence that Russell was 'paralysed' by CP? Pincock sees Russell as identifying and grappling with CP on three distinct occasions over the course of chapter V, part II of the manuscript on 'Truth and Falsehood', with a progressively deepening appreciation of its seriousness and severity. After proposing position in a complex analysis in order to provide an associated, non-permutative complex in place of a problematic, permutative complex, Russell considers the following objection:

> It may be said, of course, that 'A is earlier in γ and B is later in γ' is composed of the same constituents as 'A is later in γ and B is earlier in γ'. But these are both *molecular* complexes, and the atomic complexes which enter into them are different; the identity of constituents only appears when we carry our analysis further, to the constituents of the atomic complexes. And this remoter identity of constituents does not raise the problems with which we are at present concerned. (*TK*, 145; emphasis in the original)

Here Russell seems to recognize that he will need to appeal to unified atomic complexes in order to disambiguate two distinct molecular complexes with their constituents and form in common, but he does not yet realize that this may present him with CP, which concerns the possibility of false atomic complexes. Two pages later, Russell again raises the issue but again fails to appreciate its full significance:

> Whether any difficulties arise from the fact that the molecular complex is still permutative with respect to the constituents of its atomic constituents, is a question which must be left until we come to deal with molecular thought. But it seems fairly evident that no difficulties can arise from this fact. (147)

Third, and finally, however, seven pages later, Russell develops a more extensive treatment of the issue, in the context of which he now characterizes CP as a 'real difficulty' (154). Russell elaborates:

> Where permutative complexes are concerned, our process of obtaining associated non-permutative complexes was rather elaborate, and no doubt open to objection. One special objection is that, [1] in order to regard the associated complex as non-permutative, we have to regard its atomic constituents $x_1 C_1 \gamma$, $x_2 C_2 \gamma$, etc., as really constituents, and what is more, [2] we have to regard the

corresponding propositions as constituents of the proposition 'there is a complex γ in which $x_1 C_1 \gamma$, $x_2 C_2 \gamma$, etc.' This seems to demand a mode of analyzing molecular propositions which requires the admission that they may contain false atomic propositions as constituents, and therefore to demand the admission of false propositions in an objective sense. This is a real difficulty, but as it belongs to the theory of molecular propositions we will not consider it further at present. (ibid.)

Pincock notes that Russell develops these reflections as part of a response to one possible kind of objection to his theory of truth and falsehood. Specifically, according to this sort of objector, correspondence between belief and fact is 'arbitrary' (153) on the MRTJ. In other words, according to this objector, the MRTJ cannot credibly distinguish between true and false beliefs by correctly mapping the true ones onto corresponding complexes. Russell sees that overcoming this sort of objection through his position in a complex analysis will, however, produce 'real difficulties' related to the possibility that univocally mapping a belief to its corresponding complex, when there is more than one logically possible molecular complex composed of the same constituents and form, will involve the problematic admission of false atomic propositions. As Pincock explains:

Without assuming that $x_1 C_1 \gamma$ obtains in the belief complex, we lose the mapping from the belief complex to a single non-belief complex. That is, we require that x_1 really stand in C_1 relation to γ in the belief, even if, in the world, x_1 does not stand in the C_1 relation to any γ. The dilemma, then, is clear. Russell either must stick to ultimate constituents and so fail to define correspondence or else introduce additional constituents in the form of false propositions. I claim this objection, raised only 21 pages before the manuscript ends, is the decisive one. (2008, 128)

The implication is that Russell sensed something was awry and could 'feel in his bones' that Wittgenstein's objection was serious, but it was not until the depth of the problem became clear to him over the course of writing part II (and especially chapter V) that he became 'paralysed' by CP and so ceased work on the manuscript. But then, how is Pincock's CI consistent with Wittgenstein's extant remarks on the subject?

According to Pincock, to understand what Wittgenstein was getting at we need to familiarize ourselves with three philosophical restrictions upon or features of the MRTJ which Wittgenstein shows to be incompatible. The first restriction, or assumption, is what Pincock calls (PART):

(PART) In a propositional attitude, the entities that are the subject-matter of this attitude are also parts of the propositional attitude. (2008, 107)

As we saw in Chapter 1, on Russell's earlier theory of propositions, a proposition actually contains the 'terms' that the words used in the sentence expressing the proposition refer to. That this reflected his adherence to a mode of direct realism, in critical reaction to neo-Hegelianism and under the influence of G. E. Moore (PART), Pincock maintains, 'is such a crucial feature of Russell's conception of judgement that he maintains it even after giving up the dual-relation theory in favour of the multiple-relation theory' (2008, 208). On the MRTJ, that is, the judgement complex actually contains, as parts, those very items which are constituents of the fact complex which, if it exists, make the judgement true (the constituents exist regardless of whether the judgement is true or false). To that extent, the MRTJ bears an important affinity to Russell's earlier *PoM* theory of propositions, despite being characterized by some crucial differences.

The second key restriction, or feature, of the MRTJ according to Pincock is what he calls the principle of bivalence, or (T/F):

(T/F) Each judgement has exactly one of the following two properties: truth, falsity. (2008, 108)

Like (PART), (T/F) was a feature carried over to the MRTJ from Russell's earlier theory of propositions. According to this earlier theory, however, 'truth and falsity are simple properties of the complex things that (Russell) calls propositions' (ibid.). Within the MRTJ by contrast, and as we have seen, truth and falsehood are instead defined in terms of a relation of correspondence which either does or does not obtain between the belief complex and a corresponding complex (or fact).

Finally, according to Pincock, there is (CAT):

(CAT) All entities fall into one metaphysical category. (2008, 110)

Like (PART) and (T/F), the roots of (CAT) 'run quite deep, back at least to *Principles of Mathematics* and what is called the doctrine of the unrestricted variable' (111). In fact, for all intents and purposes, (CAT) *is* the doctrine of unrestricted variation which, as we saw in Section 1.3, played an important role both in Russell's 'ramification' of type-theory as well as in his abandonment of the substitution theory. While Stevens, as we saw in Section 2.5, invokes (CAT) to argue for his OI of Wittgenstein's objection, Pincock would reject this interpretation since he sees (CAT) as compatible with the notion that there are entities of various distinct *kinds* within the one overarching metaphysical *category*. According to Pincock, as we saw in Section 2.8, this explains how WD can be blocked without appeal to the sorts of type distinctions invoked in the SR.

But then, if Wittgenstein is not invoking type-theory in the mid-June letter, what is he actually concerned about? According to Pincock,

> When Wittgenstein writes that 'A judges that a is in the Rel[ation] R to b' must entail 'aRb. V. ¬ aRb', what he is saying is that judgement presupposes that the judgement is either true or false. Given that Russell is not able to define correspondence relations for belief complexes, this objection is conclusive if he retains (T/F) [...] In effect, Wittgenstein convinced Russell that if he was to maintain (T/F), then he must give up (CAT) in favour of a two-category metaphysics of things and facts. It appears that Russell still thought of maintaining (PART) and some kind of multiple-relation theory. But when he saw a way out that would sacrifice (PART), but preserve (T/F), he took it. (2008, 132)

The 'way out' referred to by Pincock was pursued by Russell in his work on belief in the period after his lectures on the *Philosophy of Logical Atomism*. Later in this chapter, and especially in Chapter 3, we will have an opportunity to look at those, and other, later developments in Russell's philosophy in more detail. For now, the important point to note is that, according to Pincock's CI, what Wittgenstein is saying in the mid-June letter is that (PART), (CAT) and (T/F) are incompatible. To preserve (T/F), he must give up one or more of the other two. This, according to Pincock's CI, is reflected again in Wittgenstein's remark from *NL*, quoted in Sections 2.1 and 2.7 earlier, concerning the fact that Russell's theory does not rule out as impossible the judgement that 'this table penholders the book'. Concerning this remark, Pincock writes:

> Rather than read it as involving the direction problem or the unity problem, I suggest that it is simply Wittgenstein's way of insisting on (T/F) and the need to reject (CAT). This sort of nonsensical judgement must be ruled out because that is the only plausible way to guarantee that every judgement is either true or false. Other alternatives run afoul of other principles that Russell is unwilling to give up. (134)

According to Pincock, the centrality of (T/F) to the exclusion of other doctrines such as (CAT) which conflict with it is ultimately reflected in *TLP* and especially in Wittgenstein's 'considered verdict' (ibid.) on the issue contained in *TLP* 5.5422 (quoted earlier in Section 2.7). We will revisit these claims and subject them to closer scrutiny in Section 3.6. There we will introduce and examine several reasons to doubt Pincock's claim that it was CP, and an incompatibility which it exposed between (T/F), (CAT) and (PART), which was brought to Russell's attention by Wittgenstein and which led to Russell's self-described 'paralysis'.

2.11 Landini and Giaretta on Type* Distinctions

At various points in the forgoing discussion, we have encountered, and implicitly considered, the idea that Russell may or may not have availed himself, in elucidating the 1913 version of the MRTJ defended in *TK*, of distinctions of type which differ in nature from *PM*'s type distinctions. For instance, in Section 2.1, we saw that unsymmetrical complexes such as 'A is earlier in γ' are non-permutative because no possible complex could result from interchanging the positions of A and γ, suggesting that A and γ must be of different logical and ontological types. In Section 2.5 dealing with Stevens's OI of Wittgenstein's objection, we saw that according to Stevens, precisely the problem for Russell's MRTJ was that it lacked the sorts of logical and ontological distinctions of type between particulars and universals required to block WD. Finally, in Section 2.8, we saw that according to Pincock, WD could not have been the problem which paralysed Russell, since he could easily block it by appealing to distinctions of *kind* within one general metaphysical *category* of entity. Such distinctions of kind allegedly emerged out of Russell's theory of complexes as developed in *TK* and were not to be thought of as identical with type distinctions of the sort grounded within *PM*'s theory of types. Recall that Pincock, following Landini, saw *PM*'s theory of types as stratifying *propositional functions* into types, not *entities*.

Likely, the inspiration for Pincock's identification of 'kinds' as distinct from 'types' also came from Landini, since Landini (1991, 2007) himself discusses similar sorts of distinctions and even gives them a name, type* distinctions, in order to clearly disambiguate them from *PM*'s type distinctions. Landini first introduces the idea of these alternative, type* distinctions in the context of offering a critique of the 'standard' Griffin/Sommerville reading of Wittgenstein's objection. On Griffin's view, according to Landini:

> Russell supposedly relies on the theory of types of *Principia* so that the subordinate relation is viewed as of a different logical type from that of an individual. This would rule an expression such as 'Mortality is Socrates' meaningless [...] Wittgenstein no doubt demanded that the special status of a relating relation in a complex be represented in the corresponding belief-complex. *Theory of knowledge* does reflect this in maintaining that there is a logical difference between universal and particular [...] But this logical difference, grounded in the theory

of logical form, is not a 'distinction in logical type' in the sense of the logical types set out in *Principia*. The distinction is just that universals have both an individual and a predicable nature, while other entities have only an individual nature. That a concrete particular is not a predicable might be described as a type distinction, but only in a different sense of 'type'. Hence, I do not think the connection to the *Principia* theory of types is correct. An understanding of Wittgenstein's criticism must come from another quarter. (1991, 64)

In Section 2.12 we will examine Landini's alternative understanding of Wittgenstein's objection, alluded to in this quotation, in more detail. At the moment it is important to note that, like Stevens, Landini sees *PM*'s type-theory as impotent to block the sorts of illicit substitutions which characterize WD. (In fact, Stevens's reading was clearly influenced by Landini's on this point.) According to this perspective, insofar as nonsensical beliefs such as that 'this table penholders the book' or that 'mortality is Socrates' are ruled out by distinctions of type between particulars and universals, such type distinctions are not to be identified with *PM*'s type distinctions. These stratify propositional functions not entities into types. Where Landini differs from Stevens on this issue is that while Stevens thought that Russell's MRTJ lacked the resources to make the requisite logical and ontological distinctions required to block WD, Landini sees these distinctions as inherent in Russell's theory of logical form. While the distinctions go back to *PoM* (Landini 1991, 39), they are also clearly available to Russell in the context of *TK* to block WD.

Giaretta (1997, 284) noted that the notion of 'type' developed in *TK* does not appear to be reducible to a distinction between universals and particulars, where the former have a predicable nature that the latter lack. Perhaps to account for this observation, Landini (2007, 57) subsequently expands his conception of type* distinctions to include those between entities which are and are not complex. He also explicitly links type* distinctions to the theory of complexes as well as position in a complex analysis developed and defended by Russell in *TK*. As Landini explains:

In *Theory of Knowledge*, Russell gave a final attempt to solve the narrow direction problem. He introduced what he calls 'position relations'. [...] Russell's account relies upon type* distinctions. Concrete complexes cannot occur as constituents of entities that are not complex, and universals are of a different type* from concrete complexes (facts) and entities that are not complex. Russell's characterization of unsymmetrical and non-permutative complexes depends upon distinctions of type*. But it is important to note that types* are not the types or orders of *Principia*. Russell had done away with the order/types of entities by building the structure of such a theory into *Principia*'s informal nominalistic semantics for predicate variables. The notion of types*, unlike the notion of order/types, was perfectly legitimate to Russell. Indeed, in *Principles* Russell held that the difference between universal and particular is an unanalyzable and primitive logical notion. Universals have both a predicable and an individual nature, and this is essential to the viability of the multiple-relation theory quite independently of the direction problem. The difference in type* is not coded into logical grammar. Universals are values of the individual variables (type o) of *Principia*. (57–58)

Recall that in Section 2.1 we noted that in *TK* Russell sought to resolve ND by deploying position in a complex analysis to both identify and describe non-permutative complexes associated with problematic permutative ones such as that 'A precedes B'. Thus, upon analysis, the judgement ostensibly made true by the fact, if it exists, that 'A precedes B' can actually be seen to correspond to an associated molecular complex in which 'A is earlier in γ and B is later in γ'. Though unsymmetrical, each of the atomic complexes contained within this associated molecular complex are nevertheless heterogeneous and so non-permutative, since no logically possible complex can result from interchanging the positions of their constituents. Thus, according to Landini, Russell proposed to resolve ND by appealing to type* distinctions between complexes such as γ and entities such as A and B which are not complex.

But then what purpose do type* distinctions between universals and particulars serve? According to both Landini (1991, 64) and Giaretta (1997, 285) such distinctions emerge in association with Russell's directive, within position in a complex analysis, to assign relations to a predicative position in the cognitive complex in order to evade WD. As Landini remarks:

> Wittgenstein no doubt demanded that the special status of the relating relation in a complex be represented in the corresponding belief-complex. *Theory of knowledge* does reflect this in maintaining that there is a logical difference between universal and particular. Indeed, Russell says of a complex such as *a-R-b* that 'the position of R, unlike that of the other constituents, *can* be assigned relatively to the form: this is what enables us to speak of it as the relating relation'. (1991, 64, *TK*, 146; emphases in the original)

And as Giaretta explains:

> According to a natural interpretation of what has been called 'a general pretheoretical type principle', a relating relation gets a higher type with respect to its arguments by virtue of its being relating. When a supposed complex is involved in a case of understanding, judgement or belief, no relation can be

taken as relating, considering that the supposed complex might not exist. On the other hand, the putative constituents of the supposed complex – which actually are only constituents of the understanding-, judgement- or belief-, complex – should be brought into relation with the form according to Russell's way of speaking. In particular, a relation has to be assigned the predicative position. (1997, 285)

Once R is assigned to the predicative position in a cognitive complex, according to Giaretta, it may be regarded as what he calls a 'formally relating relation' relative to the logical form contained within the complex and thus 'of a higher type than the types of the other constituents' (ibid.). A 'formally relating relation' is, essentially, the subordinate relation of the judgement complex. If the judgement is true, this relation actually relates the constituents within the complex corresponding to the judgement. As we have seen, however, for reasons outlined in Section 1.4, it cannot actually relate the other constituents of the judgement within the judgement and must therefore, problematically, be seen merely as a term of the judgement, on par with the other constituents of the judgement. This problem may be addressed, according to Russell, by assigning the relation in question to the predicative position in the logical form contained within the cognitive complex, whether it be an understanding, judgement or belief complex. This is the sense in which it is 'formally relating' as opposed to actually relating in the cognitive complex.

As a hypothesis, Giaretta proposes that when Wittgenstein referred to further premises in the mid-June 1913 letter, he meant to point out that it must be explicitly stated what constituents occupy which places in the logical form contained within the complex 'in order to warrant that the supposed complex be a possible one' (1997, 286). However, though 'it is not at all clear that Wittgenstein clearly realized' that such explicit stipulations were required, nevertheless 'in the end, Russell somehow became aware that the further assumptions hinted at or 'inarticulately' expressed by Wittgenstein were really needed' (ibid.).

In Chapter 3 I will argue that Wittgenstein did in fact clearly realize that such stipulations were required and that it was he who made Russell explicitly aware of them. Moreover, Russell's 1913 version of the MRTJ requires recourse to such stipulations precisely because, as Stevens noted, it lacks the resources necessary to block WD by appealing to distinctions of logical or ontological type between universals and particulars. Landini is quite correct to think that both universals and particulars belong to *PM*'s type o. Yet, it is precisely because universals and particulars are on this logical and ontological par that Russell must attempt to block WD by emulating (as opposed to tracking) metaphysical distinctions between them. While universals are theoretically distinct from particulars in that they have both a predicable as well as an individual nature, this predicable nature is inoperative when such universals occur as object terms (i.e. as the subordinate relation) of a cognitive complex. Thus, there are no type* distinctions of a basic or brute metaphysical nature between universals and particulars available in that context to assist Russell to block WD. That is precisely why he must appeal to illicit premises in order to assign constituents to appropriate positions in the logical form contained in the judgement. How exactly these premises are supposed by Wittgenstein to be 'illicit' will be the focus of LI and of Sections 3.1–3.2.

2.12 Landini on Wittgenstein's Critique of the MRTJ

Armed with his theory of complexes and type* distinctions in hand, WD is a 'non-starter' for Russell, according to Landini (2021, 46). The sorts of illicit substitutions, envisioned by Griffin to have posed a serious problem for the version of the MRTJ defended in *TK*, may be unceremoniously swept aside by appealing to a type* distinction between particulars and universals:

> What makes an entity a universal is precisely its capacity to unify a fact, and what makes an entity a particular is precisely its lack of having any such capacity. There is no appeal here to anything like *Principia*'s theory of types. It is simply a matter of acquaintance. Whoever is acquainted with a universal understands its nature. That has to be accepted for Russell's work in *Theory of Knowledge* to get off the ground. (ibid.)

On this view, the judgement that 'Socrates is mortal', for example, is non-permutative for Russell, since no logically possible complex can result from interchanging its constituents. The problem instead arises when attempting to address ostensibly permutative judgements such as that 'A precedes B', and more particularly in association with Russell's attempts to describe the non-permutative complexes which, if they exist, make such judgements true. While this problem bears some resemblance to the CP identified by Pincock (2008), according to Landini Pincock does not go far enough in elucidating the depth of the problem:

> In Landini (1991) I pointed out that the multiple-relation theory was an application of the theory of definite descriptions to define 'truth' as correspondence [...] Pincock (2008) acknowledged this but didn't go far with my idea. Pincock did pick up on what he called the 'correspondence problem' but did not regard it, as I did, as simply the problem of how to form a definite description of a permutative fact. (Landini 2021, 137)

Landini wishes to place great emphasis on the fact that the MRTJ is, first and foremost, a correspondence theory of truth (1991, 37). If we want to fully and properly understand the point and purpose of the MRTJ as well as Wittgenstein's critique of it, we must appreciate how Russell intended to deploy his theory of definite descriptions therein in order to describe the truth-conditions of judgements expressed by what Landini calls 'propositions$_L$':

> The hierarchy of senses of 'truth' and 'falsehood' in *Principia* is applied to what Whitehead and Russell call 'propositions'. It is a hierarchy of orders of propositions which is thereby generated, not a hierarchy of judgment-complexes. Of course, the 'propositions' here are not the objective truths and falsehoods Russell formerly endorsed. They must be declarative sentences or statements capable of truth or falsehood. [Hereafter we shall write 'proposition$_L$' when this sense, as opposed to an objective truth or falsehood, is intended.] (Landini 1991, 42)

When one asserts an atomic proposition$_L$, according to Landini, they express an elementary judgement. The MRTJ defines the foundational senses of truth and falsehood upon which the hierarchy of senses thereof is built in terms of correspondence between such elementary judgements and facts. However, the MRTJ has nothing especially to do with propositions$_L$ occurring within the scope of a propositional attitude verb. Instead the MRTJ is an extension of the theory of incomplete symbols developed in *OD* (1905) 'to contexts in which propositions$_L$ occur as grammatical subjects' (Landini 1991, 45). In such contexts, propositions$_L$ function grammatically as names, but just as there need be no entity corresponding to the name 'Apollo' occurring in the proposition$_L$ 'Apollo is wise', there need be no entity corresponding to 'p' when it occurs in a subordinate clause as in ' "p" is true' or in a truth-functional context such as p É q. Fortunately, any appearance that 'p' need refer to an entity in such contexts, and any logical or philosophical problems associated with that assumption, can be obviated through an analysis which treats 'p' as an incomplete symbol, much as 'The Present King of France' would be so treated by Russell's theory of definite descriptions as developed and applied in *OD*. For an atomic proposition$_L$ Fa, for example, 'first-truth' may be defined as follows (46):

'Fa' is true = df E!(ιp *Bel*{m,a,F} corresponds to p).

The definiens is then as follows by contextual definition (ibid.):

($\exists p$) (q) ((*Bel*{m,a,F} corresponds to q) $\equiv$ ($q = p$)).

According to Landini, this, in essence, is what Russell is doing in chapter V of part II of *TK*. He is deploying the MRTJ to provide truth-conditions for atomic propositions$_L$. Again, the MRTJ has nothing especially to do with propositions$_L$ occurring under the scope of a propositional attitude verbs. Propositional attitudes enter the picture only as part of the process of forming definite descriptions used to define truth-conditions for unasserted, atomic propositions$_L$. As Landini explains:

> I maintain that, in Russell's view, an unasserted proposition$_L$ *is* a disguised definite description and, like all such descriptions, it disappears upon contextual analysis. It is in forming the description that belief-complexes come in. For example [...] the proposition$_L$ '*a* is Red' is true just when there is a unique complex corresponding to the belief-complex $\{m,a,Redness\}$. (45)

Over and above this, however, in chapter V of part II Russell is trying to address unique problems which arise in connection with the attempt to specify such definite descriptions in the case of facts which are, at least ostensibly, 'permutative' (54; Landini 2021, 240–41). Above we saw that Russell's strategy in such cases was to specify non-permutative complexes associated with apparently permutative belief complexes. So, for example, the apparently permutative belief that 'A precedes B' will be made true by the non-permutative complex, if it exists, that 'A is earlier in γ and B is later in γ'.

Wittgenstein objects to this approach neither because it struggles to resolve ND nor, as supposed in Pincock's CI, because it generates CP. Instead, according to Landini, the issue is that it conflicts with Wittgenstein's emerging 'doctrine of showing'. Call this interpretation of Wittgenstein's objection the showing interpretation (SI). As Landini explains,

> The letters that Wittgenstein sent to Russell prior to and during the writing of *Theory of Knowledge* reveal that Wittgenstein is attacking Russell's theory of logical form on the grounds that it is unable to establish that there are non-permutative complexes. In particular, Wittgenstein is espousing what will become the 'Doctrine of showing' of the *Tractatus* [...] Undoubtedly, the famous doctrine of showing was in its infancy when Russell was writing *Theory of Knowledge*. Nonetheless, Wittgenstein's letters show the doctrine unfolding and place it, not the alleged conflict with types at the heart of his attack on the multiple-relation theory. (1991, 64–65)

The first of the letters offered by Landini in support of SI is the following one written by Wittgenstein to Russell in August 2012:

Now as to 'p v q', etc.: I have thought that possibility – namely, that all our troubles could be overcome by assuming different sorts of Relations to signs of things – over and over again! For the last 8 weeks!!! But I have come to the conclusion that this assumption does *not* help us a bit. In fact if you work out ANY such theory – I believe you will see that *it does not even touch our problem*. (*CL*, 19; quoted in Landini 1991, 65; emphases in the original)

Landini sees Wittgenstein as concerned here with the problem of unasserted propositions$_L$ occurring within molecular and general propositions. The proposal considered here by Wittgenstein, Landini argues, is one from *PM* according to which different relations of correspondence are involved depending upon whether a proposition$_L$ is atomic, molecular or quantified. In particular, the truth-conditions of a proposition$_L$ differ for these cases in the following way: 'An atomic proposition$_L$ points to a single complex, while a molecular or generalized proposition$_L$ points to many' (Landini 1991, 65). While Landini regards Wittgenstein as rejecting this proposal here, he nevertheless sees it as evidence that he and Russell were engaged in a shared programme of logical analysis, concerned with eliminating logical constants. This programme involved addressing problems surrounding the status of logical connectives and bound variables, which Landini sees Wittgenstein as alluding to in this August 1912 letter. According to Landini's interpretation, Wittgenstein's 'fundamental idea' (*TLP* 4.0312) as espoused in the *Tractatus*, the idea that there are no logical constants, was inherited by Wittgenstein from Russell.

A somewhat later letter (also, however, dating from summer 1912) clarifies Wittgenstein's point further. In it, according to Landini, Wittgenstein claims that the problems discussed earlier for unasserted propositions$_L$ occurring within molecular and quantified propositions, can be resolved by focusing on atomic propositions$_L$ and on the role played by the copula therein. Wittgenstein writes:

I believe that our problems can be traced down to the *atomic* prop[osition]s. This you will see if you try to explain precisely in what way the Copula in such a prop[osition] has meaning. I cannot explain it and I think that as soon as an exact answer to this question is given the problem of 'v' and of the app[aren't] var[iable] will be brought *very* near their solution if not solved. I therefore now think about 'Socrates is human'. (Good old Socrates!) (*CL*, 21; quoted in Landini 1991, 65; emphases in the original)

Landini sees this letter as anticipating the view, espoused in Wittgenstein's *Tractatus*, that any proposition$_L$ whatsoever, including all molecular and quantified propositions$_L$, are truth functions of elementary propositions. With respect to the more immediate historical and philosophical context, however, in addition to pointing back to concerns about unasserted propositions$_L$ addressed in the August letter quoted earlier, it also points forward to a highly significant January 1913 letter from which Landini quotes the following excerpt:

> I have changed my mind on 'atomic' complexes: I now think that Qualities, Relations (like Love), etc. are all copulae! [...] I want a theory of types to tell me that 'Mortality is Socrates' is nonsensical, because if I treat 'Mortality' as a proper name (as I did) there is nothing to prevent me to make the substitution the wrong way around. (*CL*, 25–26, quoted in Landini 1991, 66)

Several commentators, myself included, have seen Wittgenstein as concerned with WD here and as proposing to block the sorts of illicit substitutions responsible for WD by deploying a Fregean strategy according to which qualities and relations are to be construed as part of the copulae of propositions, as opposed to objects over which variables of quantification might range. Landini (1991, 66) instead sees Wittgenstein as making a point about logical form. Specifically, the point is that differences of logical form must be part of logical structure and that this must be *shown* in logical grammar.

According to Landini's SI, this same concern with the doctrine of showing then manifests roughly six months later in Wittgenstein's critique of the version of the MRTJ defended in *TK*. While Russell held, as we have seen, that concerns about the direction or 'sense' of a permutative judgement can be resolved by describing associated, non-permutative complexes to serve as the truth makers of such judgements,

> Wittgenstein disagreed. He held that no complex can be named or described. *All* meaningful propositions 'show' sense. This applies to propositions$_L$ which correspond to Russell's so called 'non-permutative' complexes as well. In every case, the proposition$_L$ is itself a 'picture' of the conditions of its truth and falsehood. (Landini 1991, 66)

This, in essence, is the point Wittgenstein is making in the notorious mid-June letter in which he claims to express his objection to Russell's MRTJ 'exactly'. Propositions intrinsically 'picture' or 'show' their truth-conditions without resort to any further premises (65). According to Landini's SI, the reference to 'no further premises' in the mid-June letter is simply a roundabout way of asserting the demands of the doctrine of showing. This explains why, according to Landini (2021, 84–85), when Wittgenstein reiterates his objection to Russell's MRTJ in *TLP* 5.5422, he says that

> the correct explanation of the form of the proposition 'A makes the judgement that p', must *show* that it is impossible for a judgement to be a piece of nonsense. (Russell's theory does not satisfy this requirement.) (emphasis added)

Wittgenstein's use of the word 'show' in this passage is, Landini insists, highly significant (2020, 225). It powerfully demonstrates that the doctrine of showing is both motivating Wittgenstein's critique of the MRTJ, as well as, given the parallels between this remark and the mid-June letter, already present in Wittgenstein's philosophy by June 1913.

Landini's SI makes several provocative and interesting points worth following up, which we will do in subsequent chapters. In Chapter 3, in particular, we will take the opportunity to look more critically at some of the challenges SI faces, most obviously those having to do with the fact that it assigns such incredibly early dates to Wittgenstein's adoption of both the picture theory and the doctrine of showing. As we shall see, a better explanation of the parallels between the mid-June letter and *TLP* is that the concerns embodied in the former foreshadow important doctrines espoused in the latter.

2.13 Lebens on the 'Representation Concern' and the Stoutian Evolution of the MRTJ

In Section 1.4 we saw that in the lead up to June 1913 the MRTJ evolved through three distinct phases: that of the 1910 version defended in 'On the Nature of Truth and Falsehood', the 1912 version defended in *PP* and the 1913 version defended in *TK*. While other scholars whose views have been canvassed thus far in this chapter see this evolution as driven by Russell's progressive attempts to resolve concerns surrounding ND, WD and UP, Lebens instead sees Russell as motivated by what he calls the 'representation-concern'. This concern, put repeatedly to Russell by his 'old philosophy teacher' G. F. Stout over the historical period in question, presses Russell to explain how the MRTJ can generate the *appearance* of unity amongst the object constituents of the judgement, without actually uniting them into an objective proposition, and while also distinguishing them from a mere list (Lebens 2017, 120). This problem is importantly distinct from the 'quasi-mereological puzzle of sticking things together' (ibid.) which, Lebens insists, should not really bother defenders of the MRTJ, at all. As Lebens explains:

> There are plenty of ways to unify a, R, and b, without thereby creating the truth-making fact that *a* is *R*-related to *b*. The real problem, once you've accounted for the unity of the proposition, is to explain why such a complex unity has the curious ability to represent things. Or put another way, the real problem is to explain how the constituents of the proposition stick together in such a way as to become representational. We called this the representation-concern. (ibid.)

In the 1910 version of the theory, according to Lebens, Russell addressed this representation-concern by appealing to the sense or direction of the subordinate relation. By allowing the subordinate relation to enter into a judgement *alongside of* a sense or direction, Lebens insists, Russell thought it would appear *as if* it were relating the other object terms of the judgement, without *actually* relating them. This would resolve the representation concern by generating something to serve as the propositional content of a judgement, which was not an objective proposition. It is the attempt to resolve the representation-concern in this manner which Russell has in mind when he says of the subordinate relation that it 'must not be abstractly before the mind, but must be before it *as* proceeding from A to B' (1910/67, 158; quoted in Lebens 2017, 122).

While Candlish (2007, 76), Griffin and others, by contrast, characterize Russell as making an appeal to the sense or direction of the subordinate relation in order to address ND, Lebens sees this reading of Russell as uncharitable. As Dorothy Wrinch (1919) pointed out, ND can instead be resolved, rather simply, by noting the non-symmetric nature of the judging relation. Lebens thinks it is implausible that Russell, a pioneer in the study of relations, would have been moved by such a trivial objection (2017, 122). Recall that each of Hanks, Pincock and Landini argued something similar about WD. WD cannot be the objection which 'paralysed' Russell, since he could resolve it easily either by appealing to his theory of types (Hanks) or his theory of complexes (Pincock, Landini).

According to Lebens, Russell's contemporary G. F. Stout was, by contrast, a much more astute reader and discerning critic of the 1910 version of the MRTJ. In his own 1910–11 paper on 'The Object of Thought and Real Being', Stout reports on a correspondence between himself and Russell in which he raised concerns about the status of the subordinate relation. In it, he pressed Russell to clarify the nature of his appeal to its 'sense' or direction. Can relational direction really exist *alongside of* a relation, or can it only be a characteristic of relations which *actually relate*? If the former, is 'direction' yet another, distinct constituent of the judgement which must now somehow be accounted for? And if the latter, how can the subordinate relation have direction or sense given that it is not actually relating anything within the judgement? Stout reports Russell responding to his concerns as follows:

> Judging alone may arrange the terms in the order Mind, A, r, B, as opposed to Mind, B, r, A. This has the same effect as if r had a sense in the judgment, and gives all that one wants without being obnoxious to your objections. (1910–11, 203)

The revision mentioned here is, as we have seen, precisely the one which Russell undertook in the context of developing the 1912 version of the MRTJ defended in *PP*. According to Lebens, while this revision 'saves' Russell from ND, it gives 'renewed vigour to the representation-concern, which now becomes *Stout's* over-riding concern' (2017, 123; emphasis in the original).

In a later (1914–15) paper the explicit topic of which is 'Mr. Russell's Theory of Judgement', therefore, Stout then addresses this reply and revision by posing what Lebens calls a 'trilemma' for the 1912 version of the MRTJ. The trilemma challenges Russell to more precisely specify and thus disambiguate between several possible interpretations of the nature of the unity apprehended by the judging subject in the act of judgement. In other words, according to this (1912) version of the theory, what precisely is the unified propositional content which, if true, corresponds to a fact? Stout offers three possible specifications, none of which he supposes Russell will find satisfactory. According to the first specification, the judgement complex itself is the unity apprehended by the subject. Since it implies that 'whenever we believe, we must at the same time be aware of the state or process of believing' (Stout 1914–15, 343), this disambiguation, Stout insists, is 'plainly absurd' (Lebens 2017, 123). According to the second specification, alternatively, the judging relation *imposes* a sense upon the subordinate relation which it otherwise would not have. In this case, allegedly, the order imposed by the judging relation is supposed to have precisely the same effect as would be the case *if* the direction of the subordinate relation entered into the judgement, without it being the case that the subordinate relation actually has sense or direction. This, however, merely reproduces the original iteration of the representation-concern which showed up in the context of the 1910 version of the MRTJ: 'a relation can only have a sense whilst *relating*' (Lebens 2017, 123; emphasis in the original). A third and final option which, according to Lebens, Stout leaves unstated,

> is to accept that the MRTJ has no response to the representation-concern; we apprehend no apparent unity when we judge. There is no single thing that we judge, when we judge. On Russell's deficient theory of judgement, propositions are no different to lists, since we have no account as to why propositions, rather than lists, are able to represent. I contend that this was Stout's real concern. (124)

Plainly, this third approach is not a live option for Russell. Over and above the comparatively trivial problems of direction, Russell must, according to Lebens, provide some more plausible account of how it is that the MRTJ generates a unified propositional content with the capacity to represent. Lebens claims that, independently of Stout, Russell recognized that the 1912 version of the MRTJ lacked the resources to resolve this representation-concern and so revised the MRTJ accordingly in 1913 to address it. Within the 1913 version of the MRTJ defended in *TK*, Russell purports to resolve Stout's representation-concern through his introduction of logical forms, which, Lebens insists, are deployed so as to create the *appearance* that the objects-terms of a judgement are united or synthesized within a proposition content, without *actually* so uniting them (2017, 132; *TK*, 116). More so than any criticisms of Wittgenstein's, it was these concerns of Stout's about representation which, according to Lebens, drove the evolution of the MRTJ from the 1910 to the 1913 version.

2.14 Lebens on the Demise of the MRTJ

Over and above providing an evolutionary history of the MRTJ, however, Lebens's principal objective is to defend it. As a defender of the MRTJ, Lebens is committed to the notion that neither Stout's representation-concern nor any of the other problems for the MRTJ we have canvassed in this chapter, whether it be ND, WD, UP or CP, are ultimately fatal to the prospects of the MRTJ to provide a viable theory of propositional content (though it may require revisions in response of some of them). But then, if the MRTJ is a viable theory, why did Russell abandon it in the face of Wittgenstein's criticisms? According to Lebens, he did not. Following MacBride (2013), Lebens suggests that

> Russell was nowhere near as moved by Wittgenstein's 1913 critique as has often been portrayed. After all, he continued to subscribe to the MRTJ until 1919. It's true that the 1913 manuscripts sputter out when Russell was supposed to turn his attention to molecular propositions, but this might not have had all that much to do with Wittgenstein. It may have been down to Russell's realization that his 1912 denial that relations relate in a direction (see §5.1) was incompatible with the MRTJ's extending to account for molecular propositions (as we saw in §2.6). As soon as he resumed his belief in relations having directions, he was able to and did continue on in his allegiance to the MRTJ. (2017, 150; cf. MacBride 2013, 209)

But then what of Russell's correspondence with both Morrell and Wittgenstein, which would seem to suggest that he was 'paralysed' by Wittgenstein's objections and felt 'ready for suicide' in the face of them? Neither Lebens, nor MacBride, are especially impressed by this evidence. According to MacBride, for instance:

> We should resist the temptation to think about Russell's dispute with Wittgenstein in the terms these letters dictate. They were written by one human being to another for a particular purpose – in this letter to excuse Russell's resort to 'casual philandery' because of Wittgenstein's criticism and Ottoline being too 'occupied' with her doctor in Lausanne to provide 'consolation'. It should hardly be controversial that Russell's more impersonal statements thought out for a philosophical audience ought to be taken as more revealing on an intellectual score. The fact that Russell, and no doubt Wittgenstein too, inwardly chose to play out certain roles in their personal relationship with one another does not constrain – condemn – us to interpret their philosophical dispute about judgement as an outward manifestation of their inner lives. (2013, 207)

When MacBride refers to 'this letter' here, he is indicating the 1916 letter to Morrell, quoted earlier in Section 1.6, in which Russell describes Wittgenstein's criticisms as an event of 'first rate importance in my life'. MacBride thinks we should treat this assertion and others like it with extreme caution, given its personal as opposed to philosophical motivations. Russell's *philosophical* writings, by contrast, show him defending the MRTJ as late as 1918, in his lectures on *The Philosophy of Logical Atomism*. Echoing these sentiments, Lebens explains:

> Our only account of Russell's immediate reaction to his meetings with Wittgenstein are gleaned from letters to his lover, Ottoline Morrell. At this stage in their relationship, Russell had a clear agenda: he wanted to evoke sympathy from Ottoline, for he knew that he was less and less an object of her amorous desire [...] Russell had a strong motive to engage in hyperbole [...] Furthermore, even if we take the letters to Ottoline seriously, and even if we accept that Wittgenstein's criticisms devastated Russell, we needn't believe that Russell's changing reaction was based purely on the *philosophical* give and take between him and Wittgenstein. Wittgenstein had a certain hypnotic hold on many of his associates. Russell was no exception. (2017, 150; emphasis in the original)

Because it is tainted by the effects of interpersonal and emotional factors, Russell's correspondence with Morrell offers dubious support for the claim that it was Wittgenstein's criticisms which persuaded Russell, logically and philosophically, to abandon the MRTJ and the 1913 *TK* manuscript. Perhaps, in any case, Wittgenstein's influence was largely psychological, not logical or philosophical. After all, in the 21 May letter to Morrell, Russell says that he could 'feel in his bones' that Wittgenstein was right, despite lacking any clear philosophical understanding of what Wittgenstein's criticism was.

When Russell did eventually abandon the MRTJ several years later, he is motivated not by Wittgensteinian concerns about nonsense judgements or extraneous premises but by a waning enthusiasm for direct realism and by Humean skepticism about the subject:

> As his realism became less direct, the MRTJ became less important to him. However, Russell tells us that he gave up the MRTJ, primarily, because he no longer believes that there is a particular thing called the self. He had to give up the MRTJ for he had lost his belief in the mental subjects of beliefs. His rejection of the subject as a particular entity has to do with his increasingly Humean tendencies, and the sense-data epistemology that accompanies it [...] By 1919, the MRTJ was dead – a victim of Russell's Humean rejection of the self; a rejection that he and Wittgenstein came to independently. (Lebens 2017, 155–56; cf. Russell 1919, 305–6)

Following Griffin (1985, 243–44), Lebens sees the direct realism characteristic of the MRTJ as being in tension with Russell's emerging, sense-data epistemology. As sense-data increasingly took centre stage in Russell's epistemology, the MRTJ receded into the background. Finally, by 1919, Russell had drawn the ultimate, Humean consequence of his sense data epistemology, the rejection of the subject, and this required him to reject mental subjects of belief and thus the MRTJ along with it.

Call MacBride and Lebens's interpretation of Wittgenstein's the irrelevance interpretation (IRI). According to IRI, Wittgenstein's objection, whatever it was, had only a psychological or emotional impact on Russell but held no genuinely philosophical or logical import. In Chapter 3, we will critically assess IRI along with each of the other interpretations described in this chapter. Of course, as we have seen, many of the commentators surveyed in Chapter 2 do recognize an important link between Wittgenstein's criticisms of the MRTJ, the demise of the MRTJ and Russell's self-reported 'paralysis'. These links will be explored as well. Before considering each of the alternative viewpoints canvassed in Chapter 2, however, in Chapter 3 I will first present my own, logical interpretation (LI) of Wittgenstein's objection and of its impact on Russell, fleshing out the details as I move on to critically consider the alternative viewpoints. Since, however, readers are likely impatient by now to hear what I have to say on these topics, I shall proceed to do so now, without further ado.

Chapter 3
RUSSELL'S PARALYSIS

3.1 The Logical Interpretation

In Chapter 2, we explicated the scholarly controversy surrounding Wittgenstein's critique of the MRTJ by surveying a selection of the most prominent and influential interpretations thereof, including those of Griffin and Sommerville, Stevens, Hanks, Pincock, Landini and Lebens. In this section, I will start out by developing my own reading of Wittgenstein's critique of the MRTJ, before moving on, in subsequent sections, to defend it in light of, and critically respond to, each of the alternative readings canvassed in Chapter 2. Responding to each of the alternatives, in turn, will also enable me to flesh out further the integral details of my reading both of Wittgenstein's objections and, ultimately, of Russell's paralysis. While many of these alternative interpretations enjoy significant merits, they also exhibit crucial flaws and inadequacies, and thus none of them provides a complete or satisfactory account of Wittgenstein's critique. By building on what is correct in these interpretations as well as identifying and rejecting their mistakes, I thus aim to articulate and defend my own interpretation of Wittgenstein's critique, which I call the logical interpretation (LI).

According to LI, Wittgenstein's critique of Russell's work in the period May–June 1913 comes in three thematically and chronologically distinctive waves (or phases). Only the second and third of these waves directly concern the MRTJ. Considering the first wave of criticism, however, will provide integral background philosophical context in terms of which to frame and understand both the nature and content of Wittgenstein's subsequent criticisms, as well as how it is he came to be interested in, and stimulated to offer criticisms of, the MRTJ in the first place, at this time in particular.

The first wave of Wittgenstein's criticisms is more broadly philosophical in nature and can be dated to on or shortly before 14 May 1913. As Blackwell and Eames note, the first reference to Wittgenstein's criticisms occurs in a 14 May letter from Russell to Ottoline Morrell, in which Russell explains that Wittgenstein 'was shocked to hear I am writing on theory of knowledge – he thinks it will be like the shilling book, which he hates' (Blackwell and Eames 1992, xix; Russell to Morrell #775). The 'shilling book' referred to here is Russell's 1912 *Problems of Philosophy*. For insight into what Wittgenstein disliked about *PP*, we can look, among other places, to a letter he wrote to Russell in summer 1912, which he concludes with the remark that 'there is nothing more wonderful than the *true* problems of Philosophy' (*CL*, 18; emphasis in the original). In significant measure, Wittgenstein disliked Russell's *PP* because, though ostensibly setting out both to convey and adjudicate the fundamental problems of philosophy, it strayed too far from what he regarded as the authentic core of philosophy, logic, in its pursuit of more peripheral epistemological and metaphysical questions. As he explains in *NL*: 'Philosophy consists of logic and metaphysics: logic is its basis. Epistemology is the philosophy of psychology' (106). Wittgenstein then reiterates this sentiment in *TLP* when he writes that the 'theory of knowledge is the philosophy of psychology' (*TLP* 4.1121). If epistemology is simply the philosophy of psychology, and logic is the basis or core of philosophy, it would stand to reason that according to Wittgenstein, epistemological problems would be resolved by logic, as opposed to logical problems being solved by appeal to epistemology. This is certainly consonant with his method as applied in *TLP*, which, essentially, is to deploy logical analysis so as to provide a final and definitive solution (*TLP* 4) to the problems of philosophy in sub-disciplines as diverse as epistemology, ethics and the foundations of mathematics.

That Wittgenstein may have had some reason to believe that Russell shared his views regarding the relative importance and centrality of logic versus epistemology and metaphysics is reflected in Russell's remark to Ottoline Morrell, in the context of a 1916 letter we looked at in Chapter 1, that 'I *had* to produce lectures for America, but I took a metaphysical subject although I was and am convinced that all fundamental work in philosophy is logical' (*ABR*, 282; emphasis in the original). Notice the correspondence between Wittgenstein's emphasis on the '*true*' problems of philosophy and Russell's stress upon the fact that he reluctantly '*had*' to produce lectures for America which did not directly deal with these logical problems. Both remarks tend to support the notion of a shared perception that logic is where the real 'action' in philosophy is at.

If Wittgenstein believed that the true problems of philosophy were logical, and that Russell's new book *TK* would be like *PP* in having an epistemological and metaphysical rather than a logical focus, it is natural to suppose that he was stimulated, on hearing that Russell would be writing such a book, to examine and reflect upon those parts of *PP* which deal most directly with what he regarded as the core, logical problems of philosophy, in anticipation of offering a critique, in relation to those problems, of Russell's new work on theory of knowledge. Likely, he hoped to convince Russell that, by his own lights, it was a mistake to attempt to tackle the fundamental, logical, problems of philosophy by examining them through the lens of epistemology. Moreover, these central logical problems must take priority, before any meaningful progress could be made on the more peripheral, epistemological and metaphysical questions. Concerns of this nature led Wittgenstein to hone in on the version of the MRTJ defended in chapter XII of *PP* as Russell's most recent, epistemologically informed attempt to grapple with concerns about atomic propositional content, concerns which Wittgenstein had himself been strenuously reflecting upon over the past several months to a year. When Russell told him about the project, he (i.e. Russell) might also have mentioned that it would involve or defend a version of the MRTJ. Doubtless, Wittgenstein intended to show Russell that he was mistaking the suburbs for the city; *PP* was on the wrong track and, to the extent that it also attempted to apply epistemological methods to the core problems of logic, and/or involved trying to resolve epistemological problems without first clarifying their inner logic, his new book must be off track as well.

In a letter dated 21 May, we thus find Russell reporting to Morrell, as we saw in Chapter 1, that Wittgenstein had come to him the previous day with a refutation of a theory of judgement which he 'used to hold'. This incident represents the second of the three waves of Wittgenstein's critique, which concerns the 1912 version of the MRTJ, and more specifically its inability to adequately account for the unity and ordering of the judgements' constituents. We saw that Stout had already raised similar concerns to Russell regarding the 1910 version of the theory and that Russell had attempted to circumvent those concerns by appealing to the judging relation itself to unify and order the constituents of the judgement. As framed by Stout, these concerns centred upon the nature of the 'sense' or 'direction' characteristic of the subordinate verb. Direction, he maintained, seems to be something a relation can only have in so far as it is actually relating. But the whole point of the MRTJ was to generate a propositional content without the subordinate relation actually relating the other object terms of the judgement into a unified and structured Russellian proposition.

At this point, Wittgenstein's concerns seem to be aligned with Stout's, though also to go beyond them in explicitly identifying WD over and above ND. This, as we saw, is reflected in how Wittgenstein frames his objection in *NL* when he says that 'every right theory of judgement must make it impossible for me to judge that this table penholders the book. Russell's theory does not satisfy this requirement' (*NL*, 103). Here, clearly, Wittgenstein means to highlight the fact that the object referred to by a substantive, 'penholder', cannot intelligibly be thought to occupy the position where a relation, such as that denoted by the prepositional verb 'is on', should go. This explains why, when he reiterates this same basic objection to Russell's MRTJ in *TLP*, he writes that the 'correct explanation of the form of the proposition, "A makes the judgement p", must show that it is impossible for a judgement to be a piece of nonsense. (Russell's theory does not satisfy this requirement.)' (*TLP* 5.5422). According to Wittgenstein, that is, the 1912 version of the MRTJ fails to rule out nonsense in so far as nothing about it prevents substituting the term corresponding to a substantive into the position where a relation corresponding to a verb should go. On the MRTJ, again, judging is a multiple relation between a judging subject and various discrete, disconnected and ontologically commensurate judgement constituents (i.e. object terms). There are no different 'types' of things on the MRTJ. Types and orders stratify propositional functions, not entities. So then why can't A judge that (a, b, c) instead of that (a, R, b)?

Though perhaps more significant than the others in this context in the sense that WD appears to have originated with Wittgenstein, WD is nevertheless only one of at least three interrelated concerns that Wittgenstein likely brought to Russell's attention on 20 May. That Wittgenstein also means to highlight ND is reflected in the fact that the garbled example from *NL* involves two problematic substitutions, not just one. The garbled judgement that 'this table penholders the book' is supposed to result from two problematic substitutions performed on the original, perfectly intelligible and well-ordered judgement that 'the book is on this table', one substitution each corresponding to WD and ND, respectively. If Wittgenstein wished to highlight WD only, then presumably a more straightforward example would be 'The book penholders this table'.

That Wittgenstein also sees both ND and WD as interconnected with the MRTJ's struggles to provide a unified propositional content is reflected in his remark in *NL* that

> when we say that A judges that etc., then we have to mention a whole proposition which A judges. It will not do either to mention only its constituents, or its constituents and form, but not in the proper order. This shows that a proposition itself must occur in the statement that it is judged; however, for instance, 'not-p' may be explained, the question what is negated must have a meaning. (*NL*, 94)

Here Wittgenstein develops an illuminating analogy between judgement and negation. The suggestion seems to be that like negation, judgement is something that operates only upon a unified propositional content. Moreover, to know what is being judged or negated the content must be precisely specified. Hence, to specify what precise propositional content is being judged, it will not do to simply mention its constituents and form. The order of those constituents must also be precisified. (Notably, Wittgenstein seems to suggest here that the precisification in question can only occur within the context of the 'proposition itself', i.e., it cannot be accomplished simply by 'mentioning' forms, constituents and positions.) Specifying the proper order of a judgement's constituents is precisely the challenge posed by both WD and ND, albeit in somewhat different ways.

From Wittgenstein's perspective, then, these three challenges for Russell's 1912 MRTJ are all interrelated. Appealing to the judging relation to resolve them is inadequate, since, in the first place, the judging relation can only apply to something which already embodies a unified and properly ordered propositional content. As we have seen, however, Russell then went on to revise the MRTJ in the 1913 *TK* manuscript to respond to these sorts of challenges. When he says in the 21 May letter to Morrell that Wittgenstein objected to a theory of judgement that he 'used to hold', this likely reflects the fact that, even prior to receiving the second wave of Wittgenstein's criticisms, he already knew he would have to make some revisions to his theory of judgement. We know, for instance, that he had been in correspondence with Stout regarding these matters as well and likely wished to strengthen the MRTJ to deal with Stout's and any other foreseeable criticisms. When he goes on in the 20 May letter to Morrell to explain that 'the correction required is not very serious' and that he will have to make up his mind 'within a week as I shall soon reach judgement', this likely reflects his having already given significant thought to, and developed some concrete ideas about, how to revise the MRTJ to address these criticisms. Yet he has not at this point settled on a considered position and recognizes some time pressure to do so relatively soon. Given that logical forms were both the focus of his fall 1912 manuscript entitled 'What is Logic?', and that they also ultimately played an integral role in the 1913 version of the MRTJ which sought to address each of Stout and Wittgenstein's concerns, it is likely that, at this point, Russell had already anticipated introducing logical forms into the 1913 version of the MRTJ but was undecided as to precisely how to do so. When he speaks of making a 'not very serious' correction to the MRTJ, he likely has in mind revising his views on, and coming to a considered position about, the precise role that logical forms would come to play.

This brings us to the third wave of Wittgenstein's criticisms, which concern Russell's attempts to deploy logical forms of corresponding complexes as constituents of judgement complexes, to resolve challenges concerning the proper ordering of the object terms of a judgement into a unified propositional content. According to LI, portions of *TK* addressing the nature of logical forms, and specifying how precisely they would be deployed so as to provide unity and ordering to judged propositional contents (chapter IX of part I and chapter I of part II), are among the 'crucial parts' of the manuscript which Russell showed to Wittgenstein during their tense meeting on 26 May. When, as reported by Russell in the letter to Morrell in the letter dated 27 May, Wittgenstein told him at that meeting 'that he had tried my view and knew it wouldn't work', Wittgenstein was likely referring to a view similar to, or perhaps even identical with, at least one of two interrelated views he describes as follows, in a January 1913 letter to Russell:

> I have changed my views on 'atomic' complexes: I now think that Qualities, Relations (like Love), etc. are all copulae! That means I for instance analyse a subject-predicate prop[osition], say 'Socrates is Human' into 'Socrates' and 'Something is human' (which I think is not complex). The reason for this is a very fundamental one: I think there cannot be different Types of things! In other words, whatever can be symbolized by a simple proper name must belong to one type. And further: every theory of types must be rendered superfluous by a proper theory of symbolism: For instance if I analyse the prop[osition] Socrates is mortal into Socrates, Mortality and $(\exists x, y)\ \varepsilon_1(x, y)$ I want a theory of types to tell me that 'Mortality is Socrates' is nonsensical, because if I treat 'Mortality' as a proper name (as I did) there is nothing to prevent me from making the substitutions the wrong way round. *But* if I analyse [it] (as I do now) into Socrates and $(\exists x)$ x is mortal or more generally into x and $(\exists x)\varphi x$ it becomes impossible to substitute the wrong way round, because the two symbols are now of a different *kind* themselves. (*CL*, 24–25; emphases in the original)

Here, clearly, Wittgenstein is proposing to obviate WD by introducing logical forms to copulate complexes. More specifically, he proposes to rule out illicit substitutions of the sort characteristic of 'Mortality is Socrates' and 'The book penholders this table' by incorporating qualities and relations into logical forms, which in turn serve as the copulae of atomic complexes. Wittgenstein's proposed logical forms are in fact quite similar to those deployed by Russell in *TK*, except for one crucial theoretical revision designed to block WD. For Russell, relations and qualities are not to be contained within the logical forms of judgements. Instead, they must be assigned to appropriate positions in the logical form as a significance constraint on sense. Elsewhere, I described Russell's proposal and strategy here as follows:

> The basic idea seems to have been that judgement would be conceived as a cognitive complex in which a subject was multiply related to various distinct items, one of which would be a logical form. The logical form would contain one or more variables or argument places. Undertaking a judgement would involve assigning objects to each of these argument places, which would in turn result in a determinate and unified cognitive complex with no empty positions (or free

variables). Different judgements would result depending upon what positions in the form were occupied by which objects. Certain combinations of constituents would be excluded in so far as they involved assigning arguments to illegitimate positions. (Connelly 2014, 7)

It is likely that when Wittgenstein says that he had tried Russell's view and 'knew it wouldn't work', he is referring to the first view discussed in his January letter to Russell, one in which logical forms are used to copulate complexes but where the logical forms do not themselves contain the relevant qualities and relations. (One notable distinction would be that Wittgenstein's is a view about atomic complexes while Russell's is a view about judgement complexes; Wittgenstein seems not to see this as a crucial distinction in this context.) Such a view, Wittgenstein recognizes, is vulnerable to WD and associated illicit substitutions such as 'Mortality is Socrates' and the like.

When in the letter to Morrell Russell insists that Wittgenstein did not 'realize the difficulties' involved in dismissing his view as 'all wrong', he is likely referring to his own long-standing concerns, related to his rejection of neo-Hegelianism in 1898, regarding the need to characterize relations as both external and fully real. We saw that in the context of *PoM* specifically and in that of his logicist programme more generally, Russell regarded fully real and external relations as indispensable to the analysis of arithmetical and geometrical order. Wittgenstein's correspondence with Russell over the period of December 1912–January 1913 shows, by contrast, that after 'a long discussion with Frege about our Theory of Symbolism' (*CL*, 22) in December, Wittgenstein subsequently became willing, by January, to accept the Fregean view that relations and qualities may not in fact be fully real, discrete and independent objects. They might instead better be construed as contained within the copulae of complexes. The idea, developed in Wittgenstein's January letter, that qualities like 'mortality' and 'humanity' are no longer to be symbolized by proper names is highly reminiscent of Frege's (1892/1985) robust distinction between concepts and objects, where the former are regarded as 'incomplete' or 'unsaturated' abstractions from propositional contents (which Frege called 'conceptual contents' (1879/1972) or 'thoughts' (1918/1977)), and only the latter can be meaningfully referred to by a proper name. For Frege, unless we appeal to a distinction between concepts and objects, where the former are 'unsaturated' or 'incomplete' and only the latter are fully real and independent, we will not be able to account for the unity of 'conceptual contents' or 'thoughts'. Unsaturated or incomplete concepts served as the metaphorical 'glue' in virtue of which thoughts or conceptual contents hold together. Objects by contrast are what are held together, or copulated, by concepts, within conceptual (i.e. propositional) contents. Russell, as we have seen, held that concepts (i.e. universals (relations or properties)) could both be objects and also serve to copulate, that is, unify, cognitive and other complexes. By January 1913, Wittgenstein seems to have rejected Russell's externalism and robust realism about concepts (i.e. universals) in favour of a view more like Frege's.

In any case, though at this point Russell suspected and 'felt in his bones' that Wittgenstein must be right, he seems not to have clearly understood Wittgenstein's objection, partly because the latter was 'very inarticulate' in expressing it. This brings us to the mid-June letter, in which Wittgenstein now claims to be able to express his objection 'exactly'. According to LI, Wittgenstein's exactly expressed objection contained in the mid-June letter specifically targets the 1913 version of the MRTJ developed in *TK*. More precisely, it targets Russell's attempt therein to resolve both WD and ND by assigning constituents to their proper positions within the logical form of a judgement. This strategy, according to Wittgenstein, runs afoul of certain basic intuitions concerning logical inference. Namely, if aRb is a significant and intelligible propositional content and thus not nonsense, then aRb v ~ aRb (or, indeed, any tautology) must follow from it automatically as it were (i.e. directly), without depending upon any supplemental premises for support. On the other hand, if aRb is nonsense, then nothing follows from it, with or without the support of other premises. So, Wittgenstein's point is that Russell's attempts to resolve ND and WD by placing significance constraints upon the admissible constituents of judgments is either useless or superfluous.

Wittgenstein's concerns about such significance constraints are in an important sense analogous to the sorts of worries that Russell expresses, in the context of developing the 1913 version of the MRTJ, about relying on the 'sense' of the relation of understanding to put the constituents of a proposition into the right order. The relation of understanding is either impotent to bring about the unity of a proposition in case its constituents are not yet united or it is superfluous in the case that they already are so united. Similarly, the judgement that aRb either already has sense independently of any significance constraints on its admissible constituents, and in that case aRb v ~ aRb follows from it directly and immediately, or it is nonsense, in which case nothing will follow from it regardless of any supplemental constraints or premises.

3.2 Revising the Standard Reading

As developed in Section 3.1, LI obviously bears a significant family resemblance to Griffin and Sommerville's standard reading (SR) outlined earlier in Section 2.2. Both place emphasis on the idea that the 'premiss' alluded to in Wittgenstein's mid-June letter refers to a significance constraint on judgements.

However, while according to SR this significance constraint is type-theoretic in nature, and modelled on *13.3 of *PM*, according to LI there is no direct connection between the significance constraint alluded to by Wittgenstein and either type-theory or *13.3. Instead, for the exemplary case of a dyadic, symmetrical judgement such as 'A is similar to B', the relevant significance constraint can be found in *TK* where Russell writes that

> the form being 'something and something have a certain relation', our understanding the proposition might be expressed in the words 'something, namely A, and something, namely B, have a certain relation, namely similarity'. (116)

Here Russell undertakes position in a complex analysis to emulate distinctions of type* between particulars and universals. In this context, position in a complex analysis is performed to block WD, though elsewhere (*TK*, part II, chapters II and V) it is used to resolve ND. While *PM* type distinctions are nominal and derive from the vicious circle principle, type* distinctions are ontological distinctions and derive from Russell's general theory of complexes. We introduced type* distinctions earlier in Section 2.11, and I will have more to say about them in Section 3.9. Type* distinctions originate in *PoM*, although it was Landini (1991, 64), as we saw, who coined the *term* 'type*' to clearly demarcate this distinct sense of type from *PM* types (cf. Landini 2007, 57–58).

In any case, while Russell clearly means the statement that 'something, namely A, and something, namely B, have a certain relation, namely similarity', as an analysis of understanding a proposition rather than as a premise in an inference, it is nevertheless clear in context that Russell believes bringing the constituents of the understanding complex into relation with the logical form of dual complexes embodies a significance constraint on propositional understanding. Wittgenstein sees this analysis as implicitly involving the following problematic inference:

P1) $(\exists x)(\exists R)(\exists y)(((x=a) \& (R=S)) \& (y=b))$

P2) aSb

C) aSb v ~ aSb

In this inference, C) represents aSb's being a significant proposition. P2) is the propositional content of the judgement that 'A is similar to B'. P1) represents a significance constraint on judgement, or propositional understanding, in which each of the constituents of the propositional content judged or understood are brought into relation with, by being assigned positions within, the logical form of a dual complex, that is, $(\exists x)\ (\exists R)\ (\exists y)\ xRy$ (i.e. 'something is related somehow to something else'). The logical form of a dual complex, as Russell tells us in chapter I of part II, is to be identified with 'the fact that there are entities that make up complexes having the form in question' (*TK*, 144). The same would obviously apply to complexes of whatever arity, and thus the logical form of a triadic complex, for instance, would be: $(\exists x)\ (\exists R)\ (\exists y)\ (\exists z)\ xRyz$. Construing logical forms in this manner allows Russell to satisfy two *desiderata*, namely (1) that there 'shall be one form, and only one, for every group of complexes which have the same form' (*TK*, 114) and (2) that it 'would be convenient to take as the form something which is not a mere incomplete symbol' (ibid.), that is, something which does not contain free (real) as opposed to bound (apparent) variables. Later, we will have the opportunity to critically consider Russell's conception of logical form, and Wittgenstein's Tractarian alternative, in more detail.

For the time being, and in any case, Wittgenstein's point in the mid-June letter is that C) should follow from P2) in the absence of P1). Following Lebens (2017), we might describe the condition identified by Wittgenstein in the mid-June letter as the 'no constraints constraint' on propositional understanding. And as Wittgenstein puts the point tersely in that context, this condition (the 'no constraints constraint') is not fulfilled by Russell's theory. While it is not especially crucial to Wittgenstein's point, it would still stand in the event that P2) were: A judges that aSb. C) is a classical tautology, and thus it must follow from any meaningful proposition, or judgement in the absence of any supplementary premises, including the significance constraint embodied in P1). Above in the context of examining Wittgenstein's comparison of Russell's view to his own as articulated in the January letter, we saw that Wittgenstein does not seem especially concerned about the alleged distinction between judgements and propositions. Indeed, he would ultimately conclude that the distinction in question is simply spurious (*NDM*, 119; *TLP* 5.542).

So again, contrary to SR, there is no direct connection between this condition and type-theoretic significance constraints of the sort embodied in *13.3 of *PM*. The significance constraint embodied in P1) earlier is thus not problematic for the 1913 version of the MRTJ because it generates an incompatibility between the MRTJ and the theory of types of *PM*. The problem alluded to by Wittgenstein is not, as was supposed by SR and described in Section 2.2, that it is circular to introduce higher-order judgements to ensure that elementary judgements are properly type and order stratified. Instead, P1) is problematic because the implication that it is required in order to infer C) from P2) violates certain basic intuitions about, and fundamental principles concerning, logical inference. In particular, for any meaningful proposition, the disjunction of that proposition and its negation must follow from that proposition in the absence of any supplemental premises. More generally, any classical tautology must follow from any meaningful proposition independently of any additional assumptions. The latter principle in particular highlights the fact that whether P2) mentions or involves a judgement or not is not especially relevant. Wittgenstein mentions judgement in the context of his mid-June letter because Russell's theory of atomic propositional content is a theory of judgement. But from Wittgenstein's perspective, Russell never should have mentioned 'judgement' in the first place and in doing so he was getting off track of the core, logical, issue, which concerns the nature and status of P2) along with other atomic propositions. This is why, in the July letter in which he says he is very sorry to hear that his objection has 'paralysed' Russell, he thinks it can only be removed by a correct theory of such propositions (not judgements).

If the exactly expressed objection contained in the mid-June letter was the objection which 'paralysed' Russell, then why, when he subsequently discusses his objections to Russell's MRTJ in *NL* and *TLP*, does Wittgenstein focus more on the criticisms developed in phase (or wave) two of his 'onslaught'? This is because these objections target the MRTJ which occurs within Russell's published writings, notably, *PP*. Wittgenstein knew that the 1913 version of Russell's MRTJ was unpublished and thus if he criticized it, no one would understand how it applied to the versions of the MRTJ which were in print. Moreover, Wittgenstein likely saw the revised version of the MRTJ contained in the 1913 *TK* manuscript more or less as an epicycle. That is, he saw it as a failed and aborted attempt to circumvent the problems inherent in 1912 *PP* version. Analogously, suppose Russell subsequently responded critically, in print, to the theory of atomic complexes Wittgenstein develops in his January 1913 letter. The scholarly community would doubtless feel this to be a 'cheap shot' and to amount to a 'straw man'. Why, they might think, did not Russell address the picture theory as developed and defended in *TLP*? Aware of the possibility of an analogous perception directed towards himself, Wittgenstein avoids public discussion of the 1913 version of the MRTJ and his criticisms thereof. In Section 3.12, in particular, and at various points elsewhere in the remainder of this chapter, I will have more to say about why Russell found the objection so paralysing and how it contributed to the demise of the *TK* manuscript.

3.3 Re-examining Stevens on EI and OI

In Sections 2.2–2.4, we saw that Graham Stevens offered two distinct criticisms of SR, which he referred to as the epistemological interpretation (EI), before moving on to offer his own, ontological interpretation (OI) of Wittgenstein's objection. In this section, we will critically assess what Stevens had to say about EI and OI, in an effort to demarcate the aspects of his account which have merit and so should be accepted from those which are misguided and so should be rejected. We will start out by looking at some of the problematic aspects of his critique of EI before identifying the aspects of this critique which are warranted. Turning to his defence of OI, we will highlight the elements of this interpretation which are correct before mentioning the respects in which OI falls short of offering a comprehensive account of Wittgenstein's critique of the MRTJ.

The first problematic aspect of Stevens's account is his characterization of SR as an 'epistemological interpretation'. There is nothing especially epistemological about SR aside from the fact that it deals with judgements. But this feature is simply carried over from Russell's MRTJ itself, which is a theory of judgement, and there is nothing particularly epistemological about their interpretation of how that theory goes wrong. By contrast, Griffin and Sommerville read Wittgenstein's objection as having a logical as opposed to epistemological character. According to SR, as we have seen, Wittgenstein meant to point out an incompatibility between the MRTJ and a fundamental element of his logical theory, the theory of types. Moreover, Wittgenstein's complaint, according to SR, is logical in nature. It has to do with inference and, more specifically, with the failure of a specified conclusion to follow from one premise in the absence of other supplemental premises.

Where SR goes wrong, as we have seen, is not in characterizing Wittgenstein's objection as epistemological as opposed to logical in nature. It is rather that, despite recognizing that Wittgenstein's complaint *is* logical in nature, SR mischaracterizes the precise details of that complaint. More specifically, as we have seen, the premise Wittgenstein refers to in the mid-June letter bears no direct connection to type-theory or to *13.3 or *PM*. The premise Wittgenstein alludes to is unique to *TK* and occurs explicitly therein on page 116. As we saw, Russell did not characterize this as a premise so much as an analysis of understanding a proposition, but Wittgenstein's objection involves construing it as an implied, though ultimately superfluous premise within an inference from a well-formed proposition to any tautology.

The next problematic aspect of Stevens's account is his first critique of SR which he, misleadingly, calls EI. We saw that according to Stevens, type-theory as developed and defended in *PM* involves two distinct, but interrelated hierarchies: the hierarchy of types and the hierarchy of orders. Following Landini, as we saw, Stevens construes each of these hierarchies as nominal rather than ontological. I accept that aspect of both Landini's and Stevens's work. What I object to is Stevens's claim that these two hierarchies have independent justifications and that only that hierarchy of orders is derived from the vicious circle principle. It will be recalled that according to Stevens, the hierarchy of types was instead grounded in an argument by 'direct inspection'. Careful attention to Russell's remarks in chapter II of the introduction to *PM*, on 'The Theory of Logical Types', however, shows that both hierarchies are meant to be derived from the vicious circle principle and that the 'direct inspection argument' is introduced to provide the hierarchy of types with supplemental, 'direct' support in addition to the 'indirect' support afforded by its derivation from the vicious circle principle. What in the scholarly literature is referred to as a 'hierarchy of orders' is, in chapter II of the introduction to *PM*, presented as a systematic ambiguity in the definition of truth and falsehood. The resultant hierarchy of senses of truth and falsehood is designed to evade a particular sort of vicious circle fallacy, which, in the illustrative case provided by Russell, has to do with the function '$\hat{p}$ is false' taking '(p). p is false' as an argument. The ostensibly offending proposition is thus identified as

{(p). p is false} is false.

According to Russell, propositions such as these are 'only possible if the word "false" really has many different meanings, appropriate to propositions of different kinds' (*PM*, 42). The systematic ambiguity of truth and falsehood he goes on to explicate in the next paragraph is designed to obviate vicious circle fallacies of this sort and is thus, in that sense, derived from the vicious circle principle.

But in that respect, the resulting hierarchy is simply one instance of a hierarchy of functions derived from the vicious circle principle. What is unique about this case is simply that the hierarchy is one of truth-functions applying to propositions. Fundamentally, however, the systematic definition of truth and falsity is merely an application, to this special case, of the very same strategy Russell has used up to this point in order to evade vicious circle fallacies, by deploying a hierarchy of propositional functions. Both the hierarchy of truth-functions and of propositional functions are thus, in this sense, to be thought of as derived from the vicious circle principle. Contrary to Stevens, neither hierarchy is 'generated' by the MRTJ. Instead the MRTJ is deployed by Russell to, inter alia, obviate paradoxes associated with vicious circle fallacies. In that sense, it is one part of an overall strategy to avoid such fallacies and so paradoxes. Hence Russell tells us that 'an analysis of the paradoxes to be avoided shows us that they all result from a certain kind of vicious circle' (*PM*, 37). Russell's use of 'all' here is telling. It suggests that paradoxes of propositions and of propositional functions have a common source, and to the extent that both sorts of paradoxes are to be avoided through the development of a hierarchy, of truth-functions and of propositional functions, respectively, both hierarchies are in that sense to be understood as derived from the vicious circle principle. Russell therefore explains that

> the paradoxes of symbolic logic concern various sorts of objects: propositions, classes, cardinal and ordinal numbers, etc. All these sorts of objects, as we shall show, represent illegitimate totalities, and are therefore capable of giving rise to vicious circle fallacies. But by means of the theory (to be explained in Chapter III) which reduces statements that are verbally concerned with classes and relations to statements that are concerned with propositional functions, the paradoxes are reduced to such as are concerned with propositions and propositional functions [...] We shall therefore proceed at once to the consideration of propositional functions. (38)

Having suggested that propositional functions are associated with paradoxes resulting from vicious circle fallacies, Russell moves on to show how such fallacies and so paradoxes can be avoided by dividing propositional functions into a hierarchy based on the vicious circle principle. He thus writes that

> a function is what ambiguously denotes some one of a certain totality, namely the values of the function; hence this totality cannot contain any members which involve the function, since, if it did, it would contain members involving the totality, which, by the vicious-circle principle, no totality can do [...] In accordance with the vicious-circle principle, the values of a function cannot contain terms only definable in terms of the function. Now given a function $\phi\hat{x}$, the values for the function are all proposition of the form ϕx. It follows that there must be no propositions of the form ϕx, in which x has a value which involves ϕx. (40)

Just as truth and falsehood must be systematically ambiguous so as to avoid vicious circle fallacies and thus paradoxes of propositions such as the liar, propositional functions must be systematically ambiguous so as to avoid vicious circle fallacies responsible for paradoxes of propositional functions, such as Russell's paradox. Both sorts of systematic ambiguity, and so hierarchies, are derived from the vicious circle principle.

The 'direct inspection argument' then comes into play to provide direct, supplementary support for the hierarchy of propositional functions thus derived:

> The considerations so far adduced in favour of the view that a function cannot significantly have as argument anything defined in terms of the function itself

have been more or less indirect. But a direct consideration of the kinds of functions which have functions as arguments and the kinds of functions which have arguments other than functions will show, if we are not mistaken, that not only is it impossible for a function $\phi\hat{z}$ to have itself or anything derived from it as argument, but that, if $\psi\hat{z}$ is another function such that there are arguments a with which both 'ϕa' and 'ψa' are significant, then $\psi\hat{z}$ and anything derived from it cannot significantly be an argument to $\phi\hat{z}$. (*PM*, 47)

Clearly, Russell does not mean 'direct inspection' to provide exclusive support for the existence of a hierarchy of propositional functions, independent of its derivation from the vicious circle principle. Instead, he means it to provide supplementary 'direct' support to the 'indirect' derivation thereof already provided. He intends 'direct inspection' to corroborate this derivation, which is obviously homologous to that of a hierarchy of senses of truth and falsehood. Indeed, the latter is presented by Russell (41–42) as simply a special case of the former, which, as we have seen, plainly involves appeal to the vicious circle principle.

From the perspective of LI, in any case, nothing ultimately hinges on whether Stevens's account of the hierarchy of types, and its independence from the vicious circle principle, is correct or incorrect. According to LI, as we have seen, type-theory bears no direct connection to Wittgenstein's critique of the MRTJ. Momentarily, we will see that Stevens's claim (following Landini) that type-theory stratifies propositional functions, not entities, into orders is indirectly relevant to LI in the sense that this implies that type-theory cannot plausibly be appealed to to block WD. On that score, Stevens is absolutely right. To see why, it will now be helpful to look at what is worth preserving within his critique of EI and his defence of OI.

Stevens is correct to home in on the logical status of the subordinate relation and on how puzzles surrounding it, especially WD, highlight the tension between Russell's MRTJ and his commitment to the unrestricted variable of quantification. To the extent that Griffin and Sommerville regard type-theory as stratifying entities, as opposed to propositional functions, into types, then this aspect of Stevens's criticism of what he calls EI is correct. Because type-theory stratifies propositional functions, not entities, into orders, it lacks the resources to block WD. To see why, we can re-examine the problematic premise P1) discussed in Section 2.2: P1) $(\exists x)\,(\exists R)\,(\exists y)\,(((x=a)\,\&\,(R=S))\,\&\,(y=b))$. The problem concerns the status of R. What kind of variable is it? If it is an unrestricted entity variable, then it should range over particulars, such as c, in addition to universals, such as S. But then, why can't the following represent a possible analysis of what Russell calls 'understanding a proposition'?

*P1) (∃x) (∃R) (∃y) (((x=a) & (R=c)) & (y=b)).

In so far as the variable R is unrestricted, it would seem that *P1) cannot be ruled out, as a possible analysis of the judgable, propositional content of a well-formed cognitive complex. Alternatively, Russell might construe R as a variable ranging over propositional functions, not entities. These, as we have seen, *can* be stratified into types, which would allow Russell to block the illicit substitution of a particular, such as c, into the offending position. This, however, would require Russell to abandon realism about relations (universals), which for various reasons surveyed earlier (notably in Section 1.1) was a nonstarter for Russell.

Stevens's OI is correct as far as it goes. Unfortunately, it does little to explain the wording of Wittgenstein's exactly expressed objection in the mid-June letter and to that extent misses crucial elements of the significance of this objection with respect to Wittgenstein's philosophical development. As we have seen, when Wittgenstein mentions a 'further premise' in that context, he is alluding to P1), and his point is that aSb v ~ aSb should follow from aSb directly, in the absence of P1), and contrary to Russell's proposed analysis of understanding a proposition. Wittgenstein's recognition of this point in particular has, as we shall see, many important consequences within the development of his early philosophy. It represents a paradigmatic and archetypal instance of the 'sense-truth regress' which Wittgenstein will go on to deploy in a variety of contexts, including those of his arguments in *TLP* for the logical independence of elementary propositions and the subsistence of objects. As mentioned, we will discuss the sense-truth regress in more detail here, in Section 4.7.

For now we will continue to work through our critical assessment of the alternative interpretations of Wittgenstein's critique canvassed in Chapter 2. As we do so, an emergent, consistent theme will be commentators mistakenly believing that Russell's MRTJ possesses the resources to block WD in the absence of P1) or its likes. Though Stevens's reading of Wittgenstein's critique is neither comprehensive nor entirely correct, it nevertheless enjoys a crucial merit, which is its recognition that Russell's MRTJ lacks these critical resources. Moreover, Stevens sees that these deficiencies are not incidental but instead derive from Russell's core logical and philosophical commitments. To that extent, and as far as it goes, Stevens's reading can readily explain Russell's paralysis in the face of Wittgenstein's critique.

3.4 Hanks on the Judging Relation and Wittgenstein's Critique of the MRTJ

Recall that Hanks's critique of SR is that it cannot explain the seriousness and severity which Russell attached to Wittgenstein's objection. The reason is that Russell could easily obviate it by appealing to type distinctions built into the judgement relation itself, without requiring recourse to any problematic, type-theoretic stipulations or significance constraints. LI accords with Hanks's UI in rejecting the notion that there is any direct connection between *PM* type-theory and Wittgenstein's critique of the MRTJ. Where LI parts company with UI is on the issue of whether Russell could so easily block WD by appealing to the type distinctions inherent in the judging relation. As we have seen, LI follows Landini and Stevens in reading type-theory as stratifying propositional functions, not entities, into types. For this and other reasons which shall be discussed momentarily, type distinctions cannot be deployed to block WD in the manner proposed by Hanks. Moreover, and relatedly, UI is incomplete relative to LI in the sense that Hanks takes Wittgenstein's critique to be restricted to only one aspect of what, according to LI, is only the second of three distinct waves of criticism. Specifically, Hanks sees Wittgenstein as pointing out that the MRTJ fails to yield a unified and truth-apt propositional content. Hanks sees this same issue of the unity of the proposition as being the focus of Wittgenstein's criticisms throughout May–June 1913 and thus claims that in explicating those criticisms, 'we can ignore logical forms and the later refinements in Russell's theory of judgement' (Hanks 2007, 127). According to LI, by contrast, in ignoring such refinements we would miss the main thrust of the third wave of Wittgenstein's criticisms, expressed first inarticulately during the 26 May meeting and then exactly in the mid-June letter.

In the remainder of this section, I will touch on each of these points of controversy and provide reasons to prefer LI over UI in light of these disagreements between the two. Ultimately, we will see that Hanks is correct to characterize Wittgenstein as concerned with the inability of the MRTJ to yield a unified propositional content. However, Wittgenstein sees this problem as enmeshed with both WD and ND, and all three are the focus of his critique of the 1912 version of the MRTJ. Moreover, and contrary to Hanks, the mid-June letter does indeed address logical forms and other refinements characteristic of the 1913 version of the MRTJ and is not, as is supposed within Hanks's UI, merely a roundabout way of restating concerns about unity, endemic to the 1912 version.

There are several reasons to reject Hanks's claim that Russell could block WD easily, by appealing to type distinctions inherent in the judging relation.

The first, as we have seen, is that type-theory does not stratify entities into types and thus cannot distinguish between a particular and a universal. From the perspective of *PM*'s type-theory, both are individuals, and thus each is within the range of *PM*'s unrestricted entity variable. Moreover, even if we grant that *PM* does stratify entities into types, it begs the question to assume that the judging relation is a predicate of type $(i, i, i, (i,i))$ (or $(3,(2))$) and not a predicate of type (i, i, i, i). Type-theory is a theory of logical syntax, not of Rylean categories. It cannot distinguish between judging and polygamy any more than it can tell us the difference between the university and the library. As Russell himself points out in *PLA*, the language set forth in *PM* 'has only syntax and no vocabulary whatsoever' (*CP*, 8: 176). In other words, the language of *PM* does not contain a judgement predicate. It contains predicates both of type $(i, i, i, (i,i))$ and of type (i, i, i, i), and leaves completely open the question of whether the judging relation has a structure characterized by the former or the latter. Russell is clearly prepared to allow for the possibility of complexes consisting of three individuals bearing a triadic relation. Hence, he writes:

> We give the name of '*a complex*' to any such object as '*a* in the relation *R* to *b*,' or '*a* having quality *q*' or '*a* and *b* and *c* standing in the relation *S*'. (*PM*, 44; emphasis in the original)

Nothing about *PM*'s logical syntax excludes the possibility that cognitive complexes could involve triadic relations between individuals, none of which is a universal. Russell would certainly like to exclude such complexes somehow, but he cannot do so by appealing to *PM*'s logical syntax. That is precisely why, in *TK*, he is motivated to introduce as significance constraints on judgements stipulations upon the constituents of judgements which do not amount to *PM* type distinctions.

Turning to *TK*, we saw in Section 1.4 that, on page 116 of the manuscript, Russell explicitly rejects the proposal, characteristic of the 1912 version of the MRTJ, of relying on the judging relation itself to unite and properly order the object terms of the judgement. His rejection of this proposal is a crucial component of his attempt to motivate the introduction of logical forms in the 1913 version of the MRTJ. It is also part of the justification for his introduction of P1) as an analysis of 'understanding a proposition', which Wittgenstein in turn construed as a significance constraint on judgements. The illustrative example used in *TK* (116) of 'A is similar to B' is not susceptible to ND since it is symmetrical and thus lacks 'sense' or 'direction'. This strongly suggests that Russell's introduction of P1) in that context is largely motivated by the attempt to block WD. If he thought that type restrictions inherent to judgement complexes could be appealed to to block WD, he never would have introduced P1) in an attempt to block WD. Wittgenstein's point in the mid-June letter is that he cannot appeal to P1) to block WD since to do so violates certain basic intuitions about, and principles regarding, logical inference.

Hanks is nevertheless correct to think that the failure of the MRTJ to yield a unified propositional content is a crucial component of Wittgenstein's critique on 20 May. Hanks does a great service by highlighting the remark from *NL* (94) quoted earlier in Section 3.1, in which Wittgenstein develops an analogy between judgment and negation, insisting that neither applies to anything aside from a unified propositional content. However, as we saw in the context of our defence of LI in Section 3.1, and as the quote appealed to by Hanks itself demonstrates, Wittgenstein sees each of these three problems, that is, WD, ND and UP, as closely interrelated. All three are part of the second wave of criticism he offers to Russell on 20 May. As we have seen, moreover, there is an additional, third wave of criticism that culminates in the mid-June letter and which specifically addresses Russell's attempts to circumvent WD by appealing to P1). Hanks's UI cannot explain why Wittgenstein refers to a supplemental premise in the context of the mid-June letter, while LI can explain it perfectly and even identify it as P1) explicitly. For this and other reasons, LI is to be preferred over UI as an interpretation of Wittgenstein's criticisms and of their paralysing effect on Russell.

3.5 Pincock on the Proposition Problem

According to LI, as we have seen, the second wave of Wittgenstein's criticisms focused on problems inherent in the 1912 version of the MRTJ, including WD, ND and UP. His third wave of criticism, by contrast, focused on refinements contained in the 1913 version, which were designed, inter alia, to address these (and likely Stout's) earlier criticisms. The refinements in question included his introduction of logical forms and, relatedly, his position in a complex analysis. In Section 2.8 earlier, we saw that Pincock characterizes WD, ND and UP each as aspects or versions of what he called the 'proposition problem' in contrast to the 'correspondence problem' (or CP). 'Proposition problem' was thus an umbrella term used to refer to the set of interrelated problems having to do with the MRTJ's alleged struggles to yield a unified, well-formed, properly ordered and sufficiently specific propositional content. Moreover, Pincock thought that the 1913 version of the MRTJ contains all the resources needed to resolve every one of these interrelated set of alleged problems, including WD, ND and UP. This claim, clearly, conflicts with LI and will be critically examined in this section. According to LI, logical forms and position in a complex analysis cannot be successfully deployed to block WD, ND and

UP without running afoul of certain basic intuitions about, and fundamental principles concerning, logical inference. In this section, reasons will be given to prefer LI over Pincock's CI, with specific reference to each of WD, ND and UP. CP will then be the subject of Section 3.6.

There are several reasons to think that Pincock's CI is incorrect. First, similarly to Hanks, Pincock claims that Russell can resolve WD by appealing to cognitive complexes themselves to rule out illicit substitutions. This strategy, as we saw, is explicitly rejected by Russell on page 116 of the *TK* manuscript. While it is therefore tempting to dismiss this claim of Pincock's out of hand, there are significant differences in the way that Hanks and Pincock see Russell as deploying cognitive complexes to block WD that are highly instructive and so worth exploring in more detail. While Hanks thought that distinctions of type were inherent in the judging relation, Pincock follows Landini in rejecting the idea that type-theory stratifies entities as opposed to propositional functions. Like both Stevens and Landini, and in accordance with LI, Pincock thus denies any direct connection between Wittgenstein's objections and *PM* type-theory. According to Pincock, however, Russell can nevertheless block WD by appealing to distinctions of kind as opposed to distinctions of type. Such distinctions of kind are grounded in Russell's general theory of complexes, not his type-theory. To block WD Russell need only avail himself of the former but not the latter.

Emerging out of Russell's general theory of complexes, according to Pincock, is the notion of heterogeneity. By appealing to heterogeneity Russell can rule out the sorts of illicit substitutions which characterize WD. As Pincock explains,

> Crucially, when we try to substitute the relation of similarity with A, we fail to get a complex. That is, this pair of constituents are *heterogenous*. More generally, any term like A is heterogenous with a property, a dual relation, a three place relation etc. (2008, 114; emphasis in the original)

As we shall see, Russell does indeed use the term 'kind' in *TK*, along with a related notion of heterogeneity. But it is worth reflecting in more detail on whether and if so how Russell's use of the term 'kind', along with his concept of heterogeneity, aligns with or tracks Pincock's notion of 'kind'. When it comes to corresponding complexes or fact complexes, Pincock seems to me to be correct to think that heterogeneity in Russell's intended sense at least approximates distinctions of kind in Pincock's sense. In other words, Russell's theory of complexes involves the idea that certain combinations of constituents are not logically possible because the constituents are not of the right 'kinds', in Pincock's sense, to occur in the relevant positions. So, for instance, near the outset of chapter VII of part I, Russell writes that

> in any complex, there are at least two kinds of constituents, namely the terms related, and the relation which unites them [...] In (say) 'A precedes B', A and B occur differently from the way in which 'precedes' occurs. On the other hand, in 'preceding is the converse of succeeding', 'preceding' occurs, *primâ facie*, in the same way in which A and B occur in 'A precedes B' [...] An entity which *can* occur in a complex as 'precedes' occurs in 'A precedes B' will be called a *relation*. When it *does* occur in this way in a given complex, it will be called a 'relating relation' in that complex. (*TK*, 80; emphases in the original)

According to this account, the complex 'A precedes B' contains at least two distinct kinds of constituents, the particulars A and B, along with the relation 'precedes'. Moreover, 'precedes' can occur in the positions in which A and B occur, although A and B cannot occur in the position occupied by 'precedes'. Finally, when 'precedes' occurs in the position that it does occur in 'A precedes B', it occurs therein as a 'relating relation', whereas when it instead occurs as one of the terms of a relating relation, as in 'preceding is the converse of succeeding', it occurs as a relation but not as one which relates. These two distinct sorts of occurrences are indicated within the sentences expressing the respective complexes using a verb 'precedes' in the first case and a verbal noun 'preceding' in the second.

There are problems, however, inherent in assimilating this notion of 'kind' to that of 'heterogeneity', having to do with cases in which relations occur as terms of relating relations. In chapter II of part II, for instance, Russell remarks that the 'relating relation in a complex is always heterogeneous to all of the other constituents' (*TK*, 123). If 'heterogeneous' means of the same as 'kind', then it is not clear how 'precedes', for instance, can be both a relating relation and the term of a relating relation. This is because, if it occurs in a complex in which it is not a relating relation, Russell might seem to be suggesting that it is heterogeneous relative to the relating relation of that complex and so cannot occur in its position within that complex. Yet later on (80) Russell affirms that it, that is, 'precedes', can occur as a relating relation. Moreover, while in this case Russell appears to characterize a constituent, that is, the relating relation, as heterogeneous relative to the other constituents, more commonly he says that it is the complexes themselves which are heterogeneous with respect to its (unsymmetrical) constituents. So, it is a bit unclear whether Pincock's notion of kind tracks Russell's notion of heterogeneity, in part because the notion of heterogeneity, and its connection with Russell's notion of 'kind', is also a bit unclear. Momentarily, we will revisit this puzzling remark on page 123 of *TK*, to see if we can make better sense of it.

Regardless of whether Pincock's notion of 'kind' perfectly mirrors Russell's notion of kind, and whether either perfectly tracks Russell's notion of heterogeneity, there does, however, seem to be a close enough approximation between these notions to attribute to Russell the view that particulars cannot occur in the position of the relating relation of a complex and thus that complexes such as 'precedes A B' are supposed to be ruled out by Russell's general theory of complexes (cf. *PLA*, 182, 225). Things get more complicated, however, when we attempt to extend these sorts of considerations to the case of cognitive complexes in particular. More specifically, and this is the second main reason to prefer LI over Pincock's CI, it is hard to see how a *general* theory of complexes can rule out specific, problematic sorts of *cognitive* complexes. For instance, how could a *general* theory of complexes rule out a cognitive complex in which four particulars stand in a tetradic relation? The relating relation of such a complex might be heterogeneous relative to the other constituents, but why would any of the other constituents be heterogeneous relative to one another, given that none of them is a relation which relates? Thus, from the perspective of a general theory of complexes, a cognitive complex in which four particulars stand in a cognitive relation would seem to be a perfectly legitimate combination. But that, in essence, is simply another way of stating WD. We saw that *PM*'s type-theory is not a theory of Rylean categories. But then we need now only note that neither is Russell's general theory of complexes. For that reason, it is hard to see how Russell's general theory or complexes can be relied upon to preclude the sorts of illicit substitutions characteristic of WD.

Indeed, it is precisely because Russell's general theory of complexes *does not* rule out, inter alia, cognitive complexes in which four particulars stand in a tetradic relation that Russell must *emulate* the required distinctions of what Pincock calls 'kind' in such cases, through a procedure by which object terms are assigned to specific positions in the logical form contained within the cognitive complex. In the context of such cognitive complexes, heterogeneity is something which emerges only *from* assigning object terms to certain positions and thus cannot be presupposed and relied upon to rule out illicit substitutions in advance and in the absence of supplementary analytical premises. In the case of cognitive complexes as opposed to fact complexes, heterogeneity is not ontological in nature but is instead conceived by Russell as being procedural, that is, relative to and generated by the procedure of position in a complex analysis. Since it occurs within chapter II of part II, which is ostensibly concerned with extending the theory of understanding developed for the specific case of symmetrical dual complexes in chapter I of part II to 'various illustrative special cases' (*TK*, 119), this may explain Russell's puzzling remark on page 123 that 'the relating relation in a complex is always heterogeneous to all of the other constituents'. He may be referring obliquely to the subordinate relation in a cognitive complex and identifying it as 'heterogeneous' relative to the procedure of assigning constituents to positions in the form contained within the judgement.

Russell's most thorough and considered treatment of this position in a complex analysis is undertaken in the context of chapter V of part II, where he is attempting to provide an analysis of the truth-conditions of judgements. In particular, he is concerned to distinguish between the truth-conditions of judgements which share their constituents and form in common and, implicitly referring back to his analysis of understanding a proposition in chapter I of part II, he tells us what heterogeneity amounts to in that as well as this context. He writes:

> It is to be observed that the relations C_1, C_2, ... Cn are not determined by the general *form*, but only by the relation R. So far as the general form 'xRy' is concerned, the position of A is the same in '*A-before*-B' as in '*A-after*-B'. It is only after the relation R has been assigned that positions can be distinguished. (*TK*, 146; emphases in the original)

In a footnote to this remark, he then goes on to provide the following gloss:

> The position of R, unlike that of the other constituents, *can* be assigned relatively to the form; this is what enables us to speak of it as the relating relation. (ibid.; emphasis in the original)

In other words, within a judgement complex, as opposed to the fact complex which exists if the judgement is true, the subordinate relation R does not actually relate the other constituents of the judgement. What allows us to speak or think of it *as if* it were a relating relation in the judgement complex is its being assigned to a particular position in the logical form of fact-complex xRy, contained within the judgement complex. Pincock notes that there are many problems with Russell's 'identification of logical forms with general facts' but that this identification 'does not seem [...] to be essential to Russell's account' (2008, 116). However, this and other passages show how essential, and problematic, this identification is.

The problem is you do not have the required heterogeneity between the subordinate relation and the other object terms of a judgement until you assign the subordinate relation to correct position within the logical form it contains. Such forms, Russell tells us, are *summum genus* or perfectly general. They thus contain no constituents but only variables. Within Russell's

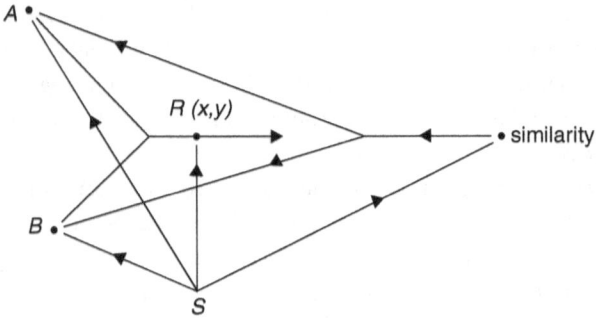

Figure 3.1 Russell's diagram of understanding.

logic, such variables are unrestricted, and thus there is no way to rule out the substitution of a particular into the position which should be occupied by a relation or universal, in the absence of supplemental premises or restrictions designed to accomplish this. Moreover, in the absence of supplemental premises or restrictions which assign a particular universal to the position of a subordinate relation in the logical form contained within the judgement complex, the nature of the other positions are ambiguous. Depending upon whether the relation is symmetrical or unsymmetrical, for example, you may either have identical or distinct positions.

Such supplemental premises or restrictions are precisely what Wittgenstein objected to in the mid-June letter. And this same basic objection applies to Russell's diagram of understanding at the end of part II chapter I which, for all essential purposes, is simply a 'map-in-space' of P1) (cf. *PLA*, 198–99). As Pincock suggests, it is true that if we grant Russell access to the network of relations depicted in his diagram of understanding (Figure 3.1), the MRTJ does indeed contain the resources required to block WD.

However, this does not involve his deploying distinctions of kind between particulars and universals, so much as it involves assigning the relevant universal to the position which is supposed to be occupied by the subordinate relation. Following Landini, Pincock accepts that both universals and particulars belong to one metaphysical category of entity, any of which may be substituted as an argument to Russell's unrestricted entity variable. But why, then, would Russell feel entitled to appeal to distinctions of kind, or heterogeneity, as a sort of 'brute metaphysical fact' (Pincock 2008, 114) which rules such substitutions out? In fact, Russell does not feel entitled to appeal to such distinctions in this context principally because, in this context, the subordinate relation is not relating. So, it is not actually combining with the other object terms and thus there is no guarantee that illicit substitutions will be prevented, by distinctions of kind which proscribe certain sorts of combinatorial possibilities. That is precisely why he introduces the network of relations depicted in his diagram of understanding in an attempt to rule such illicit substitutions out.

A key aspect of the diagram is thus its depiction of how, within the context of the network of relations depicted therein, the object terms of the judgement are brought into relation with the logical form of dual complexes. This involves stipulating the positions of each of the object terms in relation to the form. Later, in chapter V of part II, Russell will go on to describe this procedure in more detail, and at that time he will suggest that the position of the subordinate relation must be assigned first, before there are any other unambiguous positions to which to assign other object terms. Here, however, in chapter I of part II, he is abstracting from these thorny issues and deferring them until later, because he is intent on illustrating, and defending the basic and fundamental features of his theory of cognitive complexes. That is why the illustrative example he uses is of a proposition which, if true, corresponds to a structurally simple, symmetrical dual complex (*TK*, 112).

In any case, in the diagram which occurs at the end of chapter I of part II, he is simply attempting to depict the end result of the procedure described in *TK* (116), where he says that the relation of understanding cannot be relied upon to unite and order the object terms of a cognitive complex but that this can be done by bringing those object terms, in thought, into relation with the logical form of dual complexes. Thus, the diagram depicts its subject S as related to each of the other constituents of the cognitive complex, including the form, and then each of the object terms as related to the form. In virtue of this network (and it alone) similarity may thus be depicted as if 'relating' A and B. Hence Russell explains that 'in this figure, one relation goes from S to the four objects; one relation goes from $R(x, y)$ to similarity, and another to A and B, while one relation goes from similarity to A and B'. This last relation relates to what Lebens called the 'representation concern', which in 1910 was supposed to be met by the 'sense' or 'direction' of the subordinate relation and in 1912 was supposed to be achieved by the judging relation. The issue, again, is not the mereological one of combining the constituents into some complex or other; the point is to combine them in a way which represents A and B as being related by similarity, without thereby actually so relating them.

In any event, it is precisely the network of relations depicted in Russell's diagram (or 'map') of understanding that Wittgenstein intends to deny Russell access to in claiming that aSb v ~ aSb must follow from aSb in the absence of any supplemental premises. (That explains why, as we shall see in more detail in Section 3.6, the idea that one cannot make a 'map-in-space' of belief is one of two main lessons Russell draws from Wittgenstein's criticisms in the context of his analysis of belief in *PLA*.) The fact that Wittgenstein uses aRb, and develops a connection with bipolarity, suggests, again, that he sees each of WD, ND and UP as fundamentally and closely interconnected. The 'premise' Wittgenstein has in mind in the mid-June letter is precisely the part of Russell's MRTJ, described verbally in *TK* (116) and then depicted diagrammatically (118), in which the object terms of the cognitive complex are by stipulation brought into relation with the logical form of dual complexes (in the most basic, illustrative case). Though Russell does not characterize his diagram as a premise any more than he so characterizes his verbal description in *TK* (116), it is nevertheless clear from both the description and the diagram that bringing the object terms of the cognitive complex into relation with the logical form of dual complexes (in the most basic illustrative case) is presupposed in any subject's understanding of a well-formed proposition with sense. Wittgenstein's point, in a word, is that if a proposition (or judgement) is well formed, then any tautology follows from it directly and independently of any such preconditions.

The third reason to prefer LI over what Pincock's CI claims about the 1913 version of the MRTJ is that just as the latter cannot block WD in the absence of extraneous constraints or premises, it also cannot resolve ND without appealing to supplemental restrictions or premises. Pincock readily admits that Russell proposes to resolve ND by appealing to position in a complex analysis. This is another way of saying that in order to resolve ND, Russell must appeal to the stipulations which that position in a complex analysis involves. It is precisely these sorts of stipulations which Wittgenstein objected to when he said that aRb v ∼ aRb should follow from the judgement that aRb directly, in the absence of further premises. Wittgenstein's use of aRb here (as opposed, e.g., of aSb) is telling. It suggests that even if Russell could successfully resolve WD by assigning R to the position within the logical form of a dual complex where the subordinate relation must go, he would still be left with the problem of distinguishing aRb from bRa. That explains why, in *NL*, he uses the example of 'This table penholders the book' as opposed to 'The book penholders this table'. In other words, even if he finds a solution to WD, Russell still has to address ND by appealing to further stipulations in order to specify the positions of the other object terms of the judgement, within the logical form of the complex which exists in case the judgement is true. Indeed, this is precisely what Russell describes himself as doing in chapter V of part II. According to Russell, it is not until 'R' is assigned to a position in the 'general form' that there are even determinate positions for the other object terms of the judgement to be related to. Hence, he writes that 'it is to be observed that the relations C_1, C_2, ... C_n, are not determined by the general *form*, but only by the relation *R*' (*TK*, 146; emphasis in the original). Only then can we explicitly describe, and thereby disambiguate, the specific complex we are judging to be actual. While informally, and for notational convenience, we might represent our judgement by the symbol:

$R(x_1, x_2, \ldots x_n)$.

According to Russell, however, this notation makes implicit use of the spatial order of symbols and thereby conceals its more explicit logical structure:

$(\iota\gamma).\ x_1 C_1 \gamma.\ x_2 C_2 \gamma.\ \ldots\ x_n C_n \gamma.$

For our purposes, what is important is that it is only once R has been assigned to a position in the general form that the judgement even has a more explicit structure with positions to which other object terms can be assigned and so related. Admittedly, we no longer have a permutative structure and so we have made significant progress towards resolving ND on that score. But we still do not have a specific judgement until the positions of $x_1, x_2, \ldots x_n$ are assigned.

The point is: position in a complex analysis as conceived by Russell in *TK* is a rather involved procedure. The heterogeneity required to block WD only emerges out of it once R is stipulated to occupy a specific position in a logical form. Even once this stipulation is made, moreover, Russell still has work to do to resolve ND by assigning the other object terms of the judgement to specific positions in the resulting form. Contrary to Pincock's CI, the unity, well formedness, ordering and specificity of judgements is not something which, on the 1913 version of the MRTJ, naturally falls out of brute metaphysical distinctions. Instead, these things emerge, along with heterogeneity, from an intricate, successive analytical procedure which involves numerous interrelated stipulations. It is precisely these stipulations which Wittgenstein rejects in the context of the mid-June letter.

This leaves us with UP. With regards to UP, recall that in Section 2.9, we noted that Pincock claimed that Russell's MRTJ yields a unified complex just as certainly as his earlier *PoM* theory of propositions did. On this score, the principal difference between the two theories merely concerns what each regard as the truth-bearer. Within the earlier *PoM* theory of propositions, it is a structured, Russellian proposition whereas on the *TK* view, it is a unified and structured cognitive complex. Assuming it is such a unified complex, Pincock insisted, why should it not be able to have properties, including those of being either true or false?

The problem with Pincock's argument here is that it fails to clearly disambiguate the mereological problem of generating a unified complex, from the more difficult problem which Lebens dubbed the 'representation concern'. In other words, it is one thing to provide a unified complex and another to explain how it is that that complex possesses the capacity to represent facts either truly or falsely. Simply to say that a cognitive complex *can* have that property is not the same as to give an account of precisely *how*. While in the context of his earlier *PoM* theory of propositions, truth and falsehood may have been conceived as primitive, indefinable properties, but that is no longer the case for the MRTJ. In devising the MRTJ Russell appears to have thought that a cognitive complex could represent truly or falsely only in so far as it combined the object terms of the complex in a way in which they were presented to the mind *as if* being united by the subordinate relation without actually being so united. Russell developed, and critically reconsidered, several proposals to pull this off, including relying on the sense or direction of the subordinate relation in 1910 and upon the sense or direction of the judging relation in 1912. By May 1913, he settled upon deploying logical forms, and a position in a complex analysis via which the object terms of a judgement would be brought, cognitively, into relation with these logical forms. This strategy, which is described in *TK* (116) and depicted in the diagram of understanding (118), was the target of Wittgenstein's criticisms expressed first inarticulately during the meeting on 26 May and then 'exactly' in the mid-June letter. So, it is a mistake to think both that UP was not of particular concern to Russell and that it was not within the purview of Wittgenstein's critique.

3.6 Pincock on the Correspondence Problem

In Section 3.5, we examined the reasons to prefer LI over Pincock's CI as an interpretation of Wittgenstein's critique of the MRTJ, with respect to each of ND, WD and UP. While, contrary to LI, Pincock claimed that the 1913 MRTJ could address each of these worries and thus that there was no reason to think that Russell was concerned with them, we found that not to be the case. In this section, we will now train our focus in on CP and examine the many compelling reasons which exist to reject Pincock's claim that it was instead this concern that Wittgenstein brought to Russell's attention and which led to Russell's self-described 'paralysis'. The first of these reasons to be noted is that CP, which, as we saw, concerns potentially false atomic propositions occurring as constituents of molecular belief complexes, emerges only late in the manuscript. Indeed, according to Pincock, Russell's first inkling of CP does not occur until he writes page 145, which is contained in chapter V of part II. Russell did not write this material until 1 June (Blackwell and Eames 1992, xvii) while Wittgenstein had already begun to level the third wave of criticisms by 26 May. This material thus cannot be among the 'crucial parts' of *TK* which Russell showed to Wittgenstein on 26 May and to which he objected first inarticulately in conversation and then 'exactly' in the mid-June letter.

Curiously, Pincock (2008, 131) cites the fact that Russell wrote chapter V of part II after the meeting on 26 May as evidence that the CP which arises therein was discussed at the meeting. But how could Wittgenstein have objected to Russell's views as espoused in this material, if Russell had not written it yet? Moreover, in chapter V of part II, it is Russell himself who raises the CP, as opposed to it being the case that Russell wrote something therein to which Wittgenstein objected by raising the CP. Given that we know Wittgenstein objected to something contained in parts of the manuscript which Russell showed him on 26 May, why would Wittgenstein's objections actually *be* in the manuscript, as opposed to being *about* something Russell wrote in the manuscript? If, for some reason, Russell is recording Wittgenstein's objections (as discussed at the meeting) in the manuscript, then why do these objections concern Russell's correspondence theory of truth when we know that what Russell showed Wittgenstein on 26 May concerned his analysis of understanding a proposition? On the plausible and textually supported assumption that it was more or less the same objection to the MRTJ which Wittgenstein raised first on 26 May and then in the mid-June letter, by contrast, the facts tend to suggest CP as a problem that Russell encountered all on his own, in the context of his attempts to deploy position in a complex analysis in order to resolve ND. Russell had a nose for problems and paradoxes. He need not always be thought of as depending on Wittgenstein to generate or discover them.

Moreover, if CP was Wittgenstein's concern in the mid-June letter, what is the connection supposed to be with the 'premise' alluded to by Wittgenstein in the mid-June letter? What premise, or premises, might Russell have appealed to to block CP, which were *not* also supposed to bear on the proposition problem? On what grounds does Wittgenstein mean to deny Russell access to the premises required to obviate CP? According to LI, the premise alluded to in the mid-June letter occurs in *TK* (116), which is among the 'crucial parts' Russell showed to Wittgenstein on 26 May. What, by contrast, is the relevant premise in relation to CP, where is it in the manuscript and how could Russell have showed it to Wittgenstein on 26 May when there is no evidence he had any inkling of CP until 1 June?

While Pincock concedes (2008, 130) that readings of Wittgenstein's objection which take it to focus on some or other kind of proposition problem (such as ND, WD or UP) gain some support from extant correspondence and textual evidence, he claims that a more plausible reconstruction can be provided if we interpret that evidence in accordance with the idea, inherent in CI, that the crux of Wittgenstein's objection was instead CP. Pincock attempts to link CP to the mid-June letter in particular by pointing out that both involve what

Pincock calls bivalence (or (T/F)) (132). Because it will come up repeatedly in what follows, it should be noted at the outset that Wittgenstein's mentioning bivalence, or bipolarity, in a particular piece of correspondence or passage of text does not automatically link Wittgenstein's remarks there to Pincock's CP. Bipolarity, or bivalence, is a core feature of Wittgenstein's early philosophy of logic and language which connects to many different topics and themes contained therein, only some of which are directly related to his criticisms of Russell's MRTJ (cf., e.g., *TLP* 2.0211–2.0212). Allegedly, however, in the context of the mid-June letter, and in later statements of his objection in both *NL* and *TLP*, according to Pincock's CI Wittgenstein is noting an incompatibility between (T/F) and other key commitments of Russell's, including what Pincock calls (CAT) and (PART). Russell's 'paralysis' results from Wittgenstein forcing him to realize that he cannot consistently adhere to all three, according to CI. From Section 2.10 it will be recalled that (CAT) is the claim that all entities fall into one metaphysical category (Pincock 2008, 110), while (PART) is the claim that in a propositional attitude, the entities that are the subject matter of this attitude are also parts of the propositional attitude (107). Pincock's view that Russell was committed to each of these three principles is plausible and well supported. But his account of the role they play in Wittgenstein's objection, and in the demise of *TK*, is not. To see why, we have to go through Pincock's reconstruction step by step.

Evidence for the claim that Wittgenstein's mid-June letter means to target an incompatibility between these three principles is to be found, according to Pincock (2008, 132), within remarks that Russell makes in the first lecture of *PLA* (*CP*, 8: 167). There Russell points out that his 'former pupil' Wittgenstein alerted him to the fact that propositions are not names for facts. According to Pincock, these remarks are evidence of a 'fairly direct' connection 'between a rigid thing/fact distinction and the correspondence problem' (2008, 132). This is because what Russell is doing here, according to Pincock, is replacing (CAT) with a principle 'that puts things in a single category and facts in another' (133) in response to Wittgenstein's criticism.

In response to this aspect of Pincock's reconstruction, several points are worth noting. First, Wittgenstein criticized many views of Russell's, so the fact that he pointed something problematic out to Russell, and that Russell changed his view in response to it, is not automatically evidence that this particular criticism links to or is involved in Wittgenstein's critique of the MRTJ. It might easily have been the case that Wittgenstein thought Russell's view that facts can be named was wrong and, independently, that his theory of judgement was wrong as well. Second, it is not even clear that Russell needed to (or did) give up (CAT) in response to this problem. It does not follow from the fact that Russell came to agree that propositions are not names of facts, that he would therefore be compelled to give up (CAT) in favour of a metaphysical distinction between facts and things. Likewise, from the fact that Russell denies that definite descriptions are names (e.g. *PLA*, 213), it does not follow that they denote, or perhaps imply, the existence of entities of a distinct metaphysical category. Instead, they denote particulars but do so via contextual paraphrase along the lines suggested in *OD*. A more plausible strategy to address Wittgenstein's point that propositions are not names of facts, one more consistent with Russell's overall methodological and philosophical approach, would thus simply be to deny that facts are things (as opposed to saying that they are things of two different kinds). This is the approach he took, for example, with respect to both classes and propositions, when he discovered that counting them as among things led to paradoxes, given the unrestricted entity variable. In each case, in order to *preserve* (CAT), he denied that classes and propositions were things. Why would he now suddenly deny (CAT) instead? Why would he not just say that facts are not things but some sort of logical construction out of them, much as propositions and classes are also construed by him to be 'logical fictions' (*PLA*, 230) or 'false abstractions' (*PM*, 44)? That is more consistent with Russell's logical atomist methodology and, in essence, is what Wittgenstein does in *TLP* as well.

Third, and in that connection, it is not even clear that Wittgenstein rejects (CAT); so why would he point out to Russell that he needs to? In *TLP* at least, Wittgenstein appears to accept (CAT) in the form of a commitment to the idea that variables of quantification range over all and only one type of thing, namely (metaphysically simple) objects. Facts are certainly distinct from objects and things on this view but not because they belong to a distinct category of entities. Facts are not some separate type of object so much as they are merely combinations of objects (*TLP* 2.01). Hence, they cannot be named but only instead depicted by propositions.

Fourth, and in any case, even if we grant that Wittgenstein was encouraging Russell to jettison (CAT), how would that show he was pointing out CP? Could not there be other, semantic reasons why he would pressure Russell to reject (CAT), which would have little to do with the correspondence theory of truth? Fifth, and finally, the fact that Russell discusses bivalence in the passage quoted by Pincock, again, is not automatically evidence that Russell is also talking about Pincock's CP. If it exists at all, the connection between Russell's remarks in this passage and Pincock's CP is highly indirect, not 'fairly direct'. The correspondence theory of truth is not part of what Russell is talking about in this passage and, a fortiori, neither is the problem for Russell's version of that theory identified by Pincock as CP. Instead, Russell is dealing with a semantic issue, concerning how names, predicates and sentences all have 'meaning' in significantly distinct ways.

Turning now to Wittgenstein's critique of the MRTJ in *NL*, Pincock claims that when Wittgenstein insists that Russell's theory fails to make it impossible to judge that 'this table penholders the book', he is, again, simply urging Russell to reject (CAT) in order to preserve (T/F). Such judgements, according to Pincock, 'must be ruled out because that is the only plausible way to guarantee that every judgement is either true or false' (2008, 133). Allegedly, other possible alternative approaches to judgements like these, such as declaring them to be false, 'run afoul of other principles that Russell is unwilling to give up' (ibid.), including the unrestricted scope of the law of excluded middle. However, it is not clear that rejecting (CAT) is what allows Russell to preserve (T/F) here, on the assumption that is what Wittgenstein is urging Russell to do. How does rejecting (CAT) facilitate the categorization of judgements as nonsense rather than false? On Pincock's reading of what such a rejection would amount to, would it not only facilitate the categorization of facts as something distinct from things? Also, again, a connection with (T/F) does not automatically imply a connection with CP, and moreover, Wittgenstein mentions neither (T/F) nor CP in this passage. The connection to (T/F) is plausible because that is what it means for a proposition to have sense or be significant, according to both Russell and Wittgenstein (see, e.g., *PM*, 172). But the further connection to CP is a leap. CP is only one among many things within Wittgenstein's and Russell's philosophies which link to (T/F). Again, Wittgenstein's concerns here could be entirely semantic and thus have nothing to do with defining truth as correspondence.

Moreover, if this remark has nothing to do with proposition problems such as ND, then why is Wittgenstein's example 'this table penholders the book' and not 'the book penholders the table'? In other words, if ND is not at issue, then why does Wittgenstein reverse the intuitively correct order of the first and last words of the sentence? According to LI, it will be recalled, 'this table penholders the book' is supposed to result from two problematic substitutions performed on the original, perfectly intelligible utterance that 'the book is on this table', one substitution each corresponding to WD and ND, respectively. How is reversing the order of 'the book' and 'this table' meant to highlight CP according to Pincock's CI? How does the remark from *NL* (94), in which Wittgenstein develops an analogy between judgement and negation, fit into Pincock's reconstruction? There, clearly, Wittgenstein is concerned with what Pincock would categorize as 'proposition problems', including ND, WD and UP. Conceivably, Pincock could highlight a tenuous connection between negation and (T/F), but much more work would need to be done to plausibly link this remark to T/F and, a fortiori, CP.

The final epicycle of Pincock's reconstruction concerns Russell's treatment of belief in *PLA*. Before ultimately abandoning (PART) in 1919, according to

Pincock, Russell makes one last valiant effort to preserve (PART), along with (CAT) and (T/F), through the introduction of two-verb facts and the denial that one can make a 'map in space' of belief. As Pincock explains,

> Whatever the demerits of this proposal, it does seem clear that it solves the problems about correspondence that I argued bedevilled the *Theory of Knowledge* approach. For in introducing two-verb facts, Russell has found a way to have atomic complexes like A's being earlier in γ even when A is not earlier in γ. This is now noted as a puzzling fact about a belief, rather than a problem for Russell to overcome. (2008, 135)

One aspect of Pincock's reconstruction of Russell's treatment of belief in *PLA* here is correct. What is correct about Pincock's reconstruction is the idea that two-verb facts, and the impossibility of making a 'map-in-space' of belief, are noted by Russell as puzzling features of belief. However, the idea that he deploys these features to resolve CP is misconceived. Hence, regarding his discussion of belief, Russell writes:

> I hope you will forgive the fact that so much of what I say today is tentative and consists in pointing out difficulties. The subject is not very easy and it has not been much dealt with or discussed. Practically nobody has until quite lately has begun to consider the problem of the nature of belief with anything like a proper logical apparatus and therefore one has very little to help one in any discussion and so one has to be content on many points at present with pointing out difficulties rather than laying down quite clear solutions. (*PLA*, 226–27)

To summarize, Pincock may think it is 'clear' that Russell's proposal solves CP. But Russell himself thinks he is stating problems related to the analysis of belief, rather than clearly solving them. His remarks about two-verb facts and the impossibility of making a 'map-in-space' of belief are not offered as solutions to problems in the analysis of belief so much as they are presented as problems in the analysis of belief. The discovery of these problems, notably, is attributed to Wittgenstein (ibid.). Even if they were offered as solutions to something, it is a leap to say that 'something' is CP. For one thing, the nature of the alleged proposal as to precisely how two-verb facts are supposed to resolve CP is left very vague and inchoate. Moreover, if it is impossible to make a 'map-in-space' of belief (225), then how can such a map, in the form of Russell's diagram of understanding at the end of chapter I of part II of *TK*, be relied upon by Pincock (on Russell's behalf) to resolve ND, WD and UP?

Far from suggesting that CP was the problem which felled *TK*, the treatment of belief in *PLA* actually supports LI. We can see that by looking in closer detail at the difficulties alluded to by Russell in this passage. They are, in fact, Wittgenstein's criticisms of the MRTJ. Indeed, the claim that facts corresponding to statements of belief must contain at least two constituents corresponding to verbs is explicitly linked to WD by Russell and to Wittgenstein's concerns (highlighted by Stevens) about the logical status of the subordinate relation. Hence Russell insists that 'the impossibility of putting the subordinate verb on a level with its terms as an object term in the belief' (*PLA*, 226) is

> a point in which I think that the theory of judgement which I set forth once in print some years ago was a little unduly simple, because I did then treat the object verb as if one could put it as just an object like the terms, as if one could put 'loves' on a level with Desdemona and Cassio as a term for the relation 'believe'. That is why I have been laying emphasis in the lecture today on the fact that there are two verbs at least. (ibid.)

So, Russell tells us what his emphasis on two-verb facts is all about: it is his way of stating WD and the concerns it involves surrounding the logical status of the subordinate relation. When he mentions that he 'set forth in print' a theory of judgement which was 'a little unduly simple', he could be referring either to the 1912 or the 1913 version (or both), because both of them struggle with concerns regarding the logical status of the subordinate relation although they each deal with these concerns somewhat differently.

With regards to the impossibility of making a map-in-space of belief, this is a reference to the diagram of understanding that occurs at the end of chapter I of part II of *TK*. Notably, when presenting this diagram in *TK*, Russell actually refers to it as a 'map' (*TK*, 118), which links it clearly to these later comments in *PLA*. Although not getting into the technical details concerning logical forms, he is essentially merely rehearsing Wittgenstein's critique of this 'map', or diagram, which in all likelihood Russell showed Wittgenstein on 26 May 1913. What was Wittgenstein's criticism? In essence, it is that you cannot resolve WD and associated concerns regarding the logical status of the subordinate relation by drawing a diagram or 'map' in which each of the constituents of the belief are assigned to their proper positions within the logical form contained in the judgement. Why not? Because that would involve commitment to an illicit, supplementary presupposition of propositional understanding. The illicit character of this presupposition can be brought out by construing it as a premise P1) in an inference from it, along with P2) the belief that aSb, to C) aSb v ~ aSb. As we saw in Section 3.2, C) must follow from P2) in the absence of P1). Russell's takeaway from this criticism with specific reference to the diagram of understanding he showed

Wittgenstein during the tense meeting on 26 May is that it is impossible to draw a map-in-space of belief.

Contrary to Pincock's CI, finally, when Russell does eventually abandon (PART) in 1919, it is not because of an incompatibility between it and (CAT) or (T/F). Instead, it has to do with his coming to embrace neutral monism and, relatedly, rejecting mental subjects of belief. While we discussed this issue briefly earlier in Section 2.14, we will revisit it again in Section 3.9, and thus I will defer further consideration of it until then.

3.7 Russell's Diagram of Understanding

Perovic (2017) provides an in-depth exposition of Russell's diagram of understanding (Figure 3.1) and in that context, raises some important questions about the diagram. She explicitly does not use this exposition to 'advance [...] historical and interpretive theses about Russell's multiple-relation theory of judgement, its development and the reasons why he abandoned the theory' (102). Nevertheless, Perovic does draw several interesting conclusions from her exposition and makes a number of significant claims regarding Russell's diagram which bear on a main concern of this book, which is to develop and defend a reading of Wittgenstein's critique of Russell's MRTJ. Perovic's reflections also bear on a second main objective of the book, which is to familiarize readers with the relevant correspondence, documents and diagrams appreciation of which is integral to a proper understanding of Wittgenstein's criticisms. With these objectives in mind, in this section, we will consider one of Perovic's central questions about Russell's diagram and then move on to examine her claims and conclusions with respect to this question. Moreover, we will do so with a view to determining whether they provide supplemental support for LI, are consistent with it or incompatible with it. In cases where her conclusions are incompatible with LI, we will provide the reasons to prefer LI over these claims and conclusions.

The central question of Perovic's I wish to consider is: over and above the four lines of Russell's diagram which connect the subject, S, to each of $R(x,y)$, similarity, A and B, '*what is the role of additional lines that connect* similarity *to* A *and* B, *and that connect the form* R(x, y) *to* A, B, *and* similarity?' (2017, 107; emphases in the original). Perovic notes that there appears to be an incongruity with regards to how these lines are characterized by Russell and then moves on to examine several different ways one might resolve the incongruity. The incongruity consists in the fact that, when describing the diagram in *TK* (118) Russell appears to distinguish four distinct relations: one which goes from S to the four objects, another from $R(x,y)$ to similarity, yet another from $R(x,y)$ to A and B and finally a relation from similarity to A and B. Yet in *TK* (112) he describes the understanding complex later depicted in the map in *TK* (118) as involving one 'comprehensive relation' (112). After considering several flawed proposals for resolving this tension by treating each of these as distinct relations, Perovic concludes that while Russell speaks 'somewhat loosely' in *TK* (118) when he refers to four seemingly separate relations, in fact what Russell has in mind is that they are all 'parts' of

> one cognitive relation of understanding [...] By singling them out Russell was attempting to draw attention to different relationships that are established between the terms when the relation of understanding is exemplified in the complex. (2017, 111)

While we should not take the notion of 'parts of a relation' too literally since it might not make much sense metaphysically nor jive with Russell's philosophical commitments, 'there is certainly nothing incoherent about him drawing attention to parts of an understanding *complex* by appealing to different ways in which terms are related by the understanding relation' (ibid.).

Subsequently, Perovic moves on to more closely examine the nature of this comprehensive, cognitive relation and to highlight several interesting features of, and tensions within, its characterization. The first tension Perovic tries to highlight concerns the epistemic status of the logical form, for example, $R(x,y)$. At times Russell appears to characterize *acquaintance* with logical form as presupposed by propositional understanding (*TK*, 113), while elsewhere he claims that we must *understand* the form before we understand a proposition (116). This is significant, since acquaintance and understanding are two very different sorts of relations, according to Russell, which have very different sorts of objects. As Russell notes in *TK* (108), for instance, acquaintance is a dual relation whereas understanding is a multiple relation. Moreover, the sorts of things which are objects of understanding, namely propositions, can be either true or false, whereas 'an object of acquaintance is not true and false, but is simply what it is: there is no dualism of true and false objects of acquaintance' (ibid.). Later, in chapter III of part II on 'Various Examples of Understanding', Russell himself highlights this tension before concluding, as Perovic notes (2017, 116), that there is no difference between acquaintance and understanding when it comes to logical form (*TK*, 130). For our purposes, it is worth reflecting on what Russell has to say about the apparent tension in this context because it is framed in such a way as to suggest that Russell is either implicitly responding to or perhaps anticipating Wittgenstein's critique that 'facts cannot be named' (*NL*, 97–98, 107). What Russell has to say is as follows:

The case of a pure form is instructive for several reasons. To begin with, although 'something has some relation to something' is a proposition, and is true, it is nevertheless simple; hence understanding and believing, in this case; must both be dual relations. The question therefore arises: How do they differ from acquaintance? And what becomes of the opposition of truth and falsehood in such cases? [...] How can an object be at once simple and a 'fact', in the sense in which a 'fact' is opposed to a simple particular and is the sort of object whose reality makes a proposition true? Why, if pure forms are simple is it so obviously inappropriate to give them names, such as John and Peter? (*TK*, 130)

As we shall see in more detail in Section 4.3, in *NL* Wittgenstein is critical of Russell's account of logical form on the grounds that it illicitly attempts to combine features of simple and complex entities. While simples can be named, for example, facts are complex and thus cannot be named but only described by propositions with sense.

In any case, after acknowledging this tension within Russell's account of the epistemology of logical form, Perovic moves on to consider the role logical forms are supposed to play within the account of propositional understanding which Russell is attempting to convey within the map or diagram of understanding that appears in *TK* (118) at the end of chapter I of part II. In a word, Perovic concludes that its role within Russell's account is not as central as one might be led to suppose by its more or less central position in the diagram. As Perovic explains:

I do not wish to indicate, however, that the logical form $R(x, y)$ is supposed by itself to structure A, B, and *similarity* in the understanding complex. I find little evidence for that interpretation of the role of the form in Russell [...] It also seems incorrect to interpret the role of the logical form $R(x, y)$ as a template through which the understanding relation 'reaches out' and unifies the constituents of the would be complex [...] Therefore, I suggest, each of the constituents, together with the form and the understanding relation that relates them all, contributes to the particular structure of the understanding complex. (2017, 118–19; emphasis in the original)

According to Perovic, this suggestion is bolstered by Russell's description in *TK* (117) of the various ways in which different constituents occur within the understanding complex diagrammed in it (118). Additional textual support for this suggestion can, she insists, be found once again in chapter III of part II dealing with 'Various Examples of Understanding', where Russell explains that the 'classification of mental facts by the logical character of the objects involved turns out to be far more important than their classification by their own logical form' (131). Here Russell appears to be speaking of the logical form of mental facts as opposed to those occurring as constituents in cognitive complexes. This would tend to undermine to a degree its strength as a piece of evidence in favour of Perovic's claim that logical forms are not as central within Russell's account of cognitive complexes as the central positioning of $R(x, y)$ in Russell's diagram might lead one to suppose. Nevertheless, the idea that, aside from the logical form which occurs as a constituent of the cognitive complex, the logical character of other constituents also contributes to the structure of that complex is certainly consistent with LI. As we saw earlier in Section 3.6, according to LI, assigning the subordinate relation to a position within the logical form of a complex is the first step within an analytical procedure that Russell describes as 'position in a complex' analysis. The logical character of the subordinate relation contributes significantly to the structure of the cognitive complex created through that process, as we shall momentarily discuss in more detail.

Nevertheless, Perovic's denial in the earlier quotation, that it is correct to characterize a logical form as a template, and subsequent remarks concerning Russell's 'position in a complex' analysis might seem to be incompatible with LI. With respect to Russell's 'position in a complex' analysis she explains that

> it is important to note that there seems to be nothing more to Russell's notion of 'position' than 'standing in a position relation to a complex', i.e., there is no indication of positions being thought by him as analogous to empty slots or blank spaces in a complex (or on sides of relations). Thus, the image of something like '__is similar to__' is far from what he seems to have in mind when it comes to the notion of 'position'. (2017, 122; emphasis in the original)

As evidence for this claim, Perovic highlights what Russell has to say about symmetrical versus unsymmetrical complexes in chapter II of part II. There he says that 'a complex may be called "symmetrical" with respect to two of its constituents if they occupy the same position in the complex' (*TK*, 122). He gives the example of 'A and B are similar' and says that in this complex 'A and B occupy the same position' (ibid.). As we have seen, Russell's diagram of understanding at the end of chapter I of part II depicts the cognitive complex which exists when S understands that 'A and B are similar'. Yet, inspecting the diagram, we see clearly that A and B occupy two numerically distinct positions, which might seem contrary to the earlier quotation. So, what is going on?

What explains the apparent incongruity is that, while perhaps speaking somewhat loosely here just as he did in the case of describing various parts of one comprehensive relation of understanding, when Russell says in *TK* (122) that A and B occupy the same position in the complex, he means they occupy qualitatively identical positions, not a numerically identical position. And inspecting the diagram, this is precisely what it appears to show. 'A' and 'B' each have numerically distinct positions in the complex, but these two positions are qualitatively identical in the sense that there are no significant differences between the two positions with respect to how they relate to the other constituents of the complex, including the subject, similarity and $R(x, y)$. Thinking about the complex this way is then consistent with the idea that the logical form *is* like a template in some important respects and that it also contains positions analogous to empty 'slots' but that in a symmetrical complex the slots will be numerically but not qualitatively different.

Perovic appears to be correct in her assertion that within his diagram of understanding, Russell means to depict one, comprehensive relation of understanding. She also appears to be correct when she claims that there is more to the structure of the cognitive complex than is determined by the logical form it contains and that the logical nature of other constituents, notably the subordinate relation, contributes to the structure of the complex. However, it seems to me to be a mistake to deny that the logical form is analogous to a template which contains slots or blank spaces. Perovic may be correct to deny that the cognitive relation 'reaches out' and unifies the constituents of the complex 'through' the logical form. Logical forms are not synthetic, ontological, mental spectacles analogous to 3-D glasses. But what the cognitive relation of understanding does do, according to defenders of LI, is assign constituents to positions within the logical form through an analytic procedure of understanding. If LI is correct, then the logical form contained within a cognitive complex is somewhat analogous to a template with empty slots or positions to which constituents are assigned through an analytical procedure. The first step in this procedure is to assign the position of the subordinate relation. This step allegedly resolves WD. The logical nature of the subordinate relation then determines the number and nature of the other positions in the logical form. The number and nature of these positions will be determined, for instance, by the adicity of the relation and whether it is symmetrical or unsymmetrical. Depending on these factors the next phase of the analytic procedure may be more or less involved. If the subordinate relation is unsymmetrical, it will generate qualitatively distinct positions. This will generate ND and call for more in-depth position in a complex analysis, involving associated complexes, heterogeneous positions and so on. If, by contrast, the subordinate relation is dyadic and symmetrical as in the case of S understanding that 'A and B are similar', the second step of the analytic procedure involved in 'understanding a proposition' will be quite straightforward. It will involve assigning each of two constituents to one of two numerically distinct, but qualitatively identical positions within the logical form of the complex. These constituents will thereby be brought into relation with the general logical form of dyadic complexes, as Russell describes in *TK* (116) and depicts in his diagram (118). The result of this analytic procedure for the case of 'A and B are similar' is given in P1), that is, $(\exists x)\ (\exists R)\ (\exists y)\ (((x=a)\ \&\ (R=S))\ \&\ (y=b))$. Wittgenstein, as we have seen, objects to P1) along with the analytic procedure depicted in Russell's diagram of understanding on the grounds that aSb v ~ aSb should follow from aSb directly, in the absence of P1).

3.8 'Props'

An alternative account of the 'premiss' alluded to in the mid-June letter, and of its significance, is offered by Rosalind Carey, who takes Wittgenstein to be referencing a set of Russell's working notes called 'Props' (*CP*, 7: Appendix B.1) composed on 26 May 1913 or shortly thereafter (Carey 2007, 96). 'Props' consists of three pages, the first of which, as noted by E. R. Eames, is written 'on the verso of a rejected folio 197 of the book manuscript' (*CP*, 7: 195, 197). The rejected folio can be dated to 24 May, since Russell completed part I of the manuscript, up to folio 190, on 23 May. In correspondence with Morrell on 24 May, Russell reports 'embarking' on chapter I of part II on that day (Russell to Morrell, #785; Blackwell and Eames 1992, xxv). Moreover, the fact that the folio is marked 197 places it within the ten per day that Russell planned to write (Blackwell and Eames 1992, xxiv). Finally, the rejected folio contains a discussion of Meinong which was replaced by pages 107: 37–108:12, contained in chapter II of part I, placing it with other materials we know he wrote on 24 May. After showing chapter I of part II to Wittgenstein on 26 May, Russell likely composed 'Props' shortly thereafter on the back of this rejected folio.

In these notes, Carey argues, Russell develops a proposal according to which 'neutral facts' are deployed to accommodate Wittgenstein's thesis of bipolarity. On Carey's reading, the 'premiss' referred to in the mid-June letter asserts the existence of the neutral fact which comprises the judgement fact (2007, 101). Let us call Carey's reading the neutral fact interpretation (NFI). According to NFI, in 'Props' Russell is attempting to develop and articulate this proposal, while also considering the viability of Wittgenstein's alternative extensionalist approach according to which subjective propositional attitudes must be eliminated. Neutral facts are eventually found wanting as an account of bipolarity, which then leads Russell into the following dilemma, according to Carey: bipolarity can be accommodated, but only by acceding to Wittgenstein's austere extensionalism. Russell is unwilling to do this, however, as evidenced by marginalia on his copy of *NL* as well as remarks he makes in *OKEW* (Carey 2007, 108–9). Russell's unwillingness to accede to extensionalism explains why, according to Carey, Russell is 'paralyzed' by Wittgenstein's objection and abandons the manuscript but does not abandon his theory of judgement (102, 107). Not, at least, until 1919 when he embraces neutral monism and rejects mental subjects of belief. The diagrams in 'Props' represent Russell's attempts to grapple with this dilemma by undertaking to implement extensionalism and bipolarity.

More careful consideration of 'Props', by contrast, and closer inspection of the diagrams it contains reveal Russell hard at work trying to salvage the MRTJ in light of Wittgenstein's criticisms by replacing logical forms with neutral facts. Hence, when articulating the proposal contained in 'Props', Russell insists that according to it, 'judgment will still be a multiple relation, but its terms will not be the same as in my old theory. The neutral fact replaces the *form*' (*CP*, 7: 197; emphasis in the original). Within the diagrams contained in 'Props', Russell is attempting to depict the nature of the relationship between neutral facts and positive or negative facts. His thought is that by the law of excluded middle, either the positive fact $+(xRy)$ or the negative fact $-(xRy)$ must exist. In either case, the neutral fact $+/-(xRy)$ will exist, and it will 'provide a meaning for *possibility*' (7: 195; emphasis in the original). The positive judgement will correspond to the positive fact, the negative judgement will correspond to the negative fact and the neutral judgement (understanding?) will correspond to the neutral fact (7: 199).

Figure 3.2 appears on the first page of 'Props'. Carey finds it 'striking' (2007, 106) that the subject is not depicted either in this diagram or in the diagram shown in Figure 3.3. This, she thinks, is evidence of Russell experimenting with the elimination of belief states and the implementation of extensionalism. However, it is not surprising that the subject is not depicted in this diagram, since in it, Russell is not endeavouring to diagram 'understanding', as Carey supposes (103), but is instead attempting to depict the relationship between the neutral fact which occurs in the proposition and the positive fact which occurs in the world. This explains why, in diagraming the fact, a horizontal arrow is used to indicate that the relation 'R' relates x to y, whereas in diagramming the neutral fact contained in the proposition, there is no horizontal arrow and thus no suggestion that R actually relates. Instead, we find a vertical arrow which depicts a relation between the neutral fact and the positive fact.

Building on this, in Figure 3.3, Russell depicts the relation between the neutral fact, which he indicates with the $+/-$ sign, and each of the positive

116   WITTGENSTEIN'S CRITIQUE OF RUSSELL'S MRTJ

Figure 3.2 Props #1 (Russell's neutral facts).

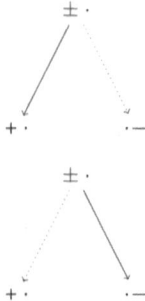

Figure 3.3 Props #2 (Russell's neutral facts).

fact and the negative fact, respectively. Figure 3.3 is not a diagram of bipolarity, as Carey supposes (2007, 104), but of the two distinct ways that a neutral fact can relate to the world, depending upon whether the relevant fact is positive or negative. Again, Russell's thought is that at least one of these facts must obtain by the law of excluded middle. If the positive fact obtains, then the relation between the neutral fact as it occurs in the proposition and the relevant existing fact will correspond to what is depicted in the top of the two diagrams in Figure 3.3. If the negative fact obtains, then the relation depicted in the bottom diagram will hold. In either case, the broken line indicates the possibility of such a relation which is nevertheless not actual because the relevant fact does not exist.

Russell concludes 'Props' by noting that the proposal it contains is plagued by 'great difficulties'. Notably, he says that there 'will only be a neutral fact when the objects are of the right types' (*CP*, 7: 199). Here Russell is referring to type* distinctions and referencing WD. We will revisit type* distinctions in greater detail momentarily, in Section 3.9. For now, however, it will be recalled that they are ontological distinctions with implications for which positions constituents of different types* can and cannot occur in within a logically possible complex. For instance, Socrates cannot occur in a complex in predicative position since he is not a property. The neutral fact can only guarantee the sense of a judgement if its constituents are of the right types. But this involves the same 'old difficulties'. Why, for instance, is +/-J(xyz) not a well-formed neutral judgement? Neutral facts cannot simply be identified with positive facts, and thus there is no guarantee that any relation they contain will actually relate. But in that case, why can they not be replaced by particulars, which also do not relate, to yield a well-formed neutral fact?

There are several reasons to think, contrary to Carey's NFI, that what appears in 'Props' is not the target of Wittgenstein's objection in the mid-June letter but is instead, in accordance with LI, an attempt to obviate the objection which Wittgenstein expressed first inarticulately on 26 May and then 'exactly' in the mid-June letter. The first reason is that there is no evidence Russell ever showed 'Props' to Wittgenstein. They are simply a set of working notes, found by archivists, and catalogued as an appendix (B.1), along with *CP* vol. 7, based on the (plausible) conjecture that they somehow belong with these materials. The second and related reason is that there *is* good evidence that Russell did show Wittgenstein chapter I of part II on 26 May, since as we saw earlier in Section 1.6, in a 27 May letter to Morrell (quoted in Griffin 1992, 446) Russell reports showing Wittgenstein a 'crucial part' of the manuscript and claims that he objected to it 'inarticulately' on that day. For several other reasons recounted in Section 1.6, it is highly likely that portions of chapter I of part II were included amongst these crucial parts. Third, there is no conclusive evidence that Wittgenstein adhered to bipolarity by June 1913.[1] Wittgenstein does not refer to 'the bipolarity of the proposition' anywhere in the extant record until he does so in *NL* (94). This and other remarks concerning bipolarity contained in *NL* were composed several months after Wittgenstein's May–June critique of Russell's MRTJ and may reflect themes which emerged out of these criticisms, rather than concerns which motivated them. Fourth, there exists no solid evidence that Wittgenstein adhered to extensionalism or sought to eliminate subjective belief states until *NDM* which, again, was composed several months (nearly a year) after Wittgenstein's May–June critique of Russell's MRTJ.

---

[1] There exists suggestive, though not conclusive, evidence that Wittgenstein may have adhered to bipolarity as early as mid-March 1913. See footnote 3.

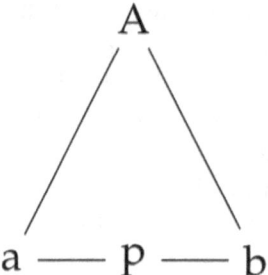

Figure 3.4 Wittgenstein's diagram of 'A believes that p'.

In Chapter 4 I will argue that extensionalism is something that appears to have emerged out of Wittgenstein's work on something called the 'ab-notation', which, as we shall explore in depth in Section 4.4, he used to study bipolarity in abstraction from truth-functionality. And while we have seen that Wittgenstein was apt to encourage Russell to focus more on propositions than on judgements, the idea of eliminating belief states is not something he explicitly proposes until April 1914, in the context of *NDM* (119). Indeed, *NL* actually contains a diagram which is supposed to depict 'A believes p' in the ab-notation (*NL*, 106). Since the subject 'A' features prominently in this diagram (Figure 3.4), it is odd that, in support of NFI, Carey cites (2007, 104) the alleged resemblance between this diagram and Figure 3.3 as evidence of Wittgenstein successfully influencing Russell to embrace a more austere extensionalist approach.

Carey follows the editors of *CP* vol. 7 in construing 'Props' as 'an attempt to take account of Wittgenstein's new theory of propositions' (*CP*, 7: 195). In response to the editor's misgivings about this construal, since 'we do not know that Wittgenstein had, by that time, made as much progress towards his new view as this suggests' (ibid.), Carey claims that 'the notes are evidence that it was' (2007, 96). This claim, however, is dubious in light of the interpretive flaws highlighted earlier, with respect to NFI's account of 'Props' and especially of the diagrams it contains. By contrast, LI is able to accommodate the evidence contained in 'Props' along with other, related evidence in a much more straightforward and convincing way. According to LI, Russell writes 'Props' on or shortly after 26 May 1913. He does this as an attempt to salvage the MRTJ in light of Wittgenstein's criticisms of his proposal, in chapter I of part II of *TK*, to block WD by assigning object terms of cognitive complexes to positions within the logical forms themselves contained as constituents of the cognitive complex. 'Props' attempts to evade Wittgenstein's critique of this proposal expressed first inarticulately in conversation on 26 May and then exactly in the mid-June letter by developing a version of the MRTJ which deploys neutral facts in lieu of logical forms in order to evade WD. Russell concludes that this proposal does not work and drops it. He does not abandon the MRTJ at this point, because he has nothing to abandon it in favour of. He eventually abandons the manuscript however because he thinks the MRTJ is not satisfactory in its current form, and thus that the book 'goes to pieces' (Blackwell and Eames 1992, xxi–xxii) at the points it introduces the MRTJ. We will discuss this issue in more detail in Section 3.12.

Contrary to Carey's NFI, Wittgenstein likely never sees 'Props' nor hears about it. His May–June critique is not driven by concerns about extensionalism and nor is bipolarity a primary motivator though it is a significant implication thereof which he would subsequently move on to explore in *NL*. Wittgenstein's May–June critique of Russell's MRTJ instead focuses on its inability to provide a theory of atomic propositional content which evades ND, WD and UP. Because it involves introducing extraneous stipulations upon the admissible constituents of cognitive complexes, it fails to resolve these issues in a way which is consistent with basic logical intuitions. Wittgenstein's 'new theory of propositions' is not something he already has on hand in May–June 1913. As we shall see in more detail in Section 4.1, the picture theory of propositions does not show up in the record until it appears in *NL* (96–97), and even there it only appears in inchoate form. The picture theory makes no explicit appearance until September 1914, in the context of *NB* (6–7).

3.9 Type* Distinctions Reappraised

In Section 2.11, we saw that each of Landini (1991, 2007, 2021) and Giaretta (1997) detected the existence of distinctions of 'type' within *TK*, which were to be carefully distinguished and clearly demarcated from *PM* types. To that end, Landini gave these distinctions a unique designation, specifically type* distinctions. While originally, Landini (1991) conceived of these distinctions, simply, as differentiating universals from particulars on the grounds that the former had both an individual and a predicable nature whereas the latter had only an individual but not a predicable nature, later, perhaps in response to Giaretta (1997), Landini (2007) then expanded the category of type* distinctions to include divisions between entities which are and are not complex. In Section 3.5, moreover, we saw that Pincock identified analogous distinctions, which he referred to as distinctions of 'kind'. Notably, Pincock drew a link between such distinctions and Russell's concept of heterogeneity.

From the perspective of a defender of LI, type* distinctions are significant because, depending upon how we construe them, they can either be seen as undermining or as supporting our reading of Wittgenstein's critique of Russell's MRTJ. If type* distinctions between particulars and universals are read as being brute or as basic metaphysical distinctions akin to Pincock's distinctions of kind, distinctions which Russell might readily avail himself of in order to block WD independently of any appeal to supplementary premises or significance constraints, then they could be seen as undermining LI. As defenders of LI, we can allow that such distinctions exist between types*, or kinds of constituents of complexes, but we cannot allow that such distinction exist between the subordinate relation of a cognitive complex and the other object terms of the complex. For our account of Wittgenstein's critique of the MRTJ to work, it must be that each of the object terms of a cognitive complex are on a logical and ontological par. On the other hand, if type* distinctions are seen as, at least in some cases, emerging *from* or out of Russell's position in a complex analysis, then they could be thought of as providing support or evidence for LI. So understood, they would show that Russell has to deploy an analytical procedure in order to *emulate* type* distinctions between universals and particulars, precisely because he *cannot* avail himself of brute metaphysical distinctions of type* in order to block WD. This analytic procedure would then embody the illicit supplemental premises or constraints which, according to LI, Wittgenstein means to deny Russell access to. For these reasons, it is crucial to any defensible reading of Wittgenstein's critique of the MRTJ that it address, as well as correctly characterize, the nature of these type* distinctions.

Thus, in this section, we will carefully consider the nature of type* distinctions between universals and particulars in *TK* and examine their status relative both to type* distinctions between complexes and entities which are not complex, as well as to Russell's associated notion of heterogeneity. I will argue that while type* distinctions of a brute metaphysical nature are appealed to by Russell in *TK*, they do not apply to the subordinate relation of cognitive complexes, because in such cases the subordinate relation does not relate. This explains why, in such cases Russell must instead attempt to emulate type* distinctions via an analytical procedure in which the subordinate relation of a cognitive complex is assigned to the correct position within the logical form contained in the cognitive complex.

With regards to Landini's characterization of type* distinctions between universals and particulars, it is important to note that it is prima facie ambiguous between the two possible interpretations outlined earlier. For instance, in Section 2.11, we saw that, in support of his claim that Russell's account relies on type* distinctions in order to block WD, Landini (1991, 64) quotes Russell's remark, in a footnote in *TK* (146), that 'the position of R, unlike that of the other constituents, *can* be assigned relatively to the form: this is what enables us to speak of it as the relating relation' (emphasis in the original). According to Landini, this quotation is evidence that Russell adheres to or accepts a logical difference between universals and particulars. But from the perspective of a defender of LI, it is crucial to think more carefully about the nature both of this evidence and of this putative logical difference. From the perspective of the defender of LI, in this remark Russell should be read as asserting that assigning R relatively to the form is what allows us to speak of it *as if* it were a relating relation (i.e. as what Giaretta calls a 'formally relating relation'), though it does not actually relate. An opponent of LI might instead prefer to read this remark as saying that it is only because of a prior, brute metaphysical distinction between universals and particulars that we are able to assign R to the position of subordinate relation.

Evidence that Landini would adhere to the latter interpretation can be found in a remark from *Wittgenstein's Apprenticeship with Russell*, in which he states that, in the case of understanding the statement 'a is red', 'the direction problem does not arise [...] [since] the corresponding complexes are non-permutative' (2007, 58). In other words, if S believes that 'a is red', then S's belief is not susceptible to WD because there can be no logically possible complex in which the positions of 'a' and 'x is red' are interchanged relative to those they have within the complex corresponding to S's belief, in the event it is true. In this regard, Landini goes on to insist, the case of 'a is red' contrasts with the case of 'a loves b'. In the case of S's belief in the latter, 'the would-be corresponding complex is permutative, and consequently Russell's characterization of the notion of "correspondence" is indirect' (59). In other words, direction problems do not arise in the case of S's belief that 'a is red', and so no analysis is called for. The putative belief that 'red is a' is ruled out, and so WD is blocked, by brute or basic type* distinctions between individuals and universals. There can be no logically possible complex corresponding to the putative belief that 'red is a', and thus there can be no such belief. In the case of S's belief that 'a loves b', by contrast, analysis *is* called for because the ostensibly corresponding complex is permutative. This is where, according to Landini, Russell's 'position in a complex' analysis kicks in to provide non-permutative complexes associated with problematic, permutative ones.

According to a defender of LI, however, to say that there can be no logically possible complex corresponding to the belief that 'red is a' (or 'mortality is Socrates') is merely another way of stating WD, as opposed to resolving it. Indeed, there cannot be a logically possible complex corresponding to the belief that 'red is a', but precisely the problem for Russell's MRTJ is that it cannot rule out beliefs which would require such logically impossible complexes to make them true. This, in a nutshell, *is* WD. In an attempt to block WD, Russell must therefore endeavour to emulate type* distinctions between universals and particulars precisely because the relevant metaphysical distinctions are inoperative with respect to the object terms of a judgement, since the subordinate relation does not relate. This is what he is attempting to accomplish, in *TK* (146), when he states that assigning the position of the relation R allows us to speak of it as the relating relation. The implication is that we could not speak of it as such unless it were first assigned to the relevant position. Similarly, again in *TK* (116), he says that assigning the position of the relation of similarity, and other constituents, relative to the logical form of dual complexes is a crucial precondition of propositional understanding. He also attempts (*TK*, 118) to provide a 'map-in-space' of the cognitive complex which results from the procedure of making these assignments. So again, on the 1913 *TK* version of the MRTJ, type* distinctions between the object terms of a judgement are something that emerge only from a rather involved analytic procedure. They are not brute, or basic logical, metaphysical or structural distinctions which can be relied upon to block WD independently of the stipulations involved in such a procedure.

That type* distinctions do not obviate the need for such an analytical procedure is even clearer in the case of Russell's treatment of ND. In that context, as we have seen, Russell deploys position in a complex analysis to define non-permutative complexes associated with problematic, permutative ones. Within this proposed solution to ND, type* distinctions only become relevant, and operative, *following* position in a complex analysis, not prior to it. It is only once this analytic procedure has been used to define non-permutative complexes associated with permutative ones that type* distinctions between relatively complex and simple entities can subsequently be relied upon to block ND. Their force and effectiveness in resolving ND thus supervenes on a prior, analytical procedure.

To the extent it acknowledges that Russell somehow became aware that the sorts of stipulations characteristic of this analytical procedure are required in order for his MRTJ to work, Giaretta's account of the role played by type* distinctions in the demise of *TK* is correct as far as it goes. However, it does not go far enough given what the extant correspondence and textual evidence allows. What better candidate for the illicit supplementary premises mentioned in Wittgenstein's June letter could there be than the aforementioned stipulations, required to resolve each of WD and ND? We know Wittgenstein was concerned with each of those thanks, inter alia, to the remark from *NL* in which Wittgenstein insists that Russell's theory cannot exclude the judgement that 'the table penholders the book' as nonsense. Does it not stand to reason, then, that Wittgenstein's exactly expressed objection to Russell's MRTJ in the mid-June letter would bear on WD and ND? On that assumption, the idea that Wittgenstein objected to stipulations illicitly invoked to block WD and ND seems almost irresistible. And thus, there is no reason to equivocate with respect to, or to qualify, as Giaretta does, the claim that it was Wittgenstein who made Russell aware that his MRTJ required illicit stipulations. According to LI, this is precisely the nature of Wittgenstein's objection as recorded in the mid-June letter.

3.10 Revisiting Landini on Wittgenstein's Critique of the MRTJ

In Section 2.12, we saw that according to Landini's SI, Wittgenstein's critique of the MRTJ was driven by his emerging 'doctrine' or 'intuition' of showing. While, as Landini acknowledges, the doctrine is not formulated *explicitly* until April 1914 (2020, 199, 211), in the context of the *Notes Dictated to Moore in Norway*, he sees it as implicit in much earlier remarks, going as far back as summer 1912. The doctrine of showing is evident, according to Landini, both in correspondence with Russell over the years 1912–13, but also within Wittgenstein's reflections on the ab-notation in, inter alia, *NL*. In essence, according to Landini's SI, the ab-notation is Wittgenstein's attempt to implement the doctrine of showing, and thus evidence of Wittgenstein's work on the ab-notation may be taken as a reliable indicator of the presence of his doctrine, or intuition, of showing (196, 223). Such evidence can readily be found both within his correspondence to Russell, as well as within the 1913 *Notes on Logic*. When Wittgenstein insists, in the June 1913 letter, that Russell's MRTJ cannot guarantee that $aRb \vee \sim aRb$ does not follow without further premises, this is a roundabout way of saying that it does not conform to Wittgenstein's doctrine of showing. Since Wittgenstein's criticism is motivated by his doctrine of showing, and Wittgenstein's doctrine of showing is merely an unsupported intuition of Wittgenstein's which Russell had no genuine reason to take seriously, we have no good reason to take Wittgenstein's critique of the MRTJ seriously either, according to SI. As Landini explains:

> The explicit purpose of the *ab*-notation was precisely to implement *Showing*. It is none other than Wittgenstein's doctrine that truth-conditions are *shown* that is precisely what imposes the requirement that nonsense truth-bearers (e.g., beliefs) be ruled out without further premises. Once we see that *showing* is what was behind Wittgenstein's criticism, we can confidently and vehemently object that Russell's multiple-relation theory doesn't require and such thing. It is high time scholars admit this and move on. Wittgenstein's criticism is altogether impotent.

That the multiple-relation theory fails the requirements of Wittgenstein's *Showing* is no relevant criticism at all. (2021, 156–57; emphases in the original)

If Landini's SI is correct, this would undermine LI, since according to LI, Wittgenstein's demand that any tautology follow from any well-formed judgement in the absence of further premises is a well-founded objection, not an unsupported intuition. Far from being impotent, it is devastating, which explains why Russell characterized it as paralyzing. It is certainly consistent with LI to hold that the saying/showing distinction *emerged from* the sorts of considerations that Wittgenstein introduces in the context of his critique of the MRTJ. But according to LI, as we have seen, what motivates the objection contained in the mid-June 1913 letter is not an intuition of showing but instead a basic logical intuition which Russell surely shared, to the effect that tautologies follow from well-formed propositions independently of supplemental support. To bolster the prospects of LI relative to SI, therefore, it will be helpful to look critically at the evidence Landini provides for assigning such early dates to the saying/showing distinction and to consider whether the correspondence and textual evidence fits better with the idea that the saying/showing distinction emerges later, as part of Wittgenstein's attempts to characterize logical form in a way that is not susceptible to the objections he levelled against Russell's MRTJ in May–June 1913.

First, even if we accept Landini's claim that Wittgenstein's reflections on the ab-notation can be taken as evidence for his adhering to the saying/showing distinction, the ab-notation does not appear in the record until *NL*, dictated in October 1913,[2] several months after Wittgenstein's critique of the MRTJ in May–June 1913.[3] Likewise, the fact that Wittgenstein used the word

---

[2] For a more detailed history of the circumstances surrounding the composition of *NL*, see Potter (2009, Appendix A).

[3] There exists suggestive, but not conclusive, evidence that Wittgenstein had an at least somewhat developed conception of the ab-notation as early as mid-March 1913. The evidence consists of (1) an anecdote told by Russell in his autobiography (*ABR*, 314–15) concerning a visit Wittgenstein paid to the Whiteheads (the subject of the anecdote is a discussion of the ab-notation between Wittgenstein and Whitehead); and (2) a 15 March 1913 letter (Russell to Morrell #721) which mentions a recent visit to the Whiteheads during which Wittgenstein and Whitehead had a discussion. While this evidence is suggestive, it is not clear how much weight can be placed on it as a means of dating the ab-notation to mid-March 1913. Writing in the late 1960s Russell is recalling, second-hand, an anecdote that was told to him by Whitehead at some point, about an event which allegedly occurred over 50 years earlier. The way the anecdote is framed makes it seem as if Russell was not present at the meeting when the correspondence with Morrell indicates he was present at the 15 March 1913 meeting. Thus, the meeting described in the anecdote, if it actually occurred at all and is not simply a blend of distinct experiences or a confabulation, may not be the same meeting as that referred

'show' in a quotation from the *Tractatus*, published in 1922, is not especially persuasive evidence that it marks a distinction Wittgenstein adhered to in June 1913. Moreover, the word 'show' as used in this context (*TLP* 5.5422) does not obviously refer to the sort of 'showing' involved in Wittgenstein's distinction between saying and showing. In this context, Wittgenstein may very well simply be talking about what a *correct explanation* of judgement must 'show', that is, explain, not what must be shown by *well-formed propositions* but not be said by them.

Second, as we will see in more detail in Section 4.4, the main purpose of the ab-notation is simply to study bipolarity, in abstraction from truth-functionality. In so doing, Wittgenstein developed and implemented a variety of related but distinct ideas. Among these are included the idea that apparently distinct but equivalent ab-functions have a common symbolic form (*CL*, 48). Another was that distinct ab-functions are cross-definable or interdefinable (*NL*, 106). A third is that all ab-functions may be reproduced by repeated applications of a single ab-function (102). Yet another was the idea that all tautologies have a common symbolic form by which they can be distinguished as against all other propositions (*CL*, 52–53). Certainly, these various ideas and themes are importantly associated within the final system presented in the *Tractatus*, but it is a mistake to simply identify them or treat them all as attempts to implement the distinction between saying and showing. Landini writes, for instance, that

> the purpose of the *ab*-Notation is to realize Wittgenstein's thesis that there is a way to show that all and only logical equivalents of quantification theory have the same expression and that tautologies are immediately revealed in the symbolism. (2021, 148)

That there exists a notation in which all logically equivalent propositions can be expressed in the same way, and that the logical form of propositions must be shown rather than said, are, however, two independent claims. As we will see in more detail in Section 4.4, the latter is an idea which appears to have emerged in Norway, as Wittgenstein continued to reflect on the unipolar character of tautologies and began to see an important connection between this discovery and his views on logical form. Landini himself provides several notations (including both Venn diagrammatic notations alongside Wittgenstein's ab-notation and variants of his truth-tabular notation (2020,

---

to in the 15 March 1913 letter. It is of course possible that Russell described some of the details wrong, details which are irrelevant to the substance of the anecdote. And it is of course possible that the ab-notation was in fact discussed at this 15 March 1913 meeting. But the evidence in question, though certainly intriguing, is hardly conclusive.

200–201)) which, allegedly, *show* the logical properties of the propositions they express. So, clearly, the idea that notations can show the logical properties of the propositions they express is a different claim than that there is one single notation in which all logically equivalent propositions can be expressed in the same way.

Landini argues that the point and purpose of Wittgenstein's N-operator notation is to implement the idea that all tautologies in particular can be expressed via one and the same form (2020, 212). (We will probe and explicate Wittgenstein's N-operator notation in much more detail in Sections 4.2 and 4.9. For now it is enough to note that N is a truth-functional operator by which it is possible, Wittgenstein claims in *TLP*, to express all meaningful propositions via series of successive applications.) In this way Landini attempts to link the N-operator to the doctrine of showing by suggesting that the purport of the N-operator is to show the logical form of tautologies. However, insofar as the N-notation provides a form particular and common to all tautologies, it does so simply as a by-product of its being designed to make it possible to express all logically equivalent propositions in the same way, since all tautologies are logically equivalent. As we shall see in Section 4.9, N is designed primarily to implement the general propositional form, not the saying/showing distinction. It does nothing to illuminate how elementary propositions show their logical form, for example, since it operates independently of their internal structure (Connelly 2017). Moreover, even if Landini's intriguing suggestion (2020, 213) that the discovery of Wittgenstein's N-operator notation can be dated to May 1915 is correct, this would still be two years following Wittgenstein's critique of the MRTJ and thus cannot plausibly be taken as evidence that on the assumption the N-operator notation implements the saying/showing distinction, the doctrine or intuition of showing is already present within Wittgenstein's May–June 1913 critique of Russell's MRTJ.

A better explanation of the saying/showing distinction, consistent with LI, is that it is an idea Wittgenstein developed while working in Norway, as an attempt to address problems inherent in the 'beastly theory of types' (*CL*, 37) without falling prey to his own objections to the account of logical form inherent in Russell's 1913 MRTJ. The idea gained supplemental support from Wittgenstein's discovery, during his exploration with the ab-notation, that tautologies are unipolar, and so lack sense, and possess a unique status relative to all other propositions. We can gain more insight into the nature of Wittgenstein's concerns about types by reflecting further on his January 1913 letter to Russell. In that letter, as we have seen, Wittgenstein motivates his new views on atomic complexes by providing the 'fundamental' reason that 'there cannot be different types of things!' (24). The exclamation mark, and its presentation as a new discovery, suggests that it is supposed to be surprising to

Russell. It is supposed to be surprising to Russell because Russell *does* adhere to distinctions between types of things. Not, perhaps, within the formal grammar of *PM*, but instead within the acquaintance epistemology developed in *PP* and, subsequently, *TK*. These distinctions, as we have seen, can be traced back to *PoM* and were dubbed type* distinctions by Landini to distinguish them from *PM*'s type distinctions. What Wittgenstein's January 1913 letter suggests, then, is that the sorts of ontological divisions embodied in type* distinctions must be done away with, along with any purported ontological divisions inherent in *PM*'s theory of types. This is why Wittgenstein insists that '*every* theory of types must be rendered superfluous by a proper theory of the symbolism' (24; emphasis added). In other words, type* distinctions should be construed nominalistically, just as *PM* types had been. The saying/showing distinction is part of Wittgenstein's attempt to implement this elimination, without falling prey to his own objections to the account of logical form contained in the *TK* version of Russell's MRTJ. It is his solution to problems plaguing 'every theory of types' not just *PM*'s theory of types.

Wittgenstein's objection in the June 1913 letter to Russell's account of logical form is that it construes the sense of an atomic proposition, or judgement, as dependent on the truth of other propositions (cf. *TLP* 2.0211–2.0212). According to LI, as we have seen, this is problematic because it violates the basic logical intuition that any tautology should follow from any well-formed proposition in the absence of additional premises. So, Wittgenstein needs an account of logical form according to which constraints thereupon must not come in the form of contentful propositions, which could be construed as illicit supplemental premises. Eventually, by April 1914 at the latest, he settled on the proposal that logical prototypes contained within propositions show the logical forms of those propositions without asserting anything about them. Because these prototypes contain real variables, they do not have content, only form. Such variables could be bound, as in Russell's proposal in *TK*, but then you would have a contentful proposition, which says something. Such a proposition, if true, would describe a contingently existing fact and not exemplify the form of facts. However, it would contain a prototype consisting of real variables, which thus *says* nothing but *shows* a logical form. Because it does not say anything, it cannot be an illicit premise in an inference to any tautology and thus does not run afoul of Wittgenstein's critique of the MRTJ contained in the June 1913 letter.

What is already implicit in this letter, along with the two letters from summer 1912 cited by Landini, is not the saying/showing distinction but instead the concerns that ultimately led to it. These concerns revolve around the attempt to give an account of logical form, which respects the distinction between real and apparent variables and is consistent with basic logical intuitions.

Ultimately, Wittgenstein's solution to these issues is embodied in each of both his saying/showing distinction and his account of the general form of a proposition. The latter, in particular, shows how logical forms of molecular propositions may be built up via truth-operations on elementary propositions and thus reduces the problem of molecular forms to that of atomic forms. But these two ideas, if interrelated, are independent. More importantly, Wittgenstein does not have either of them yet in summer 1912 or spring 2013. However, because he has already been thinking intensively about these issues in the year leading up to his critique of the *TK* version of the MRTJ, he is already armed with a criticism of Russell's proposal, which as he insisted in the context of the tense discussion on 26 May is something he 'already tried but didn't work'. His inchoate expression of this objection on 26 May, along with his more precise explanation later in the context of the mid-June 1913 letter, likely simply reflects his efforts to recall this earlier proposal and to precisify his objection to it. However, it is not until he completes the *Tractatus* that he comes to believe he has arrived at a final, definitive solution concerning these issues (*CL*, 110; *TLP*, 4). Along the path towards this final solution, important milestones include the development of the ab-notation in the 1913 *Notes on Logic*, the first explicit statement of the saying/showing distinction in the April 1914 notes to Moore and (conceivably) the May 1915 'discovery' of the N-operator. But it is a mistake to characterize any of these things as already present in the May–June 1913 critique of Russell's MRTJ. What we find in that context is Wittgenstein's rejection of a solution proposed by Russell to problems neither has yet satisfactorily resolved.

3.11 Reconsidering the Representation Concern

In Section 2.13, we saw that Lebens sought to distinguish carefully between ND and what he called the 'representation concern'. While the former, according to Lebens, is a puzzle that Russell had little reason to take seriously, the representation concern is a more serious issue for the MRTJ which led to important revisions in it. Ultimately, it led to Russell's introduction of logical forms into the 1913 version of the MRTJ.

The idea that, in response to concerns raised by Stout, important revisions to the MRTJ were undertaken by Russell over the period of 1910–13 is not inconsistent with LI. The extant textual evidence and correspondence appears to show that each of both Stout and Wittgenstein raised objections to the MRTJ which were given serious consideration by Russell and which led to important revisions. Moreover, from the perspective of a defender of LI, nothing of particular importance hinges on whether we single out Stout's concerns with a unique designation in order to more clearly differentiate them from ND (though designating them as 'representation concerns' has the potential to be problematic if it misleads us into thinking that ND, WD and UP are *not* 'representational concerns'). That said, the idea that ND was not a problem that Russell had any reason to take seriously, that it can be resolved, rather simply, by noting the non-symmetrical nature of the judging relation, is inconsistent with LI and must be addressed. From the perspective of a defender of LI, it is precisely ND which leads Russell to introduce revisions to the MRTJ which were the subject of Stout's objections. Both Stout's concerns and ND are 'representational' in nature, and Stout's representational concerns amount to more or less of an iteration or epicycle of ND. In a word, the iteration of ND posed by Stout is that if the subordinate relation does not actually relate, then how does it, or other associated constituents such as a direction or the judging relation, figure within a judgement complex in a way which allows the subordinate relation thereof to appear *as if* it relates, and the complex to thereby represent a specific, truth-evaluable content? We can acknowledge that this is an interesting and fruitful way of framing ND without committing ourselves to the mistaken idea that identifying and articulating it somehow obviates ND.

In her paper 'On the Nature of Judgement', Wrinch claims that ND can be resolved by noting that the judging relation is 'in a perfectly precise sense' (1919, 320) not symmetrical. But she never tells us what that precise sense is. Instead, she simply proceeds to assert that 'we can clearly distinguish' (ibid.) the following two judgements:

'1. I believe that *a* loves *b*', that is, 'J(I, ϕ, *a*, *b*)'

'2. I believe that b loves a', that is, 'J(I, ϕ, *b*, *a*)'

However, this assertion merely begs the obvious question: how? That, as we saw in Section 2.1, *is* ND. There, as we noted, the challenge posed by ND is to explain how the superficial distinction in order of letters on a page reflects the ordering of constituents within the judgement being expressed. According to the MRTJ, letters on a page are not constituents of judgements; instead, what they stand for are. And as Russell himself notes in *TK* (116), when it comes to ordering these constituents, the asymmetry, direction or 'sense' of the judging relation has no explanatory value. In the absence of a more robust account, listing letters on a page does little to explain how judgment constituents can be united and properly ordered in such a manner as to differentiate the content of, for example, the judgement that 'a loves b' from the judgement that 'b loves a'. In this sense, ND is obviously representational in nature.

But since ND cannot so easily be dismissed, it is plausible to think, contrary to Lebens but in accordance with Griffin, Candlish and others, that Stout's concerns, dubbed as 'representational concerns' by Lebens, are best construed as objections to Russell's attempts to resolve ND by appealing to the sense first of the subordinate relation and then the judging relation. As opposed to being properly characterized as amounting to a distinct 'representational' concern, they are better construed as iterations or epicycles of ND which, along with WD and UP, is itself a 'representational concern'. As was noted in Section 2.1, moreover, these problems persist regardless of Russell's appeals to neutral relations to avoid problematic ontological commitment to converse relations (*TK*, 85–87).

Curiously, since she claims not to regard ND as a problem, Wrinch later goes on in the paper to attempt to resolve ND through a process of 'evaluating' the logical form judgements by deploying an operator which she calls an 'evaluator' (1919, 321). Irrelevant specifics aside, this is in essence the same proposal which Russell developed in the *TK* version of the MRTJ. It involves undertaking an operation or procedure via which the constituents of judgements are assigned to positions in the logical form of the proposition judged. Though purportedly this analysis is provided by Wrinch merely for the purposes of satisfying a desire for uniformity between the account of simple and molecular propositions, it is clearly susceptible to the very same objections to the MRTJ which Wittgenstein posed first inarticulately at the 26 May meeting and then precisely in the mid-June letter. It implies that $\phi ab \vee \sim \phi ab$ does not follow from ϕab in the absence of a supplemental, analytical procedure. Nevertheless, the desire for uniformity between the atomic and the molecular case identified by Wrinch likely explains why, as Lebens himself notes, the *TK* manuscript 'sputters out' (2017, 150) at the point where Russell was supposed to turn his attention to 'molecular propositional thought'. Wittgenstein had convinced Russell that his MRTJ does not work for the atomic case and thus there was no point in trying to extend it, as is, to the molecular case. Perhaps because she is either unaware of, unfamiliar with or fails to appreciate the nature and significance of Wittgenstein's objections to the MRTJ, Wrinch attempts to undertake precisely such an extension.

3.12 The Demise of *TK* and of the MRTJ

Thus far in this chapter 3, we articulated LI in Section 3.1, before moving on, in Sections 3.2–3.11, to defend its merits relative to competitors in the scholarly literature. In this final section, we will highlight one, final, crucial merit of LI relative to several of its competitors: specifically that LI can explain the seriousness which Russell attributed to Wittgenstein's criticisms, and the severity with which he reacted to them. As defenders of the MRTJ, Lebens, Landini, MacBride, Wrinch and others are invested in minimizing the philosophical significance of Wittgenstein's objection and the concerns it raises. The fact that Russell abandoned work on the *TK* manuscript, and that subsequent correspondence appears to show that he was 'paralysed' by Wittgenstein's objection, poses challenges to these attempts at minimalization, calling for a response. We saw in Section 2.14, for example, that following MacBride, Lebens suggests that insofar as Russell was affected by Wittgenstein's criticisms, the influence was psychological, emotional and interpersonal and not logical or philosophical. This explains why, despite the exaggerated appearance of Wittgenstein's influence created by his emotionally, and interpersonally, motivated letters, Russell went on to defend a version of the MRTJ as late as 1918 in the context of *PLA*. Similarly, as we have seen, Landini argued that Wittgenstein's critique was driven by his emerging doctrine of showing, an unsupported intuition which Russell confesses he did not understand and, despite possessing a vague feeling that Wittgenstein must be right, had no legitimate logical or philosophical reason to accept. Landini's SI thus coheres with MacBride and Leben's IRI in according Wittgenstein's objection no genuine logical or philosophical significance with respect to the viability of Russell's MRTJ.

In addition to aligning better with the extant correspondence, however, LI can best explain why, although Russell ceased work on *TK* in June 1913, he continued to defend a version of the MRTJ as late as 1918. It can also better explain why Russell initially claimed not to understand Wittgenstein's criticisms but subsequently reported being paralysed by them (cf. Landini 2020, 225). What accounts for the first of these facts is that, despite Wittgenstein having severely criticized the *versions* of the MRTJ contained in *PP* as well as *TK*, Russell nevertheless continued to see Wittgenstein as an ally, engaged in a shared philosophical programme which he came to refer to as 'the philosophy of logical atomism'. This explains why he took Wittgenstein's *NL* with him to America to assist him in the composition and delivery of his logic course at Harvard in spring 1914 (Blackwell and Eames 1992, xxi). It also explains why Russell insists at the outset of *PLA* that the lectures it contains 'are very largely concerned with explaining certain ideas which I learnt from my friend and former pupil Ludwig Wittgenstein' (177). Clearly, then, Russell did not see Wittgenstein as refuting their shared, overall philosophical programme so much as specific details of particular accounts of atomic (and perhaps by extension, molecular) propositional thought. This impression could only have been bolstered by Wittgenstein, when he responded to Russell's self-described paralysis by insisting that 'it can only be removed by a correct theory of propositions' (*CL*, 34). In 1913, in other words, Wittgenstein did not himself have a correct, alternative theory of propositions, and nor did he mean to discourage Russell from continuing the search for one. Wittgenstein had no fully developed alternative to Russell's MRTJ for Russell to accede to or to abandon the MRTJ in favour of. He had inchoate *ideas* about how to account for the nature and status of atomic and molecular propositions in a manner consistent with basic logical intuitions. He dictated these in *NL*. Russell took these ideas under advisement and continued to work towards a solution of what Wittgenstein would refer to as late as March 1919 as 'our problems' (110). Russell did not abandon the MRTJ because, until 1919, there was no alternative theory to abandon it in favour of. Just ideas, gleaned from Wittgenstein, about how to develop it in light of serious and significant criticisms. And this is just what he went on to do until a viable alternative perspective presented itself to him in 1919. While MacBride and Lebens's IRI goes astray in minimizing the philosophical significance Wittgenstein's criticisms had for Russell, Lebens's account of why Russell did ultimately abandon the MRTJ in 1919 seems correct. The principal philosophical impacts of Wittgenstein's critique appear to have been that Russell ceased and ultimately abandoned work on *TK* and that Wittgenstein's criticisms left a significant and troubling gap within Russell's logical and epistemological system. As Lebens correctly notes, however, Wittgenstein's criticisms do not seem to have had Russell's abandonment of the MRTJ as a direct consequence.

With regards to Russell's claim that he did not understand Wittgenstein's criticism, this claim needs to be understood in context so as not to be mishandled. It is a response, specifically, to Wittgenstein's 'inarticulate' expression of his objection during the tense meeting on 26 May 1913. Contrary to both SI and IRI, there is no reason to think that Russell continued to struggle to understand Wittgenstein's objection following the precise expression of it in the mid-June 1913 letter and their subsequent discussion of it on 18 June. If he did not clearly understand it by that point, then why, in correspondence with Morrell, did he report having felt 'ready for suicide' on 18 June, and why did he claim to have been 'paralysed' by the objection in subsequent correspondence with Wittgenstein shortly thereafter? Why did he cease work on the *TK* manuscript more or less contemporaneously with 'Wittgenstein's onslaught'? According to defenders of LI, he did these things because, by 18 June 1913 at the latest, the nature of Wittgenstein's objections were perfectly clear to him, and at that time, he could not see how to get around them. As we saw in Section 3.6, moreover, by 1918 he still could not see how to get around them and was instead content to identify them as 'difficulties' (*PLA*, 199) within the analysis of belief. Of course, none of this need be thought of as implying that over the years 1913–18 Russell did not continue to defend the MRTJ or that he did no productive work. He continued to be both an inordinately productive thinker and a prolific writer who, much like the rest of the mass of humanity, did not have clear and compelling solutions to philosophy's most frustrating and foundational problems.

Over this same period, Wittgenstein continued to work productively as well. The fruits of his independent work, and of his collaboration with Russell on the foundations of logic, semantics and mathematics, would eventually be published in his 1922 masterpiece, the *Tractatus Logico-Philosophicus*. In Chapter 4, we will turn to explore the role played by Wittgenstein's critique of the MRTJ within his subsequent philosophical development over the next several years, culminating in the *Tractatus*. Moreover, we will examine how these criticisms foreshadow themes within his later philosophical work, as recorded in his posthumously published *Philosophical Investigations* (1953).

Chapter 4

WITTGENSTEIN ON TRUTH, LOGIC AND REPRESENTATION

4.1 The Picture Theory of Propositions

Wittgenstein's critique of Russell's MRTJ represents an important stage and episode within the development of his early philosophy, which culminates and finds its ultimate expression in the *Tractatus Logico-Philosophicus* (1922). The centrepiece of Wittgenstein's logical and semantic system as articulated in *TLP* is his picture (or model) theory of propositions. The picture theory both builds upon Wittgenstein's criticisms of Russell's MRTJ and offers an alternative to the MRTJ which is nevertheless thematically and philosophically consistent with it in many respects. Like the MRTJ, for instance, Wittgenstein's picture theory provides an account of the nature of propositional content and is also a correspondence theory of truth (David 2016). It aims to recover several features of the MRTJ while revising it to evade problems Wittgenstein sees as inherent in the MRTJ, including ND, WD and UP. Such features include direct realism, bipolarity and truth-functionality among others. It recovers Russell's direct realism by characterizing the meanings of the names contained in a proposition as the very objects that they stand for or go proxy for. It recovers bipolarity as a condition of significance or sense of propositions by characterizing propositions as intrinsically either true or false, depending upon whether the possible fact they portray either exists or does not. (The possible fact portrayed by a proposition is its sense.) It recovers truth-functionality by characterizing propositions as inherently part of a truth-functional calculus in which relations of entailment between propositions can be portrayed in truth-tables.[1] It recovers Russell's

---

[1] For more insight into the origins of the truth-tabular notation, see Anellis (2012) and Shosky (1997). Though Anellis sees Wittgenstein's truth-tabular notation as being first anticipated by Peirce in 1893, my own view is that in a more important and interesting sense it was anticipated by Cantor (1891). This is a view I develop in a paper called 'Transfinite Number in Wittgenstein's *Tractatus*', forthcoming in *Journal for the History of Analytical Philosophy*.

distinction between truth-bearers (judgement complexes) and truth-makers (fact complexes) by characterizing the *sense* of propositions as independent of their *truth*, and their truth or falsehood as being contingent upon the mind- and language-independent facts. In order to see how it purports to accomplish these things, and how it attempts to respond to difficulties inherent in Russell's MRTJ, it will be useful to trace the historical development of the picture theory out of Wittgenstein's critique of the MRTJ and into its mature expression in *TLP*.

Wittgenstein's first explicit statement of the picture theory appears in September 1914, in his *Notebooks*. There he writes that 'a proposition can express its sense only by being the logical portrayal of it [...] In the proposition a world is as it were put together experimentally. (As when in the law-court in Paris a motor-car accident is represented by means of dolls, etc.)' (*NB*, 7–8). In this remark, however, he is clarifying and developing an idea which already appears in inchoate form in his summer 1913 *Notes on Logic*. There he writes:

> In 'aRb' it is not the complex that symbolizes but the fact that the symbol 'a' stands in a certain relation to the symbol 'b'. Thus facts are symbolised by facts, or more correctly, that a certain thing is the case in the symbol says that a certain thing is the case in the world. (*NL*, 96)

Analogously, Wittgenstein writes that 'propositions [which are symbols having reference to facts] are themselves facts: that this inkpot is on this table may express that I sit in this chair' (97). In Section 3.1, we identified independent textual evidence from *NL* which shows that Wittgenstein was concerned therein with each of ND, WD and UP (94, 103). The textual evidence from *NL* we are considering now represents Wittgenstein's attempts to grapple with these problems.

Plausibly, in the two remarks above from *NL*, Wittgenstein is attempting to work out an account of propositions which will obviate ND, WD and UP by, first, eliminating 'relating relations' from the constituents of propositions and, second, de-psychologizing the proposition. On this view, the constituents of propositions will be united and appropriately ordered neither by a judging relation nor by a relating relation. Indeed, the constituents of propositions will not be objects which the words contained in the verbal expression of a judgment stand for. They will instead be symbols, which by being oriented to one another in a given way are able to depict the fact that objects they stand for are oriented to one another in a corresponding way. Importantly, they can accomplish this without containing any symbol, for example, 'R' which stands for a relating relation. The symbol 'R' in 'aRb' is merely one, inessential and eliminable way of orienting the symbols so that they picture a given fact. This is supposed to be shown more clearly by the example of the inkpot and the table. Nothing aside from the inkpot and the table (or 'a' and 'b') is needed in order to depict the fact that I sit in the chair, given that the inkpot goes proxy for me and the table goes proxy for the chair. Prepositional verbs such as 'being on' or 'being in' do not stand for constituents of reality on this view, whether universals or particulars. Instead, they are merely ways that constituents of reality may be oriented within facts. Propositions are such facts in which symbols are oriented in ways which allow the proposition to symbolize or refer to other facts.

Because facts which are propositions are made up of symbols, not the objects those symbols stand for, there is nothing especially problematic with regards to moving them around to put them in the right order. In this respect, Wittgenstein hopes to avoid problems Russell had encountered in relying on a psychological mechanism, judgement, to move constituents around and put them in the right order. Moreover, there is no constituent within a proposition corresponding to a universal, which might or might not relate the other constituents of the proposition. There is merely a symbol, for example 'R', which is a contingent and eliminable means of orienting other symbols in space in order to depict a fact. A noteworthy problem which arises from this proposal, which Wittgenstein will ultimately address in *TLP*, is how precisely the constituents of facts and propositions are united in the absence of relating relations or judging relations to do that integral work. This problem is highlighted in *NL* when Wittgenstein writes, 'Only facts can express sense, a class of names cannot' (*NL*, 105).

Wittgenstein's relatively inchoate alternative to the MRTJ proposed in *NL* is then further clarified and developed in the April 1914 *Notes Dictated to G.E. Moore in Norway* (*NDM*). There, instead of characterizing propositions as symbols having reference to facts, he says that propositions are made of names of simples and that these, as opposed to propositions, have *meaning* (*NDM*, 112). Propositions instead have *sense*, insofar as they describe reality as 'behaving' in a certain way relative to the proposition. This amounts, he claims, 'to saying that we can compare reality with the proposition [...] But [...] the possibility of comparison depends upon the conventions by which we have given meanings to our simples' (ibid.). In addition to continuing to work out the details of his proposal for recovering propositional content without appealing to relating relations, in *NDM* Wittgenstein likewise continues to work on eliminating psychological elements from his account. Wittgenstein's de-psychologizing of the proposition is made especially explicit in the final remark of the *NDM*, which is that 'the relation of "I believe p" to "p" can be compared to the relation of "p" says "p" to p: it is just as impossible that I should be a simple as that "p" should be' (*NDM*, 119). Here Wittgenstein is anticipating *TLP* 5.542, which as we shall see in Section 4.9 contains significant insights regarding Wittgenstein's conception of the general form of a proposition. The important point at present is simply that in this remark from *NDM* Wittgenstein appears to be suggesting that 'I believe' can be eliminated from an account of how propositions relate to the facts which they describe. The subject of a propositional attitude ascription is complex rather than simple, and the relation between the parts of that complex which are belief facts and the facts which those belief facts purport to describe is logical rather than psychological in nature. It thus need make no reference to a believing, meaning or thinking subject.

In *TLP* itself, Wittgenstein then goes on to provide a much more robust and detailed account of what names and simples ultimately are, such that names can stand for simples and thereby figure in elementary propositions which depict what he calls 'atomic facts' either truly or falsely. What in *NDM* Wittgenstein calls 'simples' in *TLP* he calls 'objects', which he in turn characterizes *as* simple (*TLP* 2.02). Objects, moreover, he maintains are 'unalterable' and 'subsistent' (2.0271) meaning they are not subject to change or decomposition in the manner of complexes (e.g. tables, mountains, people, etc.) which exist in space and time. Such complexes are made up of facts which, Wittgenstein insists, consist in 'the existence of atomic facts' (*TLP* 1922 2). In other words, if two elementary propositions are true, then they describe a (molecular) fact, made up of two atomic facts. Wittgenstein does not use the term 'molecular', but in his introduction Russell describes propositions which are not atomic as 'molecular' (*TLP*, xv), and for clarity it could be helpful to describe facts which are not atomic as molecular. Wittgenstein uses the German term '*Tatsachen*' to refer to 'facts' and the term '*Sachverhalten*' to refer to 'atomic facts'. This distinction roughly corresponds to our distinction between 'molecular facts' and 'atomic facts', although I think from Wittgenstein's perspective it would be more correct to say that *Sachverhalten* are *Tatsachen*, but not all *Tatsachen* are *Sachverhalten*. In other words, atomic facts are also facts but not all facts are atomic facts.

An atomic fact, in any case, is a combination of (simple) objects (*TLP* 2.01). Within atomic facts, objects 'hang one in another, like the links of a chain' (2.03). Wittgenstein's chain analogy is his attempt to explain the unity of atomic facts and elementary propositions without appealing to relating relations. Because atomic facts are made up of objects which can hang together without any additional constituent being required to hold them together, they can be represented by elementary propositions which consist of names that hang together without anything else required to hold them together. On this view, elementary propositions can contain verbs but those need not stand for any constituent of the corresponding fact, in the event the proposition is true. This is why Wittgenstein writes, in a manner reminiscent of the quote from *NL* (96) earlier, that 'instead of, "The complex sign '*aRb*' says that *a* stands to *b* in the relation *R*", we ought to put, "*That* '*a*' stands to '*b*' in a certain relation says *that aRb*"' (*TLP* 3.1432; emphases in the original). Within the elementary proposition 'aRb' in other words, the sign 'R' is an inessential element of the symbol. The same work that is done by 'aRb' could in principle be done by 'a-b', 'a b' or any convention used to orient the names contained in the elementary proposition in such a way that they may represent the configuration of objects in the fact. The letters 'a' and 'b' are examples of what Wittgenstein calls 'simple signs' or 'names' (3.202). The meanings of such names are the (simple) objects they go proxy for (3.203, 3.22). An elementary proposition is a picture that is 'a model of reality' (2.12) in which, if true, the configuration of objects in the atomic fact it depicts corresponds to the configuration of names in the proposition (3.21). The use of a verb, for example, 'R', in an elementary proposition is, according to Wittgenstein, inessential. It is merely a conventional way of orienting the names to depict a fact.

In Section 1.1 we saw that Russell thought fully real and external relations were required to capture the arithmetically and geometrically crucial phenomenon of order. Arithmetical order is characterized by Wittgenstein as involving internal relations between bases and results of series of successive operations (*TLP* 6.01–6.03). Hence, in response to Russell's 'vexed' question about whether relations are internal or external Wittgenstein writes that 'the order of the number-series is not governed by an external relation but by an internal relation' (4.1252). Geometrical order, by contrast, is recovered by Wittgenstein by distinguishing clearly between qualitative and numerical identity, which he insists cannot be defined as equivalent (5.5302). Contrary to what Russell had supposed in *PM* and elsewhere, having all properties in common is no guarantee of numerical identity according to Wittgenstein (ibid.). Instead, it is logically possible for two numerically distinct objects to have all their properties in common (ibid.). In a logically adequate notation, numerical identity is not indicated by a sign for identity but instead by identity of sign (5.53). Numerical difference between objects is marked by numerical difference of sign. It is thus possible to represent a series of ordered points on a line without appeal to signs standing for fully real and independent relations, despite Russell's erroneous inference to the contrary from what he called 'the contradiction of relativity' (see Section 1.1). Points on a line can lack any qualitative differences while nevertheless being numerically different: 'If two objects have the same logical form, the only distinction between them, apart from their external properties, is that they are different' (2.023).

Notably, external properties are not equivalent to external relations. They are instead comprised of facts consisting of objects being configured in certain ways. Hence Wittgenstein claims that objects themselves do not have properties (e.g. colours (*TLP* 2.032)), but instead that properties are produced by configurations of objects (2.0231). A helpful illustration of this idea would be colour which has a wave form or frequency. A wave form is a geometrical structure which, within Wittgenstein's logical atomism, would amount to a configuration of objects. These objects can be proxied by names, and these names can then be used to articulate a proposition, that is, a picture or model, of the wave form. No verbs are required in the proposition to represent this geometrical structure. If there are verbs occurring in the proposition, they are inessential to the depiction and in any case do not stand for any constituents of the corresponding fact. In particular, they do not stand for any external relations between the numerically distinct objects. That the objects are numerically distinct is instead indicated by using numerically distinct names.

The picture theory of propositions is intended to obviate each of UP, ND and WD as follows. UP is resolved by providing for the unity of the proposition without appeal either to relating relations or judgement relations. Simple names hang together in elementary propositions in a manner which is isomorphic to the way in which objects hang together in atomic facts. Neither a verb nor a corresponding relating relation is required to unify either the names or the objects into a fact. Like the constituents of atomic facts, the constituents of elementary propositions possess intrinsic, logical, combinatorial possibilities which allow them to combine with one another without being held together by anything else, such as an external relation corresponding to a verb. Psychological relations, like judging relations, are not required to hold together the constituents of an elementary proposition either. Instead, whatever is judged, believed, denied and so on must already be a proposition: 'Every proposition must already have a sense: it cannot be given a sense by affirmation. Indeed its sense is just what is affirmed. And the same applies to negation, etc.' (*TLP* 4.064). Or, as Wittgenstein puts the point in *NL*, 'there are only unasserted propositions' (95) (cf. *TLP* 4.064).

ND is obviated insofar as the constituents of elementary propositions are construed by Wittgenstein as linguistic items, that is, signs, rather than the objects which those signs stand for (as they had been in the MRTJ). In this case, distinguishing 'aRb' from 'bRa' really is as simple as ordering letters differently on a page, given arbitrary conventions governing the uses of words. WD is obviated since, within elementary propositions, there can be no illicit substitution of a name into a position where a verb should go. Atomic facts only contain objects, not relating relations, and elementary propositions only (essentially) contain names. Elementary propositions can contain verbs, but these verbs do not occupy positions into which one might substitute names, any more than brackets or periods do. If one did try to substitute 'c' in for 'R' within the proposition aRb, for example, the result would be a-b-c which could just as easily be expressed as aRbRc. WD thus cannot arise at the level of deep, logical grammar.

Cases where it might seem to arise at the level of surface grammar, prior to logical analysis, cannot arise either, since in such cases there will be no possible analysis which yields a truth-function of elementary propositions with sense. Given the conventional meaning of the names 'Socrates', 'Plato' and 'Aristotle', the utterance 'Socrates Plato's Aristotle' cannot be analysed as a truth-function of elementary propositions which contain simple names and depict atomic facts. However, 'Aristotle studied Plato' could be so analysed, as, for instance, an extremely lengthy conjunction of true elementary propositions which together described Aristotle's motions of holding a book, his eye movements, his thought patterns, brain waves and so on. Counterfactually, if by convention the word 'socratesed' meant the same as 'studied', then it would be intelligible to utter 'Aristotle socratesed Plato' since in that case we could give precisely the same sort of analysis just described. Words of our ordinary language are what Wittgenstein calls 'expressions' (*TLP* 3.31), which means they can only take certain sorts of arguments in order to yield an intelligible proposition, given their conventional meanings. So, while the conventional meaning we assign to words is arbitrary, '*this much* is not arbitrary – that *when* we have determined one thing arbitrarily, something else is necessarily the case. (This derives from the *essence* of notation.)' (3.342; emphases in the original). If we use 'Aristotle', 'Plato' and 'Socrates' as the names of people, then we necessarily cannot use 'Aristotle socrates Plato' to say something intelligible about them. By contrast, if we define the word 'socrates' to be equivalent to the English expression 'studied', then we can use that same utterance meaningfully.

4.2 Wittgenstein and Type-Theory

Wittgenstein's notion of an expression is integral to his proposed treatment of Russell's paradox at *TLP* 3.331–3.333. To see how, it will help to first explicate Wittgenstein's remarks about types in the lead up to his critique of the MRTJ and, relatedly, briefly discuss subsequent reflections upon Russell's paradox in *NL*. In Section 3.1, we looked at a January 1913 letter in which Wittgenstein insists that 'there cannot be different Types of things!' (*CL*, 24). In that context, we considered Wittgenstein's proposal to obviate WD by introducing logical forms to copulate complexes. We noted that when Wittgenstein told Russell during a tense meeting on 26 May that he had 'tried Russell's view and knew it would not work', he was very likely referring to a view which was similar to or even identical with the one developed in the January 1913 letter.

In the present context, however, it will be more pertinent to look at what Wittgenstein has to say about *types* in that same letter. In particular, and in contrast to Russell's view as espoused in *TK*, he appears to deny the existence of brute metaphysical distinctions, or type* distinctions between things. According to Russell's account in *TK*, as we have seen, mortality would be construed as a universal, and thus of a distinct type* from that characteristic of particulars like Socrates. This would preclude Socrates and mortality from interchanging their positions in the complex described by 'Socrates is mortal'. On the view espoused by Wittgenstein in the January 1913 letter, by contrast, 'mortality' is not a thing at all, and *this* explains why it cannot be interchanged with Socrates in a manner which would generate WD. Mortality is instead construed as part of the copula of a complex which, much like a Fregean concept, is unsaturated or incomplete. The lack of interchangeability between proper names, which stand for things, and copulae, which do not, will be tracked, Wittgenstein suggests, within a logical syntax according to which 'different kind of symbols [...] *cannot* possibly be substituted in one another's places' (*CL*, 25; emphasis in the original). While he acknowledges that the details of the proposal contained in the letter may not be precisely correct (and in fact he went on to revise it in several important respects), he nevertheless claims to be certain that 'all theory of types must be done away with by a theory of symbolism' (ibid.). As we shall see, this aspect of his treatment of type-theory survives subsequent revision to become a core feature of his analysis in *TLP*.

What does not survive is the Fregean distinction between complete and unsaturated constituents of complexes. Once we get to *TLP*, Wittgenstein maintains that complexes are made up of facts and denies, as we have seen, that facts require any copula to unite the simple objects which make them up. Wittgenstein does however continue to adhere in *TLP* to the idea articulated in this January letter that there are no different types* of things. There are only objects on this view, and they do not come in types*. While the world consists of facts, these facts are nothing over and above the objects which make them up by hanging together in certain configurations. What do come in types on the view developed in *TLP* are expressions, and it is these nominal or syntactic types which Wittgenstein then deploys in his treatment of Russell's paradox.

The basic idea behind this treatment is already present in *NL*, where Wittgenstein explains that the 'fundamental truth of the theory of types' is that a 'proposition cannot occur in itself' (96). Since a proposition cannot occur, or be contained within itself, it cannot say anything about itself (107). Building on this idea in *TLP*, Wittgenstein then insists that a propositional sign cannot contain itself, because the 'sign for a function already contains the prototype of its argument' (*TLP* 3.333). Elementary propositions are written as functions of names (4.24). Functions of names are expressions, which when presented in their general form consist of constants containing variables, for example, 'Fx', where the variable indicates the prototype of a function's possible arguments. In 'Fx', for example 'F' is constant and 'x' is variable, meaning that 'Fa', 'Fb', 'Fc' and so on are distinct propositions which result from substituting distinct names (e.g. 'a', 'b', 'c') in for the variable 'x'. 'Fx' cannot take 'Fx' as its argument, because the prototype of its argument is a name, not a function. A function which could take a function of names as its argument would have to contain a different prototype (e.g. F(φx)) and so be a different function, regardless of whether we used the same letter (i.e. 'F') as the constant within the presentation of the general form of each of the two functions. In a notation which was logically adequate and so free from ambiguity, we would never use one and the same letter to symbolize two different functions. And thus vicious circle fallacies arising from cases in which functions take themselves as arguments cannot occur in a logically adequate notation.

Neither, however, can vicious circle fallacies arise from propositions containing variables which range over propositions and thus potentially admitting themselves as arguments. While elementary propositions are functions of names, all other propositions, that is, molecular propositions, are truth-functions of these elementary propositions. Propositions may thus occur within other propositions truth-functionally, but they cannot occur in themselves since if they are elementary, they are functions of names not of propositions, and if they are molecular, they are truth-functions of elementary rather than molecular propositions. As opposed to being built up via successive applications of truth-functions, molecular propositions *are* truth-functions of elementary propositions built up via successive applications of truth-operations (*TLP* 5.234). Not to be confused with functions, which cannot take themselves as arguments, operations yield results which can in turn be taken as the base of a successive application of an operation (5.251). The proposition (p v q) v q is not constructed by substituting p v q into itself for p but is instead built up in stages by successive applications of truth-operations to elementary propositions and to propositions which result from the application of such operations. Thus the truth-operation 'v' can be applied to elementary propositions p and q to obtain the result 'p v q', which may then be taken as a base, along with q, of a second, successive application of the truth operation 'v'.

Ultimately, Wittgenstein thinks that any conceivable truth-function can be constructed via successive applications of a single truth-operation, N, to elementary propositions and, subsequently, to the N-expressions which result from applying N to elementary propositions. In Wittgenstein's N notation, p v q would be expressed as N(N(p, q)), in which N is first applied to the list of elementary propositions (p, q), and then in turn to the resulting N expression N(p, q). The proposition (p v q) v q would be constructed by taking the result of these two successive operations, that is, N(N(p, q)), along with q, as the bases of an application of N and then applying N in turn to that result. This process would yield the N-expression N(N(N(p, q)), q)), which involves nothing other than a selection or list of elementary propositions to which Wittgenstein's N-operation is applied several times in succession.

In Section 4.9, we will revisit Wittgenstein's N-operator in association with his account of the general form of a proposition. The important point to note at present is that from Wittgenstein's perspective, only symbols have 'types' and these types are reflected in the logical syntax of an adequate notation. Such a notation precludes the sorts of vicious circle fallacies responsible for generating Russell's paradox and analogous, self-referential propositional paradoxes. In an adequate logical syntax, for instance, the liar paradox is obviated since that a proposition is true or false cannot meaningfully be stated. Instead, propositions *show* how things stand *if* they are true and say that things do stand in that way (*TLP* 4.022). Like types, 'truth' and 'falsehood' are what Wittgenstein calls 'formal concepts' (4.126) or 'pseudo-concepts' (4.1272). As we shall see in more detail when we look at Wittgenstein's saying/showing distinction, such concepts are features of symbols, which can only be shown in such symbols but not literally described by them. Types of symbols are shown in variables, which embody the prototype of their possible arguments.

4.3 Logical Form

When *all* constants within an expression are turned in variables, the result is what Wittgenstein calls a 'logical prototype' or logical form (*TLP* 3.315). According to this proposal, the logical form of the symbol 'aRb', for example, would be the sign '*xRy*'. While similar to that offered by Russell in *TK*, this conception of logical form differs significantly from it in two main respects. First, according to Wittgenstein, logical forms contain neither quantifiers nor apparent (i.e. bound) variables. Second, and relatedly, they are prototypes of expressions, not general facts. In Section 3.2, it will be recalled, we noted that in *TK* Russell identifies two *desiderata* which he thinks logical forms should satisfy. First, he thinks that there should be one unitary form for all complexes of the same form (*TK*, 114). Second, and more importantly for our present purposes, he claims that it would be ideal if the form were not a 'mere' incomplete symbol (ibid.). While it is convenient for technical purposes to 'indicate the general form of a dual complex by "*xRy*"' (113), doing so, he insists, does 'not tell us what the form actually is, or whether it is anything more than a symbol' (ibid.). What Russell appears to have in mind is that logical forms should not be mere incomplete symbols because incomplete symbols do not stand for anything real. For example, as becomes clear upon contextual paraphrase, the incomplete symbol 'the present king of France' does not stand for any constituent of the proposition expressed by 'the present king of France is bald'. Russell's intuition, by contrast, is that logical forms *are* something. And thus he settles on the idea that what they are is 'the fact that there are entities making up complexes having the form in question' (114). In the illustrative case of aRb, as we have seen, the relevant fact would be described as that 'something has some relation to something' (ibid.), which could be expressed symbolically as: '(∃x) (∃R) (∃y) xRy'.

Evidence of the emergence of Wittgenstein's alternative conception of logical form can be found in *NL*, where Wittgenstein initially suggests that if we convert all of the indefinables of a proposition into variables, 'then there remains a class of propositions which is not all propositions but a type' (*NL*, 93). Later he elaborates on this proposal, claiming that if, for example, in a proposition '$\varphi(x)$' we change into variables all symbols therein 'whose significance was arbitrarily determined', this yields a class of propositions which depends 'only on the nature of the symbol "$\varphi(x)$"' and which 'corresponds to a logical type' (101). Symbols in which real variables occur are not propositions corresponding to general facts but are rather 'schemes of propositions' (100). Such schemes of propositions 'only become propositions when we replace the variables by constants (ibid.). We understand a proposition, Wittgenstein claims, when we understand its constituents and form (104). Thus we understand 'aRb' 'if we know the meaning of "a" and "b", and if we know what "xRy" means for all x's and y's' (ibid.). This of course begs ND, but at this point it will be recalled that Wittgenstein does not yet have a solution to ND. That would not come until he developed and articulated the picture theory of propositions, discussed earlier in Section 4.1.

In *NL*, Wittgenstein notes that Russell's complexes are 'unserviceable as logical types' (*NL*, 101) for the reason, among others, that they incompatibly attempt to combine the 'useful' property of being compounded with the 'agreeable' property of being simple. Here, again, Wittgenstein has in mind Russell's proposal, in *TK*, to invoke the complex general fact that there are complexes of a given form as the logical form of those complexes. In *TK*, Russell claims that, in order to avoid an 'endless regress' (113), the form must be 'something exceedingly simple' (114). Thus, though the logical form appears to have a complex structure 'it is more correct to say that it *is* a structure' (ibid.).

We saw that understanding a proposition, on this account, involves assigning constituents of a cognitive complex to positions within the structure, or logical form of the complex which exists in the event the proposition (or judgement) is true. This is unworkable, according to Wittgenstein, not only because it involves problematically combining the properties of being 'simple' and 'compound' within the logical form, but also because it implicates that whether any tautology follows from a well-formed proposition depends upon 'position in a complex' analysis. We saw that Wittgenstein brought this problem out in the June 1913 letter by characterizing the position in a complex analysis characteristic of Russell's account of logical form as an illicit supplemental premise in the inference from aRb to aRb v ~ aRb. For these and other reasons, in *NL* Wittgenstein insists that 'there is no thing which is the form of a proposition' (*NL*, 105), whether simple or compound.

Building on this critique of Russell's logical forms in *NDM*, Wittgenstein notes that 'the question whether a proposition has sense (*Sinn*) can never depend on the *truth* of another proposition about a constituent of the first' (*NDM*, 117; emphasis in the original). Logical forms thus cannot come in the form of complex, general facts corresponding to existentially quantified propositions such as '(∃x) (∃R) (∃y) xRy'. This is because, if they did, then whether 'aRb' had sense would depend upon whether (∃x) (∃R) (∃y) (((x=a) & (R=R)) & (y=b)) was true. This, as we have seen, would involve the mistaken idea that C) aRb v ~ aRb does not follow from P2) aRb in the absence of P1) (∃x) (∃R) (∃y) (((x=a) & (R=R)) & (y=b)). However, fundamental intuitions about logical inference instead suggest that C) follows from P2) in the absence of P1). The sense of aRb thus cannot depend on the truth of P1). Wittgenstein went on to invoke this 'sense-truth regress'[2] in a variety of other contexts which we will have an opportunity to discuss in more detail in Section 4.7

In any case, as a result of these criticisms Wittgenstein levelled against the conception of logical form characteristic of Russell's 1913 MRTJ, Wittgenstein himself needed some alternative account of logical form which was not susceptible to these very same objections. Such an account was not something he already had in hand when he formulated his June 1913 critique of Russell's MRTJ. Indeed, as he noted in the context of the tense meeting on 26 May, Russell's account was more or less identical to one he had recently tried to implement himself. It was only upon subsequent reflection, first in Cambridge over the summer and then in Norway over the winter, that Wittgenstein eventually settled on the distinction between saying and showing as the solution to these difficulties.

---

[2] I owe this terminology to Stuart Shanker.

4.4 Bipolarity and Extensionalism

Before we can fully and properly appreciate the distinction between saying and showing, however, it is crucial that we first explicate the themes of bipolarity and extensionalism, along with the roles they play within the development of Wittgenstein's early philosophy. This is because Wittgenstein's idea that propositions show features of language and so the world which they cannot meaningfully say applies not only to the internal logical forms of elementary propositions but to the logical forms of the molecular propositions which can be built up from these elementary propositions truth-functionally and to the logical relationships between these molecular propositions and other propositions, both elementary and molecular. It applies in particular to a class of molecular propositions known as 'tautologies' (or truth-functional truths) which, Wittgenstein insists, *show* these logical relationships but *say* nothing.

While there is considerably more to the story, in a word bipolarity is the notion than any elementary proposition is in its very nature true or false and capable of being either. Extensionalism is the generalization of this feature of elementary propositions to the molecular propositions which can be built up from them truth-functionally. The basic idea behind extensionalism is that if *any* proposition is a truth-function of bipolar elementary propositions, then *every* proposition is.

In association with our discussion of SR in Section 2.2 earlier, we saw that Russell and Whitehead claimed a proposition is 'significant' when the disjunction of that proposition and its negation is true (*PM*, 171–72). Moreover, we saw in Section 1.4 that the first of three conditions Russell claims that any adequate theory of truth must fulfil is to allow for the possibility of falsehood, in addition to that of truth (*PP*, 106). While Wittgenstein's concept of bipolarity builds on this notion, there are two key respects in which Wittgenstein tries to emphasize that his conception is distinct from Russell's account of truth and falsehood.

The first is that bipolarity is an essential rather than accidental feature of propositions, which results from the way in which they have sense. Thus, as Wittgenstein explains in *NDM*,

> 'true' and 'false' are not accidental features of a proposition such that, when it has meaning, we can say it is also true or false: on the contrary, to have meaning *means* to be either true or false: the being true or false actually constitutes the relation of the proposition to reality, which we mean by saying it has meaning (*Sinn*). (*NDM*, 113; emphasis in the original)

Perhaps referencing the remark quoted from Russell in Section 1.3, that propositions are true or false in the way that some roses are red and others are white, Wittgenstein then elaborates as follows on this point in *TLP*:

> One might think [...] that the words 'true' and 'false' signified two properties among other properties, and then it would seem to be a remarkable fact that every proposition possessed one of these properties. On this theory is seems to be anything but obvious, just as, for instance, the proposition, 'All roses are either yellow or red', would not sound obvious even if it were true. (*TLP* 6.111)

The claim that some propositions are true and some are false in the way that some roses are red and others are white is a claim Russell made in the lead up to composing *PoM* and is characteristic of his early 'Russellian' theory of propositions and not the more mature MRTJ. Nevertheless, the quotation from *NDM* would tend to suggest that, in spite of improvements in this regard achieved by the MRTJ over the *PoM* theory of propositions, from Wittgenstein's perspective Russell had failed to sufficiently emphasize and articulate the essential, as opposed to contingent, nature of the bipolarity of the proposition, even as late as 1912–13. It is not just *possible* for propositions to be false as well as possible for them to be true; it is in their very *essence* to be one or the other. As we have seen, in *TLP* Wittgenstein articulates this essential bipolarity in terms of his theory that an elementary proposition is intrinsically a picture, or a model of an atomic fact, is true if the fact exists and false if the fact does not exist. Molecular propositions are truth-functions of such elementary propositions and so are true when certain combinations of atomic facts exist and false when none of those combinations exist. This essentiality of bipolarity perhaps explains why, in a letter to Russell written from Norway in September 1913 Wittgenstein describes bipolarity as 'absolutely untangible' (*CL*, 37). By this he presumably means that bipolarity is 'untouchable' in the sense that any adequate theory of propositions, and of types (which he also mentions in the letter), must include it as an integral element.

The second key respect in which Wittgenstein wishes to emphasize that his conception of the bipolarity of propositions differs from Russell and Whitehead's idea that a proposition is significant if the disjunction between it and its negation is true is that the disjunction in question's being true is logically independent of any explicitly articulable type-theoretic distinctions between constituents of facts and propositions, regardless of whether these deal with *PM* types or type* distinctions. (In Section 4.2, we saw that by summer 1913, Wittgenstein rejects metaphysical, type* distinctions, but is working towards a proposal according to which expressions, i.e., symbols, will be distinguishable by type.) This is one key point Wittgenstein is trying to highlight in the context of the June 1913 letter in which he expresses his objection to Russell's MRTJ 'exactly'. In the context of our discussion of the June 1913 letter earlier, we noted that provided aRb is a well-formed proposition with sense, any tautology follows from it. Since 'aRb v ~ aRb' is a tautology, obviously it follows from aRb as well, assuming aRb is a well-formed proposition with sense. But then why does Wittgenstein select 'aRb v ~ aRb' as his specific example of a tautology which follows from aRb? Because over and above the point about any tautology following from any well-formed proposition in the absence of supplemental constraints upon the *PM* type, or type* of the constituents of propositions and facts, Wittgenstein wishes to emphasize the further point that propositions possess bipolarity intrinsically and independently of any such explicitly articulable type-theoretic significance constraints of the sort embodied in Russell's account of logical form.

To study this feature of propositions, in 1913 Wittgenstein devised a notation designed to explore bipolarity in abstraction from truth-functionality. This was the 'ab-notation'. The ab-notation is very similar to that illustrated by Wittgenstein in *TLP* (6.1203), except that there he no longer uses 'a' and 'b' in lieu of 'T' and 'F' in order to consider bipolarity in abstraction from truth-functionality. As he notes in a November 1913 letter to Russell, 'Whether ab-f[unction]s and your truth-f[unctio]ns are the same cannot yet be decided' (*CL*, 48). Ultimately, this question would be decided in the affirmative but not before Wittgenstein used the ab-notation extensively to study bipolarity and arrive at some interesting conclusions about molecular logical form.

In the ab-notation, every elementary proposition has two poles, 'a' and 'b'. So in the ab-notation the elementary proposition 'p' would be symbolized as a-p-b. The ab-functions of elementary propositions may then be expressed by correlating outside poles to inside poles. For instance, b-a-p-b-a expresses an ab-function of a-p-b. Specifically, it reverses the polarity of the original proposition, much as negation reverses the truth value of the proposition. Notably, if we apply this ab-function again in succession, we end up with a-b-a-p-b-a-b, which is equivalent to a-p-b much as ~~p is equivalent to p. Molecular ab-functions of two elementary propositions we would then construct by correlating the inside poles of each of those elementary propositions to those of the other, in pairs, and correlating those correlated pairs in turn with either 'a' or 'b'.

Wittgenstein was often inclined to represent these correlations two dimensionally (again, see *TLP* 6.1203), but for our purposes it is more convenient to represent them in one dimension, as he also often does. Given a-p-b and a-q-b, we would have four pairs of poles:

$((p)a, (q)a), ((p)a, (q)b), ((p)b, (q)a)$ and $((p)b, (q)b).$

By assigning 'a' or 'b' to each of these pairs we can then generate several distinct molecular ab-functions. For instance,

$$(((p)a, (q)a) - a, (((p)a, (q)b) - b, ((p)b, (p)a) - a, ((p)b, (q)b) - a)$$

would express an ab-function analogous to the each of the two, equivalent truth-functions p → q and ~p v q. The following would then express an ab-function analogous to joint negation, or ~p & ~q:

$$(((p)a, (q)a) - b, ((p)a, (q)b) - b, ((p)b, (q)a) - b, ((p)b, (q)b) - a).$$

Obviously, the same method could be used to express ab-functions of n elementary propositions by correlating 'a' or 'b' with each possible permutation of n members of the set (a,b). For example, an ab-function of three elementary propositions would correlate 'a' or 'b' with each member of the following set of ordered triples:

{(a,a,a), (b,a,a), (a,b,a), (a,a,b), (b,b,a), (b,a,b), (a,b,b), (b,b,b)} (cf. *TLP* 4.31).

The ab-function analogous to joint negation for three elementary propositions could thus be expressed as follows:

{(a,a,a) – b, (b,a,a) – b, (a,b,a) – b, (a,a,b) – b, (b,b,a) – b, (b,a,b) – b, (a,b,b) – b, (b,b,b) – a}.

If one wanted to indicate the elementary propositions whose poles 'a' and 'b' are for each of p, q and r, this could be done as follows:

{((p)a, (q)a, (r)a) – b, ((p)b, (q)a, (r)a) – b, ((p)a, (q)b, (r)a) – b, ((p)a, (q)a, (r)b) – b, ((p)b, (q)b, (r)a) – b, ((p)b, (q)a, (r)b) – b, ((p)a, (q)b, (r)b) – b, ((p)b, (q)b, (r)b) – a}.

This would express the ab-function analogous to (~p &~q) and ~r.

In summer 1913, Wittgenstein appears to have thought you could apply this same method to express 'apparent variable' propositions or what we would call 'quantified propositions'. (It appears that Wittgenstein also attempted to devise an ab-notation for identity but ultimately abandoned this attempt in favour of the proposal to eliminate the identity sign entirely which he develops in *TLP* (5.53–5.534).) In *NL*, he uses the ab-notation to define quantifiers as follows:

'for (x)φx: a-(x)-aφxb-(∃x)-b and for (∃x)φx: a-(∃x)-aφxb-(x)-b' (*NL*, 96).

Like the ab-notation for molecular functions, this notation is supposed to work by correlating the outside poles with the inside poles, but in this case the inside poles belong to functions instead of propositions. So in essence the definition of $(x)\varphi x$ correlates a with the case in which φx correlates with a for all x, and correlates b with the case in which φx correlates with b for some x. As Landini (2021, 100) has noted, when Wittgenstein goes on to conclude that 'old definitions now become tautologous' (*NL*, 96), he is referring to the definitions that Russell and Whitehead provide in *PM* *9, of negation and disjunction with respect to quantified propositions. For example, *9.01-*9.02 are supposed to define negation as it applies to quantified propositions and to correspond to equivalences characteristic of the classical Aristotelian square of opposition. Specifically, *9.01 captures the equivalence between the negation of an A sentence and an O sentence, while *9.02 captures the equivalence between the negation of an I sentence and an E sentence. When he says these definitions are 'tautologous', he presumably means that when using the ab-notation both sides of each of these definitions would be symbolized in the identical way. For instance, each of $\sim\{(x).\phi x\}$ and $(\exists x). \sim \phi x$ would be expressed in the ab-notation as follows: b-(x)-aϕxb-($\exists$x)-a. So the definition would amount to:

b-(x)-aϕxb-($\exists$x)-a. = .b-(x)-aϕxb-($\exists$x)-a,

which would be an evident tautology.

As he continued to work with the ab-notation to explore features of bipolarity, Wittgenstein became impressed by several features of ab-functions which he subsequently used to characterize truth-functions in the context of his extensionalist semantics in *TLP*. First, he noted that apparently distinct but equivalent ab-functions could be reduced to a common symbolic form. Earlier we gave the example of the equivalence between a-p-b and a-b-a-p-b-a-b, but Wittgenstein gives as an example the equivalence of b-a-b-apb-a-b-a with b-apb-a. This equivalence is analogous to that between $\sim\sim\sim p$ and $\sim p$. Wittgenstein describes this feature of the ab-notation by saying that in it, the correlation of new poles is 'transitive'. He explains this feature as follows in a fall 1913 letter he wrote to Russell from Norway:

'The correlation of new poles is to be transitive' means that by correlating one pole in the symbolizing way to another and the other to a third we have *thereby* correlated the first in the symbolizing way to the third, etc. For instance, in **a**-b-a-*b*p*a*-b-a-**b**, **a** and **b** are correlated to *b* and *a* respectively and this means that our symbol is the same as a-bpa-b. (*CL*, 48; emphasis in the original)

Wittgenstein's usual method for the inner poles was to write a-p-b rather than bpa. Here, however, perhaps because it does not matter, he switched the poles. (Elsewhere he says the orientation of the inner poles is 'arbitrary' (*NL*, 94).) The key point he wishes to bring out, however, is that **b**-a-b-*apb*-a-b-**a** and **b**-*apb*-**a** are the same symbol because their inner poles (*a* and *b*) are correlated with the same outer poles (**b** and **a**).

Second, he noted that apparently distinct ab-functions were 'cross-definable' or interdefinable. Earlier we gave the example of p → q and ~p v q, which could each be expressed in a one-dimensional ab-notation as:

(((*p*)a, (*q*)a) − a, ((*p*)a, (*q*)b) − b, ((*p*)b, (*q*)a) − a, ((*p*)b, (*q*)b) − a).

Wittgenstein gives the example of the interdefinability of 'or' and 'not'. He writes that 'the ab notation makes it clear that not and or are dependent on one another and we can therefore not use them as simultaneous indefinables' (*NL*, 95; also see *NL*, 106). He appears to have in mind that the analogous ab-functions for p v q and ~(~p & ~q) could be expressed in the ab-notation (using our one dimensional variation) as follows:

(((*p*)a, (*q*)a) − a, ((*p*)a, (*q*)b) − a, ((*p*)b, (*q*)a) − a, ((*p*)b, (*q*)b) − b).

Perhaps alluding to his earlier discussion of the definitions at *PM* *9, he notes that 'cross-definability in the realm of general propositions leads to quite similar questions to those in the realm of *ab*-functions' (106). Likely, what Wittgenstein has in mind here is that since bipolarity is an essential feature of propositions, all meaningful propositions, including general propositions, should be expressible in a version of the ab-notation.

This idea is related to the third feature of ab-functions he noticed, which was that all ab-functions could be produced out of repeated applications of a single ab-function, analogous to the Scheffer stroke or ~p v ~q. Wittgenstein explains that

> if we now find an *ab*-function of such a kind that by repeated application of it every ab-function can be generated, then we can introduce the totality of ab-functions as the totality of those that are generated by the application of this function. Such a function is ~p v~q. (*NL*, 102)

This is significant both because it anticipates the conception of a general propositional form which he subsequently identifies in *TLP*, but also because it suggests that the idea that there could be a general propositional form is something that emerged out of his use of the ab-notation to reflect on salient

WITTGENSTEIN ON TRUTH, LOGIC AND REPRESENTATION   153

features of bipolarity. Similarly, his Tractarian conception of the nature and limits of sense may have had its origin in his reflections on bipolarity via the ab-notation.

This is related to a fourth salient feature he noticed, which was that the ab-notation could be used to distinguish clearly between tautologies, contradictions and 'real' propositions or non-logical propositions. He explains how in a fall 1913 letter to Russell:

> I will first talk about those logical prop[osition]s which are or might be contained in the first 8 Chapters of Princ[ipia] Math[ematica]. That they all follow from *one* Pp is clear enough because ONE *symbolic* rule is sufficient to recognize each of them as true or false. And this is the *one* symbolic rule: write the prop[osition] down in the ab-Notation, trace all Connections (of Poles) from the outside to the inside Poles: Then if the b-Pole is connected to such *groups of inside poles* ONLY *as contain opposite poles of* ONE *prop*[*osition*], then the whole prop[osition] is a true, logical prop[osition]. If on the other hand this is the case with the a-Pole the prop[osition] is false and logical. If finally neither is the case the prop[osition] may be true or false, but is in no case logical. (*CL*, 52–53; emphases in the original)

It is a bit unclear what Wittgenstein is proposing here (see Landini (2021, 101–02; 2020, 204–10) for more details) though if it had worked it could conceivably have provided a decision procedure for first-order predicate logic. Church (1936) proved that such a decision procedure is impossible, however, which would tend to suggest that Wittgenstein's proposal must ultimately be unworkable, regardless of its precise details. Nevertheless, the general point that the ab-notation may be used to differentiate between tautologies, contradictions and non-logical propositions holds for all molecular propositions which are truth-functions (and ab-functions) of n elementary propositions for any finite n. (It may have been this fact which led Wittgenstein to suppose that an extension to quantification theory must be possible, even if the current proposal turned out 'not to be the final correct notation' (*CL*, 52).) Any truth-function of p and q which was a tautology (e.g. (p & q) → p), for instance, would correspond to the following ab-function expressed using our one-dimensional notation:

(((*p*)a, (*q*)a) – a, ((*p*)a, (*q*)b) – a, ((*p*)b, (*q*)a) – a, ((*p*)b, (*q*)b) – a).

Using our one-dimensional notation again, any truth-function of p and q which was a contradiction (e.g. (p & q) & ~p) would correspond to the following ab-function:

(((*p*)a, (*q*)a) – b, ((*p*)a, (*q*)b) – b, ((*p*)b, (*q*)a) – b, ((*p*)b, (*q*)b) – b).

While tautologies correlate all pairs of inner poles to the outer pole a, contradictions correlate all pairs of inner poles to the outer pole b. In the ab-notation, any 'real' or non-logical (i.e. contingent) proposition (e.g. p & q) would be expressed by correlating pairs of inner poles to a mix of a's and b's like so:

(((*p*)a, (*q*)a) – a, ((*p*)a, (*q*)b) – b, ((*p*)b, (*q*)a) – b, ((*p*)b, (*q*)b) – b).

The same method could be used for truth-functions of n elementary propositions for any finite n, simply by correlating each possible ordered n-tuple of elements of the set (a,b) with a or b. For instance, for three elementary propositions p, q, r, all tautological truth-functions could be expressed using our one-dimensional ab-notation as follows:

{((*p*)a, (*q*)a, (*r*)a) – a, ((*p*)b, (*q*)a, (*r*)a) – a, ((*p*)a, (*q*)b, (*r*)a) – a, ((*p*)a, (*q*)a, (*r*)b) – a, ((*p*)b, (*q*)b, (*r*)a) – a, ((*p*)b, (*q*)a, (*r*)b) – a, ((*p*)a, (*q*)b, (*r*)b) – a, ((*p*)b, (*q*)b, (*r*)b) – a}.

Here each possible correlation of inner poles of the elementary propositions a-p-b, a-q-b and a-r-b is in turn correlated with the outer a pole, which corresponds to any truth-function of p, q and r which is always, or unconditionally, true. The fact that certain molecular ab-functions are unipolar as opposed to bipolar suggested to Wittgenstein that the logical propositions which express the analogous truth-functions must possess a unique status relative to all other propositions (*NL*, 107).

4.5 Saying and Showing

Building on the insights gleaned from studying bipolarity and extensionalism via his ab-notation, and also on the reflections concerning logical form discussed in Section 4.3, Wittgenstein was led to develop a distinction between saying and showing as a means of explaining both the nature of the internal logical forms of elementary propositions, as well as the unique status of those molecular truth-functions which the ab-notation revealed to be tautological. Though the developments we have discussed in Sections 4.3–4.4, and which took place over the course of 1913, thus anticipate the distinction between saying and showing, that distinction makes its first explicit appearance within Wittgenstein's corpus at the outset of *NDM*, dictated in April 1914. There he insists that 'LOGICAL so called propositions *shew* [the] logical properties of language and therefore of [the] Universe, but *say* nothing' (*NDM*, 108;

emphases in the original). Wittgenstein refers to logical propositions as 'so-called' here to contrast them with what he calls 'real' propositions (ibid.). Real, that is, non-logical, propositions are bipolar and thus have sense. They picture an atomic or molecular fact which either exists or does not. Logical propositions by contrast are instead unipolar and thus lack sense. They are 'not *nonsense* in the same sense in which, e.g., a proposition in which words which have no meaning is nonsense' (118; emphasis in the original). Instead they apply truth-operations upon elementary propositions such that the result is unconditionally true. Since logical propositions are unconditionally true, they lack bipolarity and thus sense given that, as we saw earlier in Section 4.4, bipolarity is what it means to have sense. Though such propositions thus do not *say* anything with sense, they nevertheless show logical relationships between the propositions of which they are truth-functions.

As Wittgenstein explains, for example, take the following list of propositions φa, $\varphi a \rightarrow \psi a$, ψa (*NDM*, 108). That the third member of the list follows from the first two can be seen in the logical proposition $(\varphi a \ \& \ (\varphi a \rightarrow \psi a)) \rightarrow \psi a$. While this logical proposition is unconditionally true and thus lacks sense, it nevertheless *shows* according to Wittgenstein that ψa follows from φa and $\varphi a \rightarrow \psi a$. Another way Wittgenstein makes this point is to characterize logical propositions as 'forms of proof' or 'forms of proofs' which 'shew that one or more propositions follow from one (or more)' (109). When we look at Wittgenstein's theory of inference in Section 4.6, we will see that this relationship between logical propositions and corresponding inferences shows up in the truth-tabular notation for propositional logic, in that any inference therein can be put in the form of what is called a 'corresponding material conditional' (Bergmann et al. 2014, 100–101). If the corresponding material conditional is a logical proposition or truth-functional truth, then the inference is valid.

The distinction between saying and showing does not apply *only* to logical propositions, however. Also, Wittgenstein insists, 'every *real* proposition *shews* something, besides what it says, about the Universe: for [...] if it has sense, it mirrors some logical property of the universe' (*NDM*, 108; emphases in the original). Here Wittgenstein means to elaborate on his reflections concerning logical form and logical types which we examined earlier in Section 4.3. As we saw there, according to Wittgenstein a logical form contains only free variables and so does not say anything contentful. A logical form is a prototype, which *says* nothing, but nevertheless *shows* what sorts of *symbols* may be substituted into it to convey a proposition with sense. The logical prototype 'xRy' *shows* that the symbols a, R and b may be substituted in for its variables to express the contentful proposition 'aRb'.

If, by contrast, one tried to *say* what types of *objects* may be substituted into a given position within a judgement that aRb, for example, one would have to bind the variables within the prototype and thereby produce something like a Russellian logical form, that is, a general fact. But, as we saw earlier, the idea of aRb's having sense could depend upon the existence of such a general fact, or on the truth of a proposition asserting the existence of such a fact, runs afoul of the basic intuition that any tautology follows from aRb independently of any such fact or proposition. 'Therefore', Wittgenstein insists,

> a THEORY *of types* is impossible. It tries to say something about the types, when you can only talk about the symbols. But *what* you say about the symbols is not that this symbol has that type, which would be nonsense for [the] same reason: but you say simply: *This* is the symbol, to prevent a misunderstanding. (*NDM*, 109; emphases in the original)

In other words, while it is impossible to have a contentful theory of types since these may only be expressed with free variables, we can nevertheless use 'elucidations' in order to prevent misunderstandings or to help our interlocutor achieve understanding. According to Wittgenstein, the *Tractatus* itself consists of precisely such elucidations: 'My propositions serve as elucidations in the following way: anyone who understands me eventually recognizes them as nonsensical' (*TLP* 6.54). Such elucidations are what Wittgenstein has in mind when he says that 'in a certain sense' (4.122) we can talk about what he calls 'formal properties' (ibid.) and 'formal concepts' (4.126) such as 'object', 'complex', 'fact', 'proposition', 'function', 'number' and so on. Such words 'all signify formal concepts, and are represented in conceptual notation by variables' (4.1272). In this respect, formal concepts stand in contrast to what Wittgenstein calls 'concepts proper', such as 'tall' or 'red', which can be represented in conceptual notation by constants such as 'T' or 'G', for example, 'Ta' or 'Ga'. While we cannot meaningfully *say* that the same object 'a' is mentioned in each of these two propositions, we can show that it is by using the same name 'a' (4.1211). Nevertheless, by using words like 'object' as formal 'pseudo-concepts' (4.1272) we may engage in philosophical elucidation for the purposes of logical clarification (4.112). In so doing, however, we do not produce any contentful propositions, and thus philosophy 'is not a body of doctrine but an activity' (ibid.).

4.6 Inference

In his introduction to *TLP*, Russell describes Wittgenstein as providing 'an amazing simplification of the theory of inference' (*TLP*, xvii). In order to see why, it will help to highlight two key features of Wittgenstein's theory of inference which have come up in our examination of Wittgenstein's philosophical

aRb	~aRb	aRb ∨ ~aRb
T	F	T
F	T	T

Figure 4.1 aRb :. aRb v ~aRb.

development over the period of 1913–14 and to explore their culmination in the truth-tabular notation characteristic of the *Tractatus*. The first of these features came up in the mid-June 1913 letter in which Wittgenstein claims to express his objection to Russell's MRTJ exactly. As we have seen, the problem highlighted in that letter is that Russell's theory requires a supplemental significance constraint to explain how aRb v ~ aRb follows from aRb. The substance of Wittgenstein's objection, again, is that aRb v ~ aRb follows from aRb in the absence of any supplemental premises. The 'direct' nature of this implication becomes clearer if we examine it using Wittgenstein's truth-tabular notation as shown in Figure 4.1.

Here 'aRb' is an elementary proposition whose truth-possibilities are listed in the column furthest to the left. The molecular proposition 'aRb v ~ aRb' is a truth-function of aRb, and its truth-possibilities are listed beneath it in the column on the right. The middle column is the negation of aRb, which we use to help us calculate the truth-possibilities of 'aRb v ~ aRb'. Since 'aRb v ~ aRb' is a disjunction, it will be true on any row where either one of its disjuncts, or both, are true. On the first row, 'aRb v ~ aRb' is true because 'aRb' is true. On the second row 'aRb v ~ aRb' is true because '~ aRb' is true. Since it comes out as true on each of the truth-possibilities of the elementary proposition of which it is a truth-function, 'aRb v ~ aRb' is thus a truth-functional truth or tautology.

Wittgenstein calls the 'truth-grounds' of a proposition 'the truth-possibilities of its truth arguments that make it true' (*TLP* 5.101). In other words, each of the cases in which a row under the proposition in question contains a 'T' is a truth-ground of the proposition. A case in which a row under the proposition contains an 'F' is not a truth-ground. We can tell one proposition follows from another, Wittgenstein insists, if every truth-ground of the latter is also a truth-ground of the former (5.12). In other words, one proposition follows from another if there is no row on the table on which the latter is true and the former is false. As we can see by looking at Figure 4.1, there is no row on which 'aRb' is true and 'aRb v ~ aRb' is false, and thus 'aRb v ~ aRb' follows from aRb. Moreover, it follows in the absence of any additional premises. Notably, this would be the case for any tautology, since tautologies are truth-functional truths, and thus they come out true on all truth-possibilities. Every truth-possibility is a truth-ground of any tautology or truth-functional truth. It

p	q	p → q*	p*	q_c
T	T	T	T	T
T	F	F	T	F
F	T	T	F	T
F	F	T	F	F

Figure 4.2 *Modus ponens.*

is thus impossible for a tautology not to follow from any proposition, provided the proposition is capable of being either true or false and thus has sense.

For clarity's sake, let us examine another, slightly more complex case. In this case let us look at the following argument:

$p \rightarrow q$

p

$\therefore q$

In order to use a truth-table to assess it for validity, we include columns on the left for each of the elementary propositions contained in the argument. Then we list each of the premises and the conclusion along the top of our table and calculate their truth-possibilities based on the elementary propositions of which they are truth-functions (Figure 4.2).

In this simple *modus ponens* argument, each of p and q occur both as elementary propositions and as truth-functions of those elementary propositions which figure as propositions within the argument we are evaluating. While 'p' figures as one of the premises (premises are marked with a *), 'q' figures as the conclusion (marked with a 'c'). In these roles they serve as truth-functions of themselves (*TLP* 5), and thus we simply copy their truth-possibilities from the columns on the left. We obtain all possible combinations of truth-possibilities of p and q by listing alternating single 'T's and 'F's under 'q' and then alternating double 'T's and 'F's under 'p'. As determined by the binomial theorem provided in *TLP* (4.27), our table has two elementary propositions and thus four rows. The truth-function 'p → q' is a conditional statement. Its antecedent is 'p' since p comes before the arrow, while its consequent is 'q' since q comes after the arrow. Conditional statements are false only when their antecedent is true and their consequent is false.

Once we calculate the truth-possibilities for each of our premises and the conclusion, we can determine that this argument is valid based on the table, since there is no row on which each of the premises is true and the conclusion

p	q	p → q	(p → q) & p	(((p → q) & p) → q)
T	T	T	T	T
T	F	F	F	T
F	T	T	F	T
F	F	T	F	T

Figure 4.3 Corresponding material conditional (valid).

is false. 'If', as Wittgenstein explains, 'all the truth-grounds that are common to a number of propositions are at the same time truth-grounds of a certain proposition, then we say that the truth of that proposition follows from the truth of the others' (*TLP* 5.11). For our present purposes, the important point is that it follows directly from those premises, in the absence of any allegedly self-evident axioms, laws of inference or significance constraints. Or as Wittgenstein insists: ' "Laws of inference", which are supposed to justify inferences [...] have no sense, and would be superfluous' (5.132).

When Wittgenstein says that laws of inference would lack sense, he is alluding to the other key feature of his theory of inference that it will help to highlight and which came up earlier in our discussion of the saying/showing distinction. This is the idea that logical propositions are 'forms of proof' which show that one proposition follows from one or more others. We can see this by proving the above argument is valid using another, alternative method, namely that of corresponding material conditionals. To form the corresponding material conditional for the above argument, take the iterated conjunction of the premises, that is, ((p → q) & p), and make this the antecedent of a conditional statement of which our conclusion q is the consequent. We then evaluate the resulting conditional statement ((p → q) & p) → q) to see whether it is a truth-functional truth, that is, a tautology (Figure 4.3). If the corresponding material conditional is a tautology, then the argument is valid. If it is not a tautology, then the argument is invalid.

Here we can see that the argument is indeed valid, since the corresponding material conditional has all and only 'T's' under its main-connective, the →, in the column furthest to the right. On the left, again, we listed each of the elementary propositions of which the other molecular propositions listed along the top row of the truth-table are truth-functions. The middle two columns are there simply to help us calculate the truth-possibilities of ((p → q) & p) → q) which, in this context, is the main proposition we are interested in. Again, (p → q) is a conditional statement and thus is false only when the antecedent is true and the consequent is false, that is, on the second row. The truth-function ((p → q) & p) is a conjunction of (p → q) and p. Conjunctions are true only when both conjuncts are true and are false otherwise. This particular conjunction

p	q	p → q	(p → q) & q	(((p → q) & q) → p)
T	T	T	T	T
T	F	F	F	T
F	T	T	T	F
F	F	T	F	T

Figure 4.4 Corresponding material conditional (invalid).

is thus true on the first row but false on each of the second, third and fourth rows. Finally, ((p → q) & p) → q is a conditional statement which is false only in case its antecedent is true and its consequent is false and is otherwise true. But there is no case, or row, on which its antecedent is true and its consequent is false, and thus it is unconditionally true. An unconditionally true statement we call a 'tautology' or truth-functional truth.

By contrast, let us briefly examine the following invalid inference:

p → q

q

∴ p

This inference is an instance of a well-known fallacy called 'affirming the consequent'. We should thus be able to show that it is invalid using the method of corresponding material conditionals (Figure 4.4).

Here we can see that on the third row, the antecedent of our corresponding material conditional, that is, (p → q) & q, is true, while the consequent p is false. On that row the corresponding material conditional comes out false. Since this corresponding material conditional comes out false on one of the truth-possibilities of the elementary propositions of which it is a truth-function, it is not a truth-functional truth or tautology, and thus the inference it embodies is not valid. Likewise, the following table (Figure 4.5) proves that the same argument is invalid by showing that there is a case in which the premises are each true and the conclusion is false. In other words, not all truth-grounds shared amongst the premises, are truth-grounds of the conclusion.

In the third row, each of the premises are true but the conclusion, p, is false. Not every truth-ground shared in common among the premises is also shared by the conclusion. Each of the premises along with the conclusion are true on row 1, but on row 3 each of the premises are true and the conclusion is not true.

p	q	p → q*	q*	p_c
T	T	T	T	T
T	F	F	F	T
F	T	T	T	F
F	F	T	F	F

Figure 4.5 Affirming the consequent.

4.7 Sense-Truth Regress

In Section 4.6 we introduced truth-tables to clarify Wittgenstein's account of inference. In this and subsequent sections we will highlight several further and philosophically interesting themes within and features of Wittgenstein's logical system which are illuminated by the truth-tabular notation. These themes and features include the logical independence of elementary propositions, extensionalism, Wittgenstein's 'fundamental thought' (or *Grundgedanke*) and the general form of a proposition. Extensionalism we examined briefly earlier in association with our treatment of Wittgenstein's ab-notation, but examining it in consort with the truth-tabular notation will give us a fuller and richer understanding of it.

In this section, however, we will focus on the logical independence of elementary propositions more specifically, along with other features of Wittgenstein's viewpoint which are closely related to it, such as the subsistence of objects. We will examine how these two features of Wittgenstein's logical and semantic viewpoint arise out of the sense-truth regress. We briefly introduced the sense-truth-regress back in Section 4.3 in the context of our discussion of logical form and saw how it arose out of themes prominent in the mid-June 1913 letter. It will be recalled that one key theme within the mid-June 1913 letter was that the sense of aRb could not depend upon the truth of the significance constraint P1). In the same section, we looked at a remark from *NDM* which builds upon this idea and applies it to Wittgenstein's account of logical form. There, I promised to explore this theme in more detail later and to examine some of the further and related ways it influences Wittgenstein's early thinking. Now it is time follow that promise up.

The sense-truth regress makes its most notable subsequent appearance in *TLP* 2.021–2.0212. There it is used to explain why objects must subsist for propositions to have sense and to draw out some implications thereof for elementary propositions and their truth-functional relationships to molecular propositions. To properly understand what Wittgenstein has in mind in these remarks from *TLP*, we need to look briefly at a related remark of Russell's from *OD*. The remark comes up in the section of *OD* where Russell introduces three

p	q	p & q
T	T	T
T	F	F
F	T	F
F	F	F

Figure 4.6 Conjunction.

logical and semantic puzzles that he thinks any adequate theory of denoting should, ideally, have the capacity to resolve. There he writes:

> By the law of excluded middle, either 'A is B' or 'A is not B' must be true. Hence either 'the present King of France is bald' or 'the present King of France is not bald' must be true. Yet if we enumerated the things that are bald, and then the things that are not bald, we should not find the present King of France in either list. (*OD*, 485)

The problem alluded to here by Russell concerns denoting phrases that do not denote anything, such as 'the present King of France'. Such phrases are problematic since propositions containing them might seem to be neither true nor false and thus to constitute counterexamples to the law of excluded middle. Russell's solution was to subject such phrases to contextual paraphrase which showed how they could contribute to the meaning of propositions expressed by the sentences containing them, without actually contributing any unique constituent to the proposition.

A similar problem arises for Wittgenstein, though it is not framed in exactly the same way. For Wittgenstein the threat is not to the law of excluded middle but to bipolarity, which as we have seen is an intrinsic and essential feature of propositions. From Wittgenstein's perspective, the law of excluded middle tries to say what can only be shown in an adequate logical notation such as a truth-table. From that perspective, the problem is that Wittgenstein needs some way to guarantee that any proposition containing a non-denoting expression must be capable of being either true or false, and thus of having sense, without that sense depending on the truth of some other proposition, such as that of a proposition asserting the existence of the complex which corresponds to a denoting expression. The reason is that, unless there is some way of guaranteeing that the sense of one proposition is independent of the truth of any other proposition, the truth-tabular notation will not work. We can see this by examining the truth-table in Figure 4.6.

Just as in the ab-notation, within the truth-tabular notation, molecular propositions are represented as truth-functions of elementary propositions.

p	q	p & q
T	T	T
T	?	?
F	T	F
F	?	?

Figure 4.7 Sense-truth regress.

In Figure 4.6, the molecular proposition 'p & q' is defined so as to agree (T) and disagree (F) with certain truth-possibilities of the elementary propositions of which is a truth-function. The first row, on which 'p & q' agrees with the truth-possibilities of 'p' and 'q', is a truth-ground of 'p & q' while none of the other rows are. Moreover, as we saw earlier in Section 4.6, based on Figure 4.6 we can infer 'p & q' from the truth of both 'p' and 'q' taken together (row one) but not from that of either in isolation (rows two and three). The important point at present is simply that this truth-functional analysis of what it means for a molecular proposition to have sense, and/or to follow from some (groups of) propositions but not others, depends upon the logical independence of elementary propositions. And the logical independence of elementary propositions depends, in turn, on it being possible for one elementary proposition to have sense regardless of whether another is or is not true. For suppose that the sense of 'p' depended upon the truth of 'q'. Then rows two and four of the table would be ruled out, since in that case there could be no truth-possibilities on which p had sense but q was false (Figure 4.7).

And if rows two and four of this table are ruled out, then we can no longer use the truth-tabular notation to represent the truth-functional relationships between the molecular proposition 'p & q' and its constituent elementary propositions 'p' and 'q'. And nor can we use it to understand why 'p & q' follows from both 'p' and 'q' taken together but not each individually. Far from an 'amazing simplification of the theory of inference' or an 'uniform method of construction' (*TLP*, xvii), we would have a logical and semantic muddle.

The sense of p thus cannot depend on the truth of q and, moreover, this logical independence of p and q in turn depends upon the subsistence of objects. As Wittgenstein explains:

> Objects make up the substance of the world. That is why they cannot be composite. If the world had no substance, then whether a proposition had sense would depend upon whether another proposition was true. In that case we could not sketch any picture of the world (true or false). (*TLP* 2.021–2.012)

What Wittgenstein has to say here about objects is part of a proposal to resolve the issues posed by non-referring expressions for bipolarity, by providing a contextual paraphrase of such expressions which is similar to Russell's, but which goes further to arrive at a complete description of the complex which would exist if the expression in question in fact referred (2.0201). Such a complete description will be a truth-function of elementary propositions, themselves composed of names. The names do not have meaning, and thus the proposition does not have sense, unless the names stand for objects which, Wittgenstein insists, are timeless, indecomposable and simple. While 'the Present King of France' can surely fail to exist, if 'a' is a meaningful name, then the object it stands for *cannot* fail to subsist. This explains why he says in the earlier quotation that objects cannot be composite; if they were composite, they could conceivably decay or decompose, thus ceasing to subsist. Within Wittgenstein's metaphysical and semantic perspective, *any* purported complex corresponding to a description could fail to exist if the description is false. But *no* object referred to by a meaningful name can fail to subsist. From this it follows that whether any elementary proposition has sense depends only upon whether its constituent names have a reference and so meaning. Whether one elementary proposition has sense can therefore never depend upon the truth of some other proposition asserting the existence of any object referred to by a name. Within a logically adequate notation, according to Wittgenstein, you can never say that an object exists or does not. That an object subsists is instead shown in the meaningfulness of the name which stands for it.

The argument for the logical independence of elementary propositions and the subsistence of objects given earlier is perhaps the best and most notable example of the sense-truth regress within Wittgenstein's early philosophy. However, it is also an instance of a more general and related theme which comes up elsewhere and in a variety of contexts. What I have in mind is Wittgenstein's idea that logic and sense must be independent of facts and experience. From the perspective of Wittgenstein's early philosophy, logic is an a priori condition of sense, and thus whether a proposition has sense must be independent of whether it or any other proposition is true, and thus of whether any fact obtains. Moreover, we can know whether any proposition is logical or non-logical based purely on an examination of the symbol and independently of any factual knowledge or experience concerning what it or any other proposition says.

The idea that logic is independent of facts and experience comes up at the outset of his wartime *Notebooks*, where he writes repeatedly that 'logic must take care of itself' (*NB*, 3) and insists that this 'is an extremely profound and important insight' (ibid.). Relatedly, in the *Tractatus* itself he claims that 'logic is prior to every experience' (*TLP* 5.552) and that, unlike logic which is a priori (5.4731) 'no part of our experience is also *a priori*' (*TLP* 1922 5.634). Further, Wittgenstein insists that while 'what is certain *a priori* proves to be something purely logical' (*TLP* 6.3211), non-logical, bipolar propositions instead must be compared to reality in order to determine whether they are true or false (2.223–2.224). There are thus no such bipolar propositions which 'are true *a priori*' (2.225).

Reflecting back on the truth-tables we examined in the previous Section 4.6 and in this Section 4.7, it is obvious, moreover, that on their basis we cannot know whether 'p', 'q' or 'p & q' are true. To determine whether these propositions were true, we would need to know the sense of each of p and q and compare their sense with the facts in order to determine whether they agree or disagree. However, without any experience or knowledge of the facts, we can know a priori that 'p & q' follows from both 'p' and 'q' taken jointly but not from either taken individually. And this, according to Wittgenstein, shows that 'all inference takes place *a priori*' (*TLP* 1922 5.133).

4.8 The Fundamental Thought (*Grundgedanke*)

In *TLP* 1922 (4.0312) Wittgenstein writes that 'my fundamental thought is that the "logical constants" do not represent. That the *logic* of facts cannot be represented' (emphasis in the original). This 'fundamental thought' or *Grundgedanke* brings together and crystallizes a number of different ideas which we have considered thus far in this chapter, including those concerning logical form, the unique status of logical propositions, the saying/showing distinction and the a priori nature of inference. While the *Grundgedanke* would be transmuted and transformed by reflection on these various ideas, and these ideas, as we have seen, in many respects emerged out of Wittgenstein's May–June 1913 critique of the MRTJ, it would be a mistake however to say that Wittgenstein's fundamental thought emerged out of Wittgenstein's May–June 1913 critique. This is because the *Grundgedanke* actually makes its first appearance within the extant correspondence in a June 1912 letter to Russell. There Wittgenstein writes that

> Logic is still in the melting pot but one thing gets more and more obvious to me: The propositions of Logic contain ONLY *apparent* variables and whatever may turn out to be the proper explanation of apparent variables, its consequence *must* be that there are no logical constants. Logic must turn out to be a totally different kind than any other science. (*CL*, 14–15; emphases in the original)

As Wittgenstein himself appears to acknowledge, the proposal contained in this letter is inchoate. However, what Wittgenstein seems to have had in mind is that since logical propositions are perfectly general, they contain only bound (apparent) variables, which occur under the scope of a universal quantifier. They thus do not deal with anything in particular, and so logic has no specific content, or objects for constants to denote. Of course, if there are no logical constants, then an obvious question concerns the nature and status of the symbols contained within logical propositions (e.g. (p) (p v ~ p)). If '(p)', 'v' and '~' are not constants and do not stand for anything, how and what do they mean? What do they contribute to the meanings of logical and non-logical propositions, and how?

The attempt to answer these questions led Wittgenstein into an eliminativist programme, which culminates in his characterization of the general form of a proposition in terms of successive applications of an operation, N($\bar{\xi}$), which, like all operations, 'shows itself in a variable' (*TLP* 1922 5.24). In the context of pursuing this programme, Wittgenstein would develop a very different conception of logical propositions than that contained in the June 1912 letter quoted earlier. As we have seen, already by 1913 Wittgenstein was beginning to characterize logical propositions as unique in being tautological, rather than perfectly general. They were revealed to be tautological through Wittgenstein's reflections on bipolarity, for which he devised the ab-notation. Significantly, the ab-notation shows how to eliminate many supposed logical constants, including ~, &, v and →. Likely inspired by his success in eliminating these symbols, Wittgenstein appears to have experimented, less successfully, with attempts to replace quantifiers and the identity sign with an equivalent ab-notation. Presumably, he thought this must be possible since bipolarity is the essence of sense, and thus it would have to be possible to express any sense one could convey with quantifiers and identity using the ab-notation instead, given that the ab-notation captures all there is to bipolarity. Hence, in a November 1913 letter to Russell he insists that while the ab-notation for identity is not yet 'clear enough [...] it is obvious that such a Notation can be made up' (*CL*, 54). However, the elimination of quantifiers and identity would prove to be more challenging than Wittgenstein anticipated and would have to wait until his discovery of the N-operator, which we will discuss in more detail in the next section (4.9). In the remainder of this section I want to highlight some of the ways in which the *Grundgedanke* specifically shows up in the *Tractatus*.

Building on his work with the ab-notation, in *TLP* Wittgenstein goes on to use the truth-tabular notation to show that logical connectives are interdefinable and so eliminable. In *TLP* (5.42) he therefore writes that the 'interdefinability of Frege's and Russell's "primitive signs" of logic is enough to show that they are not primitive signs' (cf. *NL*, 98). As examples of such

WITTGENSTEIN ON TRUTH, LOGIC AND REPRESENTATION   167

p	q	p → q	~p	~p ∨ q
T	T	**T**	F	**T**
T	F	**F**	F	**F**
F	T	**T**	T	**T**
F	F	**T**	T	**T**

Figure 4.8 Interdefinability.

primitive signs Wittgenstein provides ~, v and →. The truth-tabular notation shows, for example, that p → q is equivalent to ~p v q (Figure 4.8).

In the truth-table in Figure 4.8, each of the columns for the two propositions we are interested in comparing, 'p → q' and '~p v q', can be seen in bold. On the left-hand side of our table, as usual, we have listed the truth-possibilities of the two elementary propositions 'p' and 'q' of which these two propositions are truth-functions. Appearing in between the two bolded columns is '~p', which is there to help us calculate the truth-arguments for the truth-function '~p v q', since it is a disjunction of '~p' and 'q'. Disjunctions are true just in case either one of their disjunctions, or both, are true. They are false only when both disjuncts are false. On the second row, '~p' is false and q is also false, making '~p v q' false. On every other row the disjunction is true. On the first row it is true because q is true. On the third it is true because both 'q' and '~p' are true. On the fourth it is true because '~p' is true.

Once we have calculated the truth-arguments for the truth-function '~p v q' and listed those truth-arguments in the column under the proposition, we can see that it is exactly the same truth-function as p → q. Moreover, as Wittgenstein highlights in *TLP* (4.442), we could easily express this truth-function using a truth-table, which has no logical connectives in it whatsoever. In our table, we simply need to list the cases in which the truth-function agrees with the truth-possibilities of 'p' and 'q' in order to convey the truth-function we are interested in. Following Wittgenstein, this can be done as shown in Figure 4.9.

What Wittgenstein wants us to notice is that using this truth-table, we are able to represent the truth-function ordinarily expressed as 'p → q' without making use of the sign '→' or any other allegedly primitive signs. From this it is obvious, Wittgenstein thinks, that →, ~, v, & and so on are in principle eliminable, and thus not genuinely primitive signs. Exploiting this idea (*TLP* 5.101), Wittgenstein shows how to express each of the 16 truth-functions of two elementary propositions in a one-dimensional notation which eliminates the need for any of the standard sentential connectives. For example, Wittgenstein writes 'p & q' as (TFFF) (p, q) and '~p & ~q' as (FFFT) (p,q). As we shall see in

p	q	
T	T	T
T	F	
F	T	T
F	F	T

Figure 4.9 The *Grundgedanke*.

p	q	(p & q) ≡ (q & p)			~p	p ∨ ~p	p & ~p	~(p & ~p)
T	T	T	**T**	T	F	**T**	F	**T**
T	F	F	**T**	F	F	**T**	F	**T**
F	T	F	**T**	F	T	**T**	F	**T**
F	F	F	**T**	F	T	**T**	F	**T**

Figure 4.10 Truth-functional truth.

more detail in the next section (4.9), by building on and generalizing the latter truth-function in particular (along with the general idea of a one-dimensional, truth-functional notation), Wittgenstein hopes to deploy his N($\bar{\xi}$) operator to capture the general form of a proposition and so express any meaningful proposition, including those ostesibly involving Russellian quantification.

Before moving on to do so we need to highlight another important, and related, way in which the *Grundgedanke* shows up in the Tractarian, truth-tabular notation. In Section 4.6 we saw that by putting any *modus ponens* argument in the form of a corresponding material conditional, we could then calculate its truth-arguments for each of the truth-possibilities of the elementary propositions of which it is a truth-function. Using a truth-table to do so, we found that when put in this form, *modus ponens* comes out as a truth-functional truth or a tautology. For our present purposes, the important point to note is that, according to Wittgenstein, all logical propositions come out as truth-functional truths or tautologies when expressed using the truth-tabular notation. In the truth-table in Figure 4.10, I provide some representative examples for illustrative purposes.

In bold I have highlighted three truth-functional truths and listed the truth-arguments for each of these truth-functions, also in bold, beneath their main connective. As usual, our elementary propositions 'p' and 'q' are listed in the two columns furthest to the left. In the column next to the right, I have calculated the truth-arguments for the proposition (p & q) ≡ (q &p) based on the truth-possibilities of its elementary propositions. In order to do this, I first calculated the truth-arguments for each of the two conjunctions of those elementary propositions (i.e. 'p & q' and 'q & p') which flank the sign for material bi-conditional statements, namely '≡'. Each of these conjunctions is true only on the first row, while they come out as false on every other row. Material bi-conditional statements, whose main connective is always '≡', come out as true if the two propositions which flank the '≡' have the same value on a given row and come out false if the two propositions do not have the same truth-value on that row. Since 'p & q' and 'q & p' have the same truth-value on every row, '(p & q) ≡ (q &p)' comes out as a truth-functional truth or tautology. This particular tautology corresponds to the inference rule known as 'commutation'.

The next column to the right, for '~p', is used to help us calculate the truth-arguments under the main connective of the column next to the right, for 'p v ~p'. We have seen that disjunctions come out as true for every truth-possibility on which one or the other of their disjuncts, or both, is true. In this case, 'p' is true on rows one and two whereas ~p' is true on rows three and four. The disjunction thus comes out as true on every row and so is a truth-functional truth or tautology. This particular tautology is an instance of the logic law of excluded middle.

The next column, 'p & ~p', is included to help us calculate the truth-arguments for our final proposition on the right. The truth-function 'p & ~p' is a conjunction, which thus comes out as true for any truth-possibility according to which each of its conjuncts are true and comes out false otherwise. As we can see by examining the columns for each of 'p' and '~p', there is no row of the table upon which they both come out as true. The truth-function 'p & ~p' thus comes out as false on every row and so is a truth-functional falsehood or contradiction. Applying negation to this molecular proposition yields ~(p & ~p), for which I have listed the truth-arguments on each truth-possibility in the column furthest to the right. Because negation simply reverses the truth-value of whatever it applies to, '~(p & ~p)' comes out as true on every row and is thus a truth-functional truth or tautology. This particular truth-functional truth is an instance of the logical law of non-contradiction (cf. *PT* 6.1121).

Aside from showing how the tautologousness, or truth-functional truth, of a proposition may be calculated on the basis of truth-possibilities of elementary propositions, the table in Figure 4.10 also highlights several features of logical propositions which exemplify Wittgenstein's 'fundamental thought'. The first is that although each of these logical propositions seems to correspond to a distinct logical law or rule of inference, they all have the very same truth-conditions. Because they all have the same truth-conditions, they all say the same thing: 'in fact all propositions of logic say the same thing, to wit, nothing' (*TLP* 5.43). The logic of facts thus cannot be represented, according to Wittgenstein, because the attempt to do so yields nothing but contentless tautologies. Whether a proposition is a tautology can be seen in its truth-function, which amounts to a list of truth-arguments on which a proposition agrees with its truth-possibilities. There are no logical constants because all logical operators are interdefinable and can be eliminated in favour of the truth-tabular notation. Unlike names, which are genuine primitive signs and have an indefinable, independent meaning by virtue of standing for something, namely an object, logical operators are definable in terms of other signs, have no independent meaning and stand for nothing.

It is worth highlighting, finally, that the idea that logical constants do not stand for anything and that logical propositions do not represent anything are each distinct from if related to the doctrine that logical form is shown in propositions but not said by them. From the perspective of a defender of LI, this distinction is important to keep in mind since if it is not, one might argue that the presence of the *Grundgedanke* in the summer 1912 correspondence with Russell is evidence for Landini's claim that Wittgenstein's intuition, or doctrine of showing, appeared much earlier in the timeline than spring 1914. Wittgenstein's June 1912 letter in which he denies that there are logical constants and insists that there can be no representation of the logic of facts might then erroneously be thought to lend credence to Landini's claim that Wittgenstein's doctrine of showing appears much earlier in the timeline and should be thought of as the driving force behind Wittgenstein's critique of the MRTJ. Landini himself claims (1991, 65) that the idea that there are no logical constants was inherited by Wittgenstein from Russell. So, it does not seem available to Landini to mount this sort of attack on LI, since Landini thinks Russell had no reason to take Wittgenstein's critique seriously, given his own philosophical commitments. If Wittgenstein's objection highlighted one of Russell's own philosophical commitments, Landini could not dismiss the objection so easily (Russell himself clearly did not). Nevertheless, if Landini or one of his defenders were to mount this sort of challenge to LI, it would run into the additional roadblock identified earlier. Specifically, it would involve a failure to distinguish clearly between the *Grundgedanke* and the saying/showing distinction. Though these ideas are associated in Wittgenstein's final system, they are nevertheless distinct and have different points of origination within the timeline of the development of Wittgenstein's thought.

4.9 The General Propositional Form

The notion of a general propositional form emerged out of Wittgenstein's reflections on bipolarity via the ab-notation. In experimenting with this notation to study bipolarity in abstraction from truth-functionality, Wittgenstein discovered several interesting features of molecular ab-functions, which we highlighted earlier in Section 4.4. Though as we have seen, Wittgenstein did not wish to prejudge the issue of whether ab-functions were identical to truth-functions, it was always his strong presumption that reflection on molecular ab-functions, and on their construction in the ab-notation would yield important insights into the nature and construction of molecular truth-functions. This presumption manifests itself in the following passage from *NL*, where Wittgenstein highlights some interesting features of molecular truth-functions which show up in reflection upon the ab-notation:

> To every molecular function a WF scheme corresponds. Therefore we may use the WF scheme itself instead of the function. Now what the WF scheme does is, it correlates the letters W and F with each proposition. These two letters are the poles of atomic propositions. Then the scheme correlates another W and F to these poles. In this notation all that matters is the correlation of the outside poles to the poles of the atomic propositions. Therefore not-not-p is the same symbol as p. And therefore we shall never get two symbols for the same molecular function. (*NL*, 94)

For our purposes, the important feature of molecular truth-functions which is highlighted in this passage is that in a TF notation of the sort Wittgenstein describes, equivalent molecular truth-functions will be symbolized in exactly the same way. Wittgenstein's example here is the molecular truth-function not-not-p which, as he says, is equivalent to p. In the ab-notation, each of these two propositions would be expressed as a-p-b. Following Wittgenstein's proposal in the earlier quotation, by substituting 'T' for 'a' and 'b' for F, we obtain T-p-F. Expressed in the manner shown in *TLP* (5.101), each of these two propositions would be expressed as (T, F) (p).

The idea that equivalent truth-functions have a common symbolic form, however, is not the same as the idea of a general propositional form. That is the idea of a notation in which *all* propositions can be expressed in a common form, not just equivalent propositions. The idea that equivalent molecular truth-functions have a common symbolic form is certainly the germ of the idea of a general propositional form, but extending this idea to cover all meaningful propositions involves substantially more work, as we shall see. The next step for Wittgenstein was to show how all molecular truth-functions may be constructed by the repeated application of one, particular truth-function. Such a function must obviously be more sophisticated than simple negation, for instance, since negation will simply reverse the truth-value of the proposition it is applied to and, if applied again, will reverse it again, back to what it was. In his introduction to *TLP*, Russell notes that Scheffer had shown 'that all truth-functions of a given set of propositions can be constructed out of either of two functions' (*TLP* xv). The two functions are ~p v ~q (the stroke (p|q) and ~p & ~q (the dagger (p↓q)). In the passage that follows from *NL*, Wittgenstein references the former:

> Since the *ab*-functions of *p* are again bi-polar propositions, we can form ab-functions of them, and so on. In this way a series of propositions will arise, in which in general the *symbolizing* facts will be the same in several members. If now we find an *ab*-function of such a kind that by repeated application of it every ab-function can be generated, then we can introduce the totality of ab-functions as the totality of those that are generated by application of this function. Such a function is ~p v ~q. (*NL*, 102; emphasis in the original)

Here Wittgenstein builds upon the idea that equivalent molecular ab-functions will have a shared symbolic form as expressed in the ab-notation, to arrive at the idea that there is a single truth-function which, if applied repeatedly, can be used to express any truth-function. The proposal Wittgenstein offers here is that any truth-function can be constructed by repeated application of the Scheffer stroke to elementary propositions. For example, ~p can be expressed using the stroke as p|p, and p → q would be expressed as (p|p)|((q|q)|(q|q)).

In the earlier passage from his introduction to *TLP* Russell goes on to claim that Wittgenstein 'makes use of' the dagger (i.e. ~p & ~q or p↓q) to construct all truth-functions. While this may convey the general idea behind Wittgenstein's proposal to the novice, it is not strictly correct. This is because although similar in some respects, the N-operator which Wittgenstein deploys within his characterization of the general form of a proposition in *TLP* (6) is importantly distinct from each of both the stroke and the dagger. While it is more akin to the latter than the former, it would be more strictly correct if Russell had said that Wittgenstein 'builds on' as opposed to 'makes use of' the dagger. The most significant difference is that while the dagger is a binary operator and thus in any given application yields a truth-function of two arguments, N operates upon arbitrarily large numbers of propositions and so can, in any single application, express a truth-function of any arbitrarily large number of arguments. This makes it a much more convenient tool with which to express the truth-functional equivalents of quantified propositions. Before showing how this is done, it will be helpful to briefly explain the symbol Wittgenstein provides in *TLP* (ibid.), which, as he says there, is the general form of a truth-function and thus the general form of a proposition.

Within this symbol, ([p, ξ, N(ξ)]), Wittgenstein specifies a procedure whereby all possible truth-functions may be constructed via successive applications of a single, truth-functional operator, specifically N, to arbitrarily, and indefinitely, large selections of elementary propositions. According to Wittgenstein's symbol for the general form of a truth-function, we thus start with all elementary propositions (p̄), and from there, generate truth-functions by applying N successively, first to selections of those elementary propositions (ξ̄) and then to N-expressed truth-functions of those elementary propositions. To say that a truth-function is 'N-expressed' is, simply, to indicate that it is symbolized using successive iterations of N alone, exclusive of other, equivalent combinations of truth-functional operators such as '~' (i.e. negation) or '&' (i.e. conjunction). Notably, N functions similarly to joint negation (e.g. ~p & ~ q), except that it may be applied to more than two propositions at a time. Indeed, N is defined such that it may take an indefinite and arbitrarily large number of arguments, from one to an infinite number of arguments. For example, if we wanted to express (~p & ~ q) & ~r using Wittgenstein's N notation, we could do so as follows: N(p,q,r). If we wanted to express (~p & ~ q) & (~r & ~s), we could do so as follows: N(p,q,r,s). And so on.

In Section 4.2, we have already shown how to use N to construct several common truth-functions. Now let us examine how Wittgenstein purports to use the arbitrarily large domain size of N to recover Russellian quantification. By allowing N to take an arbitrarily large number n of arguments, and by allowing those arguments to be each of an arbitrarily large number n of substitution instances of a propositional function such as fx, for example, we may then use N to express something equivalent to Russellian quantification over an arbitrarily large or even infinite domain. As Wittgenstein explains in *TLP* (5.52), for instance, 'If ξ has as its values all the values of a function fx for all values of x, then N(ξ̄) = ~(∃x).fx.' In other words, if we substitute for x in fx, a distinct name for every object we wish to quantify over, and then place each of the elementary propositions which result within the brackets under the scope of the N operator, like so: N(fa, fb, fc, fd, ..., fn), then we will thereby express something that is equivalent to the negation of (∃x).fx. To N-express the equivalent of (∃x).fx, then, we need simply to apply an additional 'N' to the front of this N expression in succession as follows: N(N(fa, fb, fc, fd, ..., fn)).

Like (∃x).fx, {N(N(fa, fb, fc, fd, ..., fn))} is equivalent to a truth-functional expansion, a disjunction which takes each of an arbitrarily large number of substitution instances of the propositional function fx as disjuncts. The equivalent truth-functional expansion can thus be given in the form of a disjunction as follows: fa v fb v fc v fd v ... v fn. In Section 4.2 we saw how to express the conjunction of p and q using the N operator (i.e. as N(N(p), N(q))), and we can now build on this to show how N may be used to recover universal quantification. For instance, we may express (∀x) fx by using N to recover something equivalent to the conjunction of each of the substitution instances of fx, like so: N(N(fa), N(fb), N(fc), N(fd), ..., N(fn)). This N-expression is then equivalent to the following, conjunctive, truth-functional expansion: fa & fb & fc & fd & ... & fn.

For illustrative purposes, in our exposition we have followed Wittgenstein (*TLP* 5.52, 5.501) in focusing on how N may be used to recover quantification into monadic propositional functions. In *TLP* (5.501), Wittgenstein briefly indicates one way in which we might expand this same basic method to capture quantification over propositional functions of higher arity. Specifically, the third of the three kinds of description he identifies, by which we may select arguments for presentation to the N operator (i.e. stipulate terms to occur within the brackets under the scope of an iteration of N) involves 'giving a formal law that governs the construction of the propositions' (ibid.). In that case, what will occur in the brackets under the scope of one or more iterations of N will be 'all the terms of a series of forms' (ibid.). Here Wittgenstein seems to have in mind the sorts of formal series described in *TLP* (4.1252), which involves a number of objects (a, b, c, etc.) being ordered in a series by iterations of a dyadic relation R. In this case, the propositional function 'xRy' serves as a sort of prototype or recipe which can be used to gather together substitution instances of a dyadic, as opposed to monadic propositional function, for presentation to the N-operator. With regards to each of the second and third kinds of description identified in *TLP* (5.501), there would seem to be no barrier to using the same basic procedures, or others like them, to gather together substitution instances of triadic, quadratic or other propositional functions of even higher arity in order to use N to recover quantification over such propositional functions, via the method of truth-functional expansion exposited earlier.

In each case we would use the propositional function we are interested in to produce a list of elementary propositions, each of which was a substitution instance of that propositional function obtained by substituting a name in for each variable in the proposition function. A distinct name would be used for each distinct object in the domain we are quantifying over, and we will never substitute the same name in for two distinct variables within the same propositional function. For example, if we wanted to N express $(\exists x)(\exists y).fxy$, we could do so by using N to truth-functionally expand over an arbitrarily large domain of n members. If we call the first member of this domain 'a', the nth 't', and the n-1th 's', then we may N-express our truth-functional expansion as follows:

N(N(fab, fac, fad, ..., fba, fbc, fbd, ..., fts)).

Notably, due to Wittgenstein's use of exclusive quantifiers to help eliminate the identity sign, substitution instances such as 'faa', 'fbb,' 'ftt' and so on will not appear in this N-expression. It is of course possible to place such substitution instances under the scope of N, but in doing so we would be expressing a different quantification. For instance, using Wittgenstein's exclusive quantifiers we could express the associated quantification as follows (cf. *TLP* 5.32):

($\exists x$) ($\exists y$).fxy.v. ($\exists x$) ($\exists x$).fxx.

This would then be recovered by the following N-expression:

N(N(fab, fac, fad, ..., fba, fbc, fbd, ..., fts, faa, fbb, ..., ftt).

Assuming we leave the last four letters of the alphabet for use as variables rather than constants, then if our domain is larger than 22 members we might run out of letters. To address this problem, however, we could just indefinitely add primes to our small roman letters from a-t (e.g. a') to create enough constants until we reach the required number n of constants.

There are some important problems with this proposal, which we will discuss in the next section (4.10), when we look at Wittgenstein's transition away from the Tractarian logical and semantic system towards his later philosophical perspective. What is important to highlight at the moment is that the symbol Wittgenstein provides in *TLP* (6), for the general form of a proposition, is a variable with which he attempts to implement the idea that all meaningful language can be constructed via a single truth-functional operator, N, independently of any other signs or operators, such as the identity sign, truth-functional connectives or quantifiers. Wittgenstein thus describes the symbol he provides in *TLP* (ibid.), containing N, as 'the one and only general primitive sign in logic' (5.472). It is also significant that Wittgenstein describes the variable he offers in *TLP* (6) as the 'general form of a truth-function'. This is because it is designed to implement a related idea, known as 'extensionalism', according to which all meaningful language is truth-functional, and more specifically, any meaningful proposition is a truth-function of elementary propositions.

We already discussed this idea briefly in relation to Wittgenstein's ab-notation in Section 4.4 but noted in Section 4.7 that our understanding of it can be augmented by considering the truth-tabular notation.

With respect to extensionalism, the important feature to highlight about this table (Figure 4.11) is that each of the propositions listed in the row along the top are truth-functions of the elementary propositions p and q listed in the column furthest to the left. Each of them is a bipolar proposition which agrees with certain truth-possibilities of the elementary propositions (marked by a 'T' under its main connective) and disagrees with others (marked by an 'F' under its main connective. Extensionalism is simply the claim that all meaningful propositions are like this. Extensionalism 'extends' bipolarity from specific propositions to all propositions by claiming, in essence, that if any proposition is a truth-function of elementary propositions, then every proposition is. This feature of propositions is reflected in the fact that all meaningful propositions can be constructed via repeated applications of either of the two

p	q	p → q	p & q	p ∨ q	p↓q	p|q
T	T	T	T	T	F	F
T	F	F	F	T	F	T
F	T	T	F	T	F	T
F	F	T	F	F	T	T

Figure 4.11 Extensionality.

p	q	p ∨ ~p	p & q	p ∨ q	p↓q	p & ~p
T	T	**T**	T	T	F	**F**
T	F	**T**	F	T	F	**F**
F	T	**T**	F	T	F	**F**
F	F	**T**	F	F	T	**F**

Figure 4.12 The limits of sense.

truth-functions listed in the columns furthest to the right, p↓q and p|q. For instance, p ∨ q may be expressed using the ↓ symbol as (p↓q)↓(p↓q). Using the ↓, p & q can be expressed as (p↓p)↓(q↓q).

When, in his introduction to *TLP* Russell describes the process indicated by Wittgenstein's symbol for the general form of a proposition, he notes that, over and above depending on Scheffer's proof of the truth-functional completeness of ↓, it relies on Wittgenstein's 'derivation of general propositions from conjunctions and disjunctions' (*TLP*, xvii). What Russell has in mind here is the process we described earlier, where, in order to use his N-operator to recover quantification, Wittgenstein builds upon and generalizes the fact that ↓ may be used to express conjunctions and disjunctions. He does this by using N to express the equivalent of conjunctive or disjunctive truth-functional expansions which are themselves equivalent to quantification over arbitrarily large domains.

Removing p → q and p|q from the table in Figure 4.11 and replacing them with, respectively, a tautology and a contradiction will help us visualize extensionalism under a slightly different, but highly illuminating aspect (Figure 4.12).

Truth-functional truths such as p ∨ ~p and truth-functional falsehoods such as p & ~p are limiting cases of propositions in that they come out as true or false, respectively, on each of the truth-possibilities of the elementary propositions of which they are truth-functions. They are not 'nonsense' in the sense that they are not legitimate combinations of signs but instead 'lack sense' in the sense that they are not bipolar and thus do not depict a fact which might either exist or not. The table in Figure 4.12 is designed to highlight that, within Wittgenstein's system, tautologies and contradictions constitute the 'limits of sense', and thus every proposition which has sense and is thus bipolar lies in between these limits. Truth-functional truth and truth-functional falsehood circumscribe the range within which lies all significant discourse. Extensionalism is the idea that there is nothing 'beyond' these limits. Every meaningful proposition is a truth-function which lies within the range circumscribed by tautologies and contradictions.

Wittgenstein considers a potential counterexample to this thesis in *TLP* (5.541). Specifically, he considers propositions of the form 'A believes that p', otherwise known as propositional attitude reports. He claims that superficially, propositional attitude reports might appear to describe a situation in which a proposition (e.g. 'p') stands in some sort of relation to an object A (e.g. a human mind or subject). Notably, he claims that proposition attitude reports were actually construed this way within Russell's theory of knowledge. Proposition attitude reports are, notoriously, problematic for extensionalism since they seem not to preserve truth-value upon the substitution of truth-functionally equivalent components. Adapting an example which Russell uses in *OD* (485) we could stipulate that 'p' is to mean 'Scott is the author of *Waverly*', and 'q' is to mean 'Scott is Scott'. Since p and q are each true under this interpretation, then we should be able to substitute one for the other within any truth-function, without changing its truth value. For example, if p is true, then p v r must be true since disjunctions are true as long as one of their disjuncts is true. Since q is also true, substituting it in for p in p v r should not alter the truth-value of the resulting proposition, q v r. And it does not: q v r is true since q is true, and disjunctions are true as long as one of their disjuncts are. This reflects the fact that p v r is a truth-function, and more specifically a truth-function (disjunction) of p and r.

Now contrast that with the case of 'George IV wonders whether p'. In that case substituting q in for p will not preserve the truth-value of the original statement, despite the fact that p and q are both true and so alike in truth-value. As Russell notes, 'An interest in the law of identity can hardly be attributed to the first gentleman of Europe' (*OD*, 485). Thus, it may very well be that while 'George IV wonders whether p' is true, 'George IV wonders whether q' is false. And from this it might seem to follow that propositions can meaningfully occur within contexts which are not truth-functional, contrary to extensionalism. If this were the case, then the symbol Wittgenstein provides at *TLP* 6 could not plausibly be thought to indicate the general form of propositions (though it might still indicate the general form of truth-functions).

In *TLP* (5.542), Wittgenstein endeavours to obviate this problem by way of a logical analysis of the problematic sentence form 'A believes that p'. In a manner analogous to Russell in *OD*, Wittgenstein claims that the superficial surface grammar of these sentences disguises a deeper logical form and that once this form is revealed through logical analysis and contextual paraphrase, the problematic appearance presented by these sentence forms will be dissipated. 'It is clear', he explains,

> that 'A believes that p', 'A has the thought that p', 'A says p' are of the form ' "p" says p': and this does not involve a correlation of a fact with an object, but rather the correlation of facts by means of the correlation of their objects. (ibid.)

This analysis builds upon the analysis of 'statements about complexes' which Wittgenstein provides in *TLP* (2.0201), which we discussed briefly earlier in Section 4.7. The idea is that the expression 'A' at the level of surface grammar encodes a complete description of the complex A. For instance, when 'George IV' occurs in a sentence at the level of surface grammar, this encodes a complete description of George IV which occurs at the level of depth grammar, and which could, in principle, be revealed through logical analysis. Amongst the propositions making up this complete description would be those describing his thoughts, beliefs and/or utterances. These would consist of existing facts in the world, just like anything else. His thought might consist of his brain waves, for example, and the particular thought George IV had about whether Scott was Waverly might consist in a selection of such brain waves, which could in principle have been modelled by an fMRI or EEG scan, had such technology been available in his time. Wittgenstein's idea is that, in principle, we could read off from such a representation of the thought what the content of that thought is. Obviously, representations of other's thoughts were not as accurate in the past as they are in the present or as they are likely to be in the future. But according to Wittgenstein their logical form is similar. They report correlations between facts which are *representations* and facts which are *represented*. And this will not involve describing any relation between a fact and an object. Instead it will involve correlating two facts by means of a correlation of their objects, that is, of simple names with simple objects.

4.10 Transition

Thus far in this chapter, we have examined several topics, concepts and themes within Wittgenstein's early philosophy, including the picture theory of propositions, bipolarity, logical independence, inference, extensionalism and the general propositional form. To the extent that they do so originate, we have probed the origins of these ideas within Wittgenstein's formative interchanges with Russell, while placing a special focus within our account of the development of Wittgenstein's early philosophy, on the role played therein by, and import of, Wittgenstein's May–June 1913 critique of Russell's MRTJ. In so doing we found these topics, concepts and themes to be highly interdependent, interrelated and integrated, each an integral aspect of one deeply unified, and highly systematic, approach to concerns within the philosophies of logic and language.

Wittgenstein's shift from this earlier way of thinking to his later way of thinking gained its initial impetus from doubts about the viability of certain of these themes and concepts, notably extensionalism and relatedly the logical independence of elementary propositions. Wittgenstein began to experience these doubts over the years 1929–30, when he returned to philosophy after a lengthy, self-imposed hiatus following the completion of *TLP* at the end of World War I. From there, the shift rapidly accelerated, and Wittgenstein's thought evolved into a new and illuminating philosophical perspective. This new perspective was not so radically new, however, as to render everything about his earlier philosophy obsolete. In this section, we will briefly explore two of the main reasons which motivated Wittgenstein's shift from his earlier to his later philosophical perspective, before moving on in Section 4.11 to examine some of the important continuities between the two perspectives, with a special focus on those which tie Wittgenstein's later philosophy with his May–June 1913 critique of Russell's MRTJ.

Sometime during the years 1930–31, once the shift and evolution in his thought was sufficiently advanced for him to be able to articulate the nature of the doubts which had led him to abandon the Tractarian system, Wittgenstein made the following remark to his student Desmond Lee, which concerns *TLP* (1.12):

> 'For the totality of facts determines both what is the case, and also all that is not the case.' This is connected with the idea that there are elementary propositions, each describing an atomic fact, into which all propositions can be analysed. This is an erroneous idea. It arises from two sources. (1) Treating infinity as a number, and supposing that there can be an infinite number of propositions. (2) Statements expressing degrees of quality. This is red contradicts This is white. But the theory of elementary propositions would have to say that if p contradicts q, then p and q can be further analysed, to give e.g. r,s,t, and v,w, and ~ t. The fact is self-sufficient and autonomous. (King and Lee 1980, 120)

In this remark, Wittgenstein highlights two problematic assumptions, or 'sources', of the interrelated and central Tractarian ideas of extensionalism and of a general propositional form. We saw that according to the author of the *Tractatus*, all meaningful language is truth-functional and thus that every meaningful proposition is a truth-function of elementary propositions which describe atomic facts. According to *TLP* (1.12), such facts constitute a totality, which can in principle be completely described by truth-functions of those elementary propositions. As we have seen, such truth-functions can be represented either in the truth-tabular notation Wittgenstein introduces in *TLP* (4.31) or in the N($\bar{\xi}$) notation Wittgenstein introduces later in *TLP* (5.502).

The first problematic assumption identified by Wittgenstein, that 'infinity is a number', relates to his attempts to use N($\bar{\xi}$) to recover Russellian quantification over infinite domains. Wittgenstein addresses this problem in greater detail in a lecture on 25 November 1932, in which G. E. Moore records Wittgenstein as identifying 'a most important mistake in the *Tractatus*' (Stern et al. 2016, 216), which is 'muddling up a sum with the limit of a sum' (217). In this context, Wittgenstein claims that 'if *all* general propositions were identical with logical products or logical sums […] then any *general* proposition could be written' (ibid.) using N. The notes do not contain the letter 'N', but it is clear that his N-operator is what he means by the expression '($\hat{\xi}$)[-------T}', which he says represents the 'negation of all propositions that are values of ξ' (ibid.). Continuing on, he says that in the *Tractatus*, he mistakenly supposed 'that ($\exists x$) fx = fa v fb v fc *& so on* was of laziness, when it wasn't'. Moreover, he insists that if the '& so on' were 'of laziness', then 'it could be replaced by an enumeration' (ibid.).

What Wittgenstein appears to have had in mind here is that the Tractarian account of quantification involves conceiving infinity as type of number known as a 'limit ordinal'. Within transfinite number theory, a limit ordinal is a transfinite number which has no immediate predecessor, but which has immediate successors that are also transfinite. The first transfinite limit ordinal ω is defined not as a *member* of the natural number series but instead *as the series* of natural numbers in its totality (see Steinhart 2009, 151–52, 163). The limit ordinal ω thus has no immediate predecessors, but it does have an immediate successor, $\omega +1$. In any case, the important point is that in the *Tractatus*, Wittgenstein appears to have thought that if there were an infinite totality of elementary propositions, each of which described one member of an infinite totality of atomic facts, you might in principle be able to write the whole list of such elementary propositions down, and there would be a last entry on the list, which would be the ωth entry on the list.

What he is saying in the aforementioned remark from Moore's lecture notes is that this idea is confused. In his words, it muddles up the idea of an ordinary sum with that of the limit of a sum. In an ordinary, arithmetical sum which has a final term, you can enumerate all of the terms of the sum. For instance, in $1 + 1 = 2$ the final term of the sum is '1'. When you are dealing with a sum which approaches a limit, by contrast, you cannot enumerate all of the terms it contains because they are infinite, and so endless, in number. So, for example, as in the case of 1+ 1, 2 is also the sum of $1 + \frac{1}{2} + \frac{1}{4} + \ldots =$. Both sums 'terminate' in the number 2 in the sense that 2 is the 'answer' or solution to both sums. But from this it does not follow that, like 1 + 1, this second sum has a final term. On the contrary, in the second case 2 is the 'answer' in the sense that it is the limit of a sum with an endless number of terms. In his *Tractatus*, Wittgenstein seems to have wanted to be able to treat truth-functional expansions as if they could be infinite in length while still having a 'limit' in the sense of an end, or terminus.

This explains why, when Ramsey (1931, 74) describes Wittgenstein's analysis of universal quantification (e.g. 'For all x, x is red') in terms of conjunction, he provides as his illustration of that analysis, a terminal, truth-functional expansion (i.e. '*a* is red and *b* is red and ... and *z* is red'). It also explains why Wittgenstein writes in the *Big Typescript* that

> my understanding of the general proposition was that $(\exists x).$ fx is a logical sum, and that although its terms weren't enumerated there, they could be enumerated (from the dictionary and the grammar of language). (*BT*, 249)

As Wittgenstein later realized, however, this notion involved a mistake analogous to conflating these two distinct sorts of arithmetical sums. In the portion of Moore's notes from the 1932 lecture quoted earlier, Wittgenstein is telling us that, on the basis of this confusion, he mistakenly presumed that the terms of an infinite, truth-functional expansion could be treated as if they were enumerable. If they were, this would make it possible, for instance, to complete the N-expression corresponding to $(\forall x)$ fx as follows:

N(N(fa), N(fb), N(fc), N(fd), ..., N(fω)).

Here 'ω' simply refers, for the sake of convenience, to the ωth name on the list of names substituted into fx in order to generate an elementary proposition for presentation to N. This N-expression would then be equivalent to the following, conjunctive, truth-functional expansion:

fa & fb & fc & fd & ... & fω.

But what Wittgenstein later realized is that if the list a, b, c, d, ..., ω is endless, then you cannot, even in principle, write the whole, relevant truth-functional expansion down, whether using N or any other notational device. In order to recover Russellian quantification, N would need to be supplemented with some sort of quantificational operator, such as a set forming operator (see

Geach 1981, 1982). But then N would not be the sole primitive sign. And propositions would not have a completely general form because you would not be able to generate them all by applying the same operation, iteratively and in succession to selections of elementary propositions. Sometimes you would need to introduce into this process a completely new and foreign operator, such as a set-forming operator.

The second problematic assumption identified in the remark to Desmond Lee quoted earlier is the independence thesis for elementary propositions. In the remark, this thesis is described as the view that atomic facts are 'self-sufficient and autonomous'. Correlated with this is the idea that elementary propositions are logically independent. Earlier in Section 4.7 we reflected on the truth-tabular notation as a means of highlighting how both extensionalism and Wittgenstein's account of inference depend upon the logic independence of elementary propositions. In this context, we can build on those reflections in order to exposit the more specific problem for the independence thesis articulated by Wittgenstein in the remark to Desmond Lee. This problem is sometimes called the 'colour-exclusion problem', but as Wittgenstein notes it is a more general problem concerning statements expressing degrees of quality. The same basic problems would apply, for example, to the pair of statements 'the water is cool' and 'the water is warm'. Wittgenstein's example is that of the pair of propositions 'this is red' and 'this is white'. The problem with this pair of propositions is that, presuming they refer to the same thing, they cannot both be true (though they can both be false). This pair of statements and others like them in the relevant respect are called 'contraries'. The 'colour-exclusion problem' essentially concerns pairs of elementary propositions which are contraries. If two elementary propositions cannot both be true, then the first row of any truth-table representing truth-functions of those two propositions will be ruled out. For example, if p is 'this is red' and q is 'this is white', then we cannot use the characteristic truth-table for conjunction in order to display how p & q is a truth-function of the elementary propositions p and q. We might try, as shown in Figure 4.13.

But then we would fail to capture the idea that p & q is true when each of p and q is true, and we would be unable to use our table to show that p & q follows from both p and q taken together but not from either individually.

Wittgenstein considered various strategies to resolve this problem *via* logical analysis. The approach he alludes to in the remark to Desmond Lee quoted earlier is more or less the same as that pursued in *TLP* (6.3751), which involves further analysing the pair of contrary propositions to yield a hidden contradiction. In that case, 'this is red' and 'this is white' would not be elementary propositions but would instead upon analysis be truth-functions of elementary

p	q	p & q
?	?	?
T	F	F
F	T	F
F	F	F

Figure 4.13 The colour-exclusion problem.

propositions. For example, 'This is red' might be r & s & t, whereas 'This is white' would be v & w & ~t. Since upon analysis 'this is red' contains 't' and 'this is white' contains ~t, the two propositions would turn out to be contradictory, while no pair of elementary propositions contained in their ultimate truth-functional analysis would be contraries. However, Wittgenstein eventually became dissatisfied with this approach, perhaps because as Frank Ramsey highlighted (1923, 474), it appears to involve a confusion between physical and logical necessity.

4.11 The Later View: Continuities amidst Contrasts

In any case, in the early 1930s Wittgenstein came to see the Tractarian logical and semantic framework as both unworkable and irreparable. For the reasons outlined earlier among others, he would reject core features of his early philosophy of logic and language, including both extensionalism and the idea of a general propositional form. Over time, he came to view language, by contrast, as a motely of various and diverse linguistic practices situated in contingent and evolving social and natural life-forms (PI §§19, 23). According to this later philosophical perspective, careful phenomenological description of language in its proper social and practical context reveals that, far from exhibiting the determinacy, rigidity and systematicity of a formal, truth-functional calculus, it can be much more clearly and profitably understood philosophically in light of comparison with games, whose rules and routines are often (though not always) much less formal, rigid, determinate and systematic. Despite these important shifts in Wittgenstein's perspective on language and logic, however, there remained a number of deep and significant continuities between the later and earlier views. In this penultimate section I will highlight some of these continuities, with a focus on those with relevance to, or whose provenance can be traced to, Wittgenstein's critique of Russell's MRTJ.

The main relevant continuity between the early and later perspective, out of which several others can be seen to emerge, is that embodied in the 'linguistic turn' characteristic of early and mid-twentieth-century analytic philosophy. Glock and Kalhat (2018) describe the linguistic turn as

> a radical reconception of the nature of philosophy and its methods, according to which philosophy is neither an empirical science nor a supraempirical enquiry into the essential features of reality; instead it is an a priori conceptual discipline which aims to elucidate the complex interrelationships among philosophically relevant concepts, as established in linguistic usage, and by doing so dispel conceptual confusions and solve philosophical problems. The linguistic turn originated with Wittgenstein's *Tractatus Logico-Philosophicus* (1921).

Glock and Kalhat's characterization of the linguistic turn as something which originates in Wittgenstein's early philosophy aligns well with the views I will articulate in the remainder of this section. It also coheres nicely with my overall interpretation of Wittgenstein's critique of the MRTJ and of its significance within the history of analytic philosophy. (Momentarily I will argue that the linguistic turn as characterized by Glock and Kalhat was inaugurated by Wittgenstein's critique of the MRTJ.) For that reason, I have chosen this interpretation of the linguistic turn over other alternative characterizations, notably that of Michael Dummett (1981, 1991).[3] Though these characterizations need not be incompatible if we think of them as referring to distinct but related linguistic 'turns', or methodological recalibrations within the history of philosophy, from the perspective of a proponent of an alternative account of *the* linguistic turn the significance of Wittgenstein's critique of the MRTJ would doubtless appear to be somewhat different.

If, for instance, following Dummett one thought the 'first example' (1991, 111) of the linguistic turn was to be found in §62 of the *Grundlagen*, where Frege endeavours to disclose features of those objects which he has identified as numbers by deploying his context principle to analyse attributions of number (i.e. statements), then, based on the remainder of this section, one might believe that Wittgenstein's critique of Russell's MRTJ did not perhaps inaugurate but was nevertheless another highly important episode within the movement known as the linguistic turn, one which influenced the historical trajectory of the linguistic turn in integral respects. If, following Bergmann one thought of the linguistic turn as 'the fundamental gambit as to method, on which ordinary and ideal language philosophers (OLP, ILP) agree' (1960, 607), then based on the remainder of this section one might view Wittgenstein's

---

[3] Additional alternative accounts of the linguistic turn can be found in Hacker (2013), Bergmann (1953/67, 60; 1960) and Rorty (1967). A critique of Dummett's reading of the linguistic turn as originating in Frege can be found in Weiner (1997).

critique of the MRTJ as the point within the linguistic turn at which OLP and ILP began, despite their more fundamental methodological agreement, to diverge in identifiable ways.

Notably, despite wishing to emphasize the crucial methodological importance of ideal language philosophy within the linguistic turn in a way which Glock and Kalhat would not, Bergmann (1953/67, 63) nevertheless coheres with Glock and Kalhat (as well as Hacker (2013)) in thinking of the linguistic turn as something which originates in Wittgenstein's early philosophy. Moreover, the editorial selections made in Rorty's (1967) canonical anthology *The Linguistic Turn* tend to suggest that the linguistic turn is a twentieth-century movement, which does not directly involve Frege at all. Thus, Dummett's characterization of the linguistic turn as something which originates in Frege's *Grundlagen* appears to be an outlier. It appears that Dummett took the term 'linguistic turn' which was already in circulation, used to refer to a twentieth-century philosophical movement not directly involving Frege, and retroactively applied it to, or 'read it back into', Frege's late nineteenth-century writings. Though my own view is that this is not prohibitively unreasonable, Weiner (1997) has given reasons to think that this retroactive application is problematic.

While it is beyond the scope of this book to provide a detailed account of, and to critically adjudicate, the scholarly controversy surrounding the linguistic turn, I have chosen to focus on Glock and Kalhat's description because, as indicated, it is most coherent with what I will have to say and the most conducive to the reading I want to give. What I have to say in this section will thus provide supplementary support to Glock and Kalhat's account of the linguistic turn. It will not however provide a definitive defence of this account over the alternatives, a formidable and worthwhile undertaking but one which is well beyond the scope of this book. Hopefully, absent such a definitive defence, readers can nevertheless agree that Wittgenstein's critique of Russell's MRTJ inaugurates *a* linguistic turn of sorts regardless of whether it can be accurately characterized as *the* linguistic turn.

From the perspective of Glock and Kalhat's account, Frege and Russell doubtless provided crucial philosophical background for, and stimulus to, Wittgenstein to undertake this linguistic turn. Yet each of these thinkers' interest in language was subordinate to and derivative upon their primary, epistemological project of providing foundations for mathematics in logic. It was instead Wittgenstein who fundamentally recalibrated the trajectory of early analytic philosophy, away from an epistemological inquiry into the foundations of mathematics and towards a therapeutic investigation into linguistic usage, for the purposes of resolving philosophical confusion. It was Wittgenstein who sought to sharply demarcate philosophy from science and to rigorously demonstrate the unintelligibility of 'supraempirical' metaphysical speculation. In undertaking this recalibration, moreover, Wittgenstein deviated from Frege and Russell in methodologically crucial ways, most notably in his rejection of their attempt to devise and deploy a logically perfect language for epistemological purposes.

The genesis of the linguistic turn as characterized by Glock and Kalhat can thus already be found in Wittgenstein's May–June 1913 critique of Russell's MRTJ, eight years prior to the publication of *TLP*. More specifically, to a significant extent Wittgenstein's critique already embodies the rejection of the 'ideal language philosophy' at the heart of Frege and Russell's epistemological projects. While both Russell and the logical positivists would subsequently attempt to merge Wittgenstein's ideas with their own, for use within the projects of 'ideal language philosophy' and 'scientific philosophy', the linguistic turn undertaken by early Wittgenstein would ultimately instead culminate in his later philosophy, which would in turn heavily influence 'ordinary language philosophy' (or 'natural language philosophy' (Hacker 2013)). As Glock and Kalhat (2018) note,

> In his introduction to the *Tractatus*, Russell took Wittgenstein to be 'concerned with the conditions which would have to be fulfilled by a logically perfect language' […] In doing so, he sought to recruit Wittgenstein to the ranks of 'ideal language philosophy' as represented by Frege and himself, which holds that natural languages are logically defective and need to be replaced by an ideal language – an interpreted logical calculus – for the purposes of science and 'scientific philosophy'. This, however, was a misreading. For Wittgenstein is explicit that 'all propositions of our everyday language, just as they stand, are in perfect logical order'.

The idea that 'all propositions are already in perfect logical order', expressed explicitly in *TLP* (5.5563), is already implicit in Wittgenstein's mid-June critique of Russell's MRTJ. For according to that critique, as we have seen, if aRb entails aRb v ~ aRb, that is, has sense and is significant, then it does so independently of any stipulations designed to ensure it conforms to the requirements of an appropriately type-regimented ideal language. (The point holds whether the type-regimentation involves *PM* types or type* distinctions, though in the specific context of Wittgenstein's mid-June letter the latter is the relevant sense of 'type'.) Insofar as it has sense at all, aRb is thus already in 'perfect logical order' just as it is.

Moreover, as much as Wittgenstein remained tethered to Russell's direct realism to a very significant degree in the context of his early philosophy, in retrospect, within his mid-June 1913 critique of Russell's MRTJ he was already taking the initial steps which would lead him to break from it entirely in the context of the later philosophy. In so doing, he shifted his philosophical focus, and that of others later influenced by him, towards linguistic usage, which is a hallmark of the linguistic turn. In January 1913, as we saw, Wittgenstein viewed logical forms as constituents of complexes, in a manner which anticipates Russell's *TK* theory of logical form in significant respects. Yet by mid-June 1913 Wittgenstein is beginning to see logical form as something contained within the logical syntax, or logical grammar, of language itself. From this vantage point, an illuminating way of framing Wittgenstein's mid-June 1913 critique of the MRTJ is to say that logical form cannot be external to and imposed upon language but must be internal and intrinsic to it.

As Wittgenstein's early philosophy continued to evolve and develop he began to see logical grammar as something which constrains, but also shows itself in the use of, an expression. This of course anticipates his later view that grammar, or rules of grammar, constrain and are manifest in the use of expressions. The later view, that grammar shows itself in the use of an expression, is not contraposed to the claim that it can be meaningfully stated. And nor is grammar something hidden deep beneath the surface of ordinary language and revealed through logical analysis. Instead grammar is to be found within the rules governing our prototypically social, disciplined linguistic practices. Such rules are both syntactic and semantic and can either be explicitly stated in dictionaries, for example, or shown in the normative activities of human beings (or of creatures whose behaviour is sufficiently like that of human beings). Yet grammatical rules are in essence what logical grammar becomes once it is fully divorced from Russell's direct realism and ideal language philosophy.

Wittgenstein's final and decisive break with Russellian direct realism comes in the form of his 'interpretation argument' (Williams 1999), which demonstrates among other things that semantic and syntactic rules cannot be simply 'read off' mind- and language-independent features of reality (PI §292). Scientific and supraempirical enquiry will thus be of limited utility in reflecting philosophically on normative phenomena like meaning and will instead tend to engender confusion. A paradigm case of such confusion would be the endlessly problematic identification of universals as the meanings or referents of general terms. But analogous problems arise due to misunderstandings concerning the meanings of singular terms or proper names. Both sorts of problems and the confusions from which they derive are supposed to be endemic to the Augustinian picture of language which Wittgenstein introduces in PI §1 and then moves on to criticize.

According to this picture of the essence of human language 'the individual words in language name objects – sentences are combinations of such names

[...] Every word has a meaning. This meaning is correlated with the word. It is the object for which the word stands' (PI §1). However the meaning of a proper name, for instance, cannot simply be identified with the object it stands for, since any object will possess a variety of perceptually and conceptually salient features which could, given a distinct normative practice, be the salient feature that we should interpret a speaker as intending to pick out with an ostensive definition of a name (PI §28). Proper names do not lack meaning if they lack reference, so long as they possess a rule-governed use within a linguistic practice, a use which can be explained via ostensive definition among other methods (PI §§29–30). To give the meaning of a proper name is thus to give general directions for its use (cf. Strawson 1950, 327). Likewise, propositions can still have sense though they contain proper names without reference. Sense is not fundamentally a matter of bipolarity or extensionalism but of use in rule-governed linguistic activities.

The truth of a proposition, moreover, cannot be reduced to a relation of isomorphic correspondence between a picture and a fact, since there are many different ways of interpreting and so applying a picture (PI §139). The 'correct' way to interpret the meaning of a picture or of a sentence is given in the normative criteria governing the uses of its constituent words. 'Sense' and 'truth' are such words and thus, as opposed to involving mysterious intentional relations of isomorphism and modelling between thoughts and facts, are instead applied correctly or incorrectly within prototypically social, disciplined linguistic practices governed by rules. If we want to eliminate philosophical confusion, we must, as opposed to devising formal theories of philosophically interesting concepts such as 'sense' and 'truth', instead examine and reflect upon these practices along with uses of these and other words within them.

As noted by Glock and Kalhat (quoted earlier), the linguistic turn is thus ultimately a revolution not simply in the understanding of important philosophical concepts, but one which concerns the nature of philosophy and philosophical method itself. According to this 'radical reconception' of philosophy and its methods, philosophy 'is not a body of doctrine but an activity' (*TLP* 4.112). While Wittgenstein's conception of the nature of this activity would evolve along with his changing perspective upon language and logic, its goal would remain the same: to dispel philosophical confusion. In the early period, logistical analysis was deployed to achieve the 'logical clarification of thoughts' (ibid.). By undertaking such clarification, we would be able to demonstrate to anyone who tried to say anything metaphysical and so unscientific that 'he had failed to give a meaning to certain signs in his propositions' (6.54). One among other modes in which this might occur would be as the result of combining signs in ways which, given their conventional meanings, are inconsistent with logical syntax (e.g. 'Socrates is identical' (5.473)). In the later period, by contrast, phenomenological description was used to elucidate the workings of concepts (e.g. family resemblance concepts) with a view to preventing philosophically problematic misunderstandings, as well as to expose and eliminate troublesome metaphysical misinterpretations of words which do not conform to their ordinary uses: 'What we do is to bring words back from their metaphysical to their everyday use' (PI §116).

In Section 4.4, we examined how the key theme of bipolarity developed out of Wittgenstein's critique of Russell's MRTJ and specifically out of the idea that the bipolar truth-possibilities of a proposition are both entailed by and constitute the sense of propositions. Using the ab-notation to reflect on bipolarity in abstraction from truth-functionality, Wittgenstein discovered many interesting combinatorial features of molecular truth-functions. This included the discovery of a class of propositions, tautologies, which are true under all conditions. Wittgenstein came to see unconditional truth, or tautologousness, as the defining feature of a distinctive class of propositions, logical propositions, whose truth was independent of all possible experience and which were thus knowable a priori. Such propositions were clearly demarcated from empirical propositions which could turn out to be either true or false and thus were knowable only on the grounds of experience.

Likewise, in the context of Wittgenstein's later philosophy, he identifies a class of propositions, which he calls 'grammatical propositions', that are distinct from empirical propositions. Grammatical propositions are sometimes confused with empirical propositions which can be a source of philosophical confusion (PI §251). Unlike empirical propositions, however, it makes no sense to negate grammatical propositions, which are knowable a priori. Such propositions either state or are derived trivially from grammatical rules. Examples would include 'every rod has a length' (ibid.), 'this body has extension' (PI §252) and 'another person can't have my pains' (PI §253). Failing to appreciate the grammatical nature of these propositions, or conflating them with empirical propositions, leads us into quagmires of the sort which characterize traditional metaphysics and epistemology.

For instance, while 'another person can't have my pains' is derived trivially from a grammatical rule concerning first-person sensation reports, that is, 'first-person sensation reports attribute sensations to the person who utters them', it has been misinterpreted to imply that sensations take place in an epistemologically private, and metaphysically distinctive, inner space or medium. The dubious epistemic nature of this posited space, that is, the mind, then tends to suggest the existence of a problem concerning other minds, namely: how can we know whether they exist? The problem is dissolved however when we examine the grammar of sensation talk and realize that sensations are states, not of mind (like belief or doubt) but of living bodies (PI §281). Because numerically specific instances of pains are usually, though not always, had by one living creature at a time, sensation reports are typically first-personal and thus governed by the associated grammatical rules. One use of 'another person can't have my pains' is to simply convey these grammatical rules without describing any facts. If it makes no sense to deny that 'another person can't have my pains', then 'another person can't have my pains' conveys no substantive empirical or metaphysical content and cannot be the basis of an interesting philosophical theory or thesis. However, in cases in which it does make sense to deny that 'another person can't have my pains', for example, conjoined twins, corresponding injuries (PI §253), then the utterance in scare quotes is being used differently, to deny an empirical proposition. In that case, it means something different, and what it denies is simply a contingent, empirical and observable fact. In the case of conjoined twins what is erroneously denied is that they cannot jointly share one numerically specific pain experience. In the case of corresponding injuries what is erroneously denied is that two people cannot have the qualitatively same type of pain. Sports injuries and conjoined twins might be interesting topics of scientific research, but such research cannot yield deep insight into necessary metaphysical features of reality any more than can supraempirical enquiry of the sort characteristic of traditional metaphysics and epistemology.

The demarcation between grammatical and empirical propositions which characterizes Wittgenstein's later philosophy, and which was the heir of his earlier distinction between logical and empirical propositions, goes along with a distinctive conception of the nature of the relationship between philosophy and science which represents a final important point of continuity between the two perspectives. Wittgenstein himself alludes to this point of continuity when in PI he says that 'it was true to say that our considerations could not be scientific ones' (PI §109). Here he is referring to his remark from *TLP* that 'philosophy is not one of the natural sciences' (*TLP* 4.111). According to the author of *TLP*, philosophy 'sets limits to the much disputed sphere of natural science' (4.113) and aims at the logical clarification of scientific propositions. Yet the logical propositions with which philosophy deals are 'construed wrongly' (6.111) if they are assimilated to natural scientific propositions. Unlike the empirical propositions characteristic of natural science, which can be true or false and are contingently one or the other depending upon whether the empirical facts they describe either exist or do not, and are known to be true only on the grounds of experience, logical propositions lack content and are thus true and knowable independently of any facts or of experience. Similarly, in PI, Wittgenstein claims that, in contrast to the natural scientist, it is 'not of any possible interest' to the philosopher 'to find out empirically' that realty is different than we conceived it to be (PI §109). In contrast to the natural sciences, philosophy does away with explanation and theory construction. In its place the philosopher engages in phenomenological description of 'the workings of our language' (ibid.) with a view to 'arranging what we have always known' (ibid.) to alleviate confusion and misunderstandings.

The germ of the idea that philosophy is an investigation into the workings of language, rather than into any empirical, supraempirical or extra-linguistic facts, is already present in Wittgenstein's mid-June 1913 critique of Russell's MRTJ. For as we have seen, the main thrust of that critique according to LI is that aRb has sense independently of the general facts which Russell construed as logical forms and which he described as knowable through a mode of supraempirical, 'logical experience' (*TK*, 97). The sense of aRb cannot depend upon the existence of the supraempirical fact described as $(\exists x)\ (\exists R)\ (\exists y)\ (((x=a)\ \&\ (R=R))\ \&\ (y=b))$, in which the constituents of aRb are assigned to positions within the logical form of dual complexes. While Wittgenstein may have begun his 'apprenticeship' (Landini 2007) with Russell as a disciple of the latter's 'scientific method in philosophy' (*CP*, 8: 55–73), by mid-June 1913 he was already in the process of making a monumental 'linguistic turn' which would render the scientific method of dubious utility within both his early and later philosophical investigations.

4.12 Conclusion

In this book I have set out to achieve four main objectives. The first was to develop my reading of Wittgenstein's May–June 1913 critique of the MRTJ, which I call the 'logical interpretation' (LI). The second was to defend LI against the most prominent competing readings in the scholarly literature, including SR (Griffin and Sommerville), OI (Stevens), UI (Hanks), CI (Pincock), SI (Landini), NFI (Carey) and IRI (Lebens and MacBride). After explicating most of these competing interpretations in Chapter 2 (the one exception was NFI which was instead dealt with in Section 3.8 on 'Props'), in Chapter 3 I then articulated LI and defended it against each of these competing interpretations. This was done in part to flesh out additional, significant details of LI but also to highlight the reasons to prefer LI over each of these competing interpretations.

According to LI, as we have seen over the course of the book, Wittgenstein objects to Russell's failure, in the context of the MRTJ, to provide a unified, unambiguously ordered and appropriately type* regimented propositional content which does not depend for its sense on the truth of a significance constraint that assigns constituents of a judgement to positions within the logical form of the complex it corresponds to, in the event the judgement is true. Among the advantages LI enjoys over its competitors, include that it can readily explain the self-described 'paralysis' Russell experienced in response to Wittgenstein's objection. It also explicitly identifies the 'premise' referred to in the June letter to Russell in which Wittgenstein claims to express his objection 'exactly'. Moreover, it aligns well with Wittgenstein's insistence on the fundamentally logical character of philosophical problems. And it helps greatly to explain and contextualize the emergence of several crucial themes within Wittgenstein's early, logical philosophy. Such themes include, notably, the saying/showing distinction, which emerged from Wittgenstein's attempts to give an account of logical form that was not susceptible to his own critique of Russell's MRTJ.

The third main objective of the book was to situate Wittgenstein's critique of Russell's MRTJ within the broader context of each of Wittgenstein and Russell's philosophical development. To that end, crucial historical and philosophical background of Wittgenstein's critique was introduced in Chapter 1, which focused largely on Russell's philosophical development over the period of 1898–1913, but also briefly touched on the very early stages of Wittgenstein's philosophical career during his initial residence at Cambridge over the years 1911–13. Russell's subsequent development over the years of 1913–19 was dealt with in Sections 2.14 and 3.12, both of which addressed the (independent) demise of each of *TK* as well as Russell's MRTJ. These themes were also discussed in Section 3.6, which looked at integral associations between *TK* and *PLA* as a means of developing an improved appraisal of Russell's *TK* diagram of understanding, one which bolsters the prospects of LI relative to those of Pincock's CI. Wittgenstein's philosophical development subsequent to May–June 1913 was the main focus of Chapter 4, in which we explored how themes such as bipolarity, extensionalism and independence emerged out of Wittgenstein's critique of Russell's MRTJ and then culminated in Wittgenstein's *TLP*. In Section 4.10 we then looked at the transition from Wittgenstein's early to his later philosophy, before examining key points of continuity between the early and later views in Section 4.11, with a special focus on those points the provenance of which could be traced to Wittgenstein's May–June 1913 critique of Russell's MRTJ.

In summary, over the course of the book we saw that Wittgenstein's critique of Russell's MRTJ had a profound effect on the philosophical development of each of these two great twentieth-century thinkers. It marked the historical moment at which Wittgenstein emerged onto the scene as an independent and impactful philosopher of keen insight and extraordinary influence. It shaped the development of several core concepts, themes and distinctions within Wittgenstein's philosophy both early and late. Within the early period this includes Wittgenstein's influential picture theory of propositions, his independence thesis and his saying/showing distinction, along with his thought on logical form, type-theory, bipolarity, extensionalism and the general propositional form. Within the later view this would include his idiosyncratic conception of grammar, his distinction between grammatical and empirical propositions, his semantic reflections on the use of expressions and his linguistic turn within philosophical method.

With respect to Russell's philosophical development, Wittgenstein's critique left a significant breach in his epistemology that, over time, would contribute to his ultimately abandoning the MRTJ in favour of neutral monism in 1919. As we saw in Section 3.6, it also directly influenced Russell's analysis of belief in *PLA*. Moreover, several of Wittgenstein's ideas which emerged out of his critique and which he set out in *NL* Russell sought to incorporate into both his 1914 lectures on logic at Harvard and his 1918 lectures on the *Philosophy of Logical Atomism* in London. These included Wittgenstein's thought on facts and propositions and in particular on atomic, molecular and general propositions. The themes of extensionalism and the general propositional form, which as we saw earlier were shaped in important ways by Wittgenstein's critique of the MRTJ, would influence Russell's thinking about the foundations of mathematics to such an extent that he would address them in the introduction to his second edition of *PM* (1925). Russell would of course also write a highly influential introduction to Wittgenstein's *TLP*, which specifically addresses, among other topics, Wittgenstein's critique of his MRTJ. Concerning the linguistic turn inaugurated by Wittgenstein's critique of his MRTJ, Russell would take up the mantle of ideal language philosophy and as its champion, come to grapple with the many foot soldiers of the natural language philosophy inspired by Wittgenstein's later philosophical approach.

The fourth main objective of the book was to introduce students and scholars of early analytic philosophy to, and familiarize them with, the relevant historical events, textual evidence, scholarly controversies, letters, notes and diagrams associated with Wittgenstein's critique of Russell's MRTJ. The relevant historical events were the focus of Chapter 1, while the scholarly controversy surrounding Wittgenstein's objection was the focus of Chapter 2. Key passages from relevant correspondence and texts were introduced in each of Chapters 1–4, while relevant notes and diagrams came into particular focus in Sections 3.6–3.8.

In the course of pursuing these objectives we have also, and to some extent, begun to illuminate the significance of Wittgenstein's critique of Russell's MRTJ within the broader context of the historical and philosophical development of the analytic tradition. In that regard, however, over and above answering some integral questions, we have also perhaps raised several questions for further investigation. We noted that Wittgenstein's critique could be seen to inaugurate a linguistic turn in analytic philosophy and also that controversy surrounding the proper characterization of the linguistic turn leads directly into consideration of the fundamental methodological and metaphilosophical debates which engaged analytic philosophers over the course of the twentieth century and that continue to do so to this day. Moreover, at the outset, we noted that Wittgenstein's critique of Russell's MRTJ concerns several of the weightiest and most fundamental topics in philosophical semantics, a claim that was surely vindicated over the course of the book.

Beyond inspiring interest in Wittgenstein's criticisms, the scholarly controversy surrounding them and the philosophies of Wittgenstein and Russell, I hope that this book has shed light on these fundamental issues and that it may also reinvigorate interest in these broader methodological and metaphilosophical questions. While the Vienna Circle logical positivists saw great potential within his 'far-reaching ideas' (Carnap et al. 1929/73, 311), Wittgenstein himself also hoped to stimulate such original thought in others (PI, viii). As we have seen repeatedly over the course of this book, among these stimulating and seminal ideas are doubtless included those associated with Wittgenstein's momentous and ingenious May–June 1913 critique of Russell's MRTJ.

REFERENCES

Works by Russell

The Autobiography of Bertrand Russell. With an introduction by Michael Foot. London: Routledge (1967/98).
The Collected Papers of Bertrand Russell
  Vol. 2: *Philosophical Papers, 1896–99.* Ed. Nicholas Griffin and Albert C. Lewis. London: Unwin Hyman (1990).
  Vol. 3: *Toward the 'Principles of Mathematics', 1900–02.* Ed. Gregory H. Moore. London: Routledge (1993).
  Vol. 4: *Foundations of Logic 1903–5.* Ed. Alasdair Urquhart and Albert C. Lewis. London: Routledge (1994).
  Vol. 8: *The Philosophy of Logical Atomism and Other Essays, 1914–19.* Ed. John G. Slater. London: George Allen & Unwin (1986).
An Essay on the Foundations of Geometry (1st paperback ed.). Cambridge, UK: Cambridge University Press (1897/2011).
My Philosophical Development. London: George Allen & Unwin (1959).
'On Denoting'. *Mind* 14(56): 479–93 (1905).
'On Propositions: What They Are and How They Mean'. In *Logic and Knowledge: Essays 1901–1950*, 283–320. Ed. R. C. Marsh. London: George Allen & Unwin (1919/56).
'On the Nature of Truth and Falsehood'. In *Philosophical Essays*, 147–59. New York: Simon and Schuster (1910/67).
Our Knowledge of the External World as a Field for Scientific Method in Philosophy. Chicago, IL: Open Court (1914).
'The Philosophy of Logical Atomism'. In *Logic and Knowledge: Essays 1901–1950*, 321–44. Ed. R. C. Marsh. London: George Allen & Unwin (1918/56).
*Principia Mathematica to *56.* Co-authored with Alfred North Whitehead. Cambridge, UK: Cambridge University Press (1910–13/97).
The Principles of Mathematics. New York: W. W. Norton (1903/37).
The Problems of Philosophy. Scotts Valley, CA: Create Space International (1912/2017).
Theory of Knowledge: The 1913 Manuscript. London: Routledge (1992).

Works by Wittgenstein

The Big Typescript: TS 213, German-English Scholar's Edition. Ed. and trans. C. Grant Luckhardt and Maximilian A. E. Aue. Malden, MA: Blackwell (2005).
Cambridge Letters: Correspondence with Russell, Keynes, Moore, Ramsey, and Sraffa. Ed. Brian McGuiness and G. H. von Wright. Oxford, UK: Basil Blackwell (1995).

Notebooks 1914–1916, 2nd ed. Ed. G. H. von Wright and G. E. M. Anscombe. Oxford, UK: Basil Blackwell (1961).

'Notes on Logic'. In *NB* (Appendix I, 94–108).

Philosophical Investigations, 3rd ed. Trans. Elizabeth Anscombe. Englewood Cliffs, NJ: Prentice Hall (1953/2001).

Prototractatus. Ed. B. F. McGuiness, T. Nyberg and G. H. von Wright. London: Routledge (1997).

Tractatus Logico-Philosophicus. Trans. C. K. Odgen. London: Routledge & Keegan Paul (1922).

Tractatus Logico-Philosophicus. Trans. D. F. Pears and B. F. McGuiness, with an introduction by Bertrand Russell. London: Routledge (1967).

Works by Other Authors

Anellis, Irving H. 2012. 'Peirce's Truth-Functional Analysis and the Origin of the Truth-Table'. *History and Philosophy of Logic* 33: 87–97.

Bergmann, Gustav. 1953/67. 'Logical Positivism, Language, and the Reconstruction of Metaphysics'. In Richard Rorty (ed.), *The Linguistic Turn: Recent Essays in Philosophical Method*. Chicago, IL: University of Chicago Press, 1967, 63–71.

———. 1960. 'Strawson's Ontology'. *Journal of Philosophy* 57(19): 601–22.

Bergmann, Merrie, James Moor and Jack Nelson. 2014. *The Logic Book*, 6th ed. New York, NY: McGraw-Hill.

Blackwell, Kenneth, and Elizabeth Ramsden Eames. 1975. 'Russell's Unpublished Book on Theory of Knowledge'. *Russell: The Journal of Bertrand Russell Studies*, Old Series No. 19: 3–14.

———. 1992. 'Introduction'. In *ToK*.

Bostock, David. 2012. *Russell's Logical Atomism*. Oxford, UK: Oxford University Press.

Candlish, Stewart. 2007. *The Russell/Bradley Dispute and Its Significance for Twentieth-Century Philosophy*. New York: Palgrave Macmillan.

Cantor, Georg. 1891. 'On an Elementary Question in the Theory of Manifolds'. In William Ewald (ed.), *From Kant to Hilbert: A Source Book in the Foundations of Mathematics*, vol. 2. Oxford, UK: Clarendon, 920–22.

Carey, Rosalind. 2007. *Russell and Wittgenstein on the Nature of Judgement*. London, UK: Continuum Books.

Carnap, Rudolf, Hans Hahn and Otto Neurath. 1929/73. 'The Scientific Conception of the World: The Vienna Circle'. In R. S. Cohen and M. Neurath (eds), *Empiricism and Sociology*. Dordrecht: Reidel, 299–318.

Church, Alonzo. 1936. 'A Note on the *Entscheidungsproblem*'. *Journal of Symbolic Logic* 1: 40–41.

———. 1974. 'Russellian Simple Type Theory'. *Proceedings of the American Philosophical Association* 47: 21–33.

Connelly, James. 2014. 'Russell and Wittgenstein on Logical Form and Judgement: What Did Wittgenstein Try That Wouldn't Work?' *Theoria* 80(3): 232–54.

———. 2017. 'On Operator N and Wittgenstein's Logical Philosophy'. *Journal for the History of Analytical Philosophy* 5(4): 1–25.

David, Marian. 2016. 'The Correspondence Theory of Truth'. In Edward N. Zalta (ed.), *The Stanford Encyclopedia of Philosophy*, Fall ed. https://plato.stanford.edu/archives/fall2016/entries/truth-correspondence/.

REFERENCES

Dummett, Michael. 1981. *Frege: Philosophy of Language*, 2nd ed. Cambridge, MA: Harvard University Press.
———. 1991. *Frege: Philosophy of Mathematics*. Cambridge, MA: Harvard University Press.
Elkind, Landon, and Gregory Landini, eds. 2018. *The Philosophy of Logical Atomism: A Centenary Reappraisal*. Cham, Switzerland: Palgrave Macmillan.
Fine, Kit. 2000. 'Neutral Relations'. *Philosophical Review* 199: 1–33.
Frege, Göttlob. 1879/1972. 'Conceptual Notation: A Formula Language of Pure Thought Modelled upon the Formula Language of Arithmetic'. In Terrell Ward Bynum (trans. and ed.), *Conceptual Notation and Related Articles*. Oxford, UK: Clarendon Press, 103–66.
———. 1892/1985. 'On Concept and Object'. In Brian McGuiness (ed.), *Collected Papers on Mathematics, Logic and Philosophy*. Oxford, UK: Blackwell, 182–94.
———. 1918/1977. *Logical Investigations*. Edited by P. T. Geach; translated by P. T. Geach and R. H. Stoothoof. Oxford, UK: Basil Blackwell.
Galaugher, Jolen B. 2013. 'Substitution's Unsolved "Insolubilia"'. *Russell* 33: 5–30.
Geach, Peter T. 1981. 'Wittgenstein's Operator N'. *Analysis* 41: 168–70.
———. 1982. 'More on Wittgenstein's Operator N'. *Analysis* 42: 127–28.
Giaretta, Pierdaniele. 1997. 'Analysis and Logical Form in Russell: The 1913 Paradigm'. *Dialectica* 51: 273–93.
Glock, Hans-Johann, and Javier Kalhat. 2018. 'The Linguistic Turn'. *Routledge Encyclopedia of Philosophy*. https://www.rep.routledge.com/articles/thematic/linguistic-turn/v-1.
Griffin, Nicholas. 1985. 'Russell's Multiple Relation Theory of Judgment'. *Philosophical Studies* 47: 213–47.
———. 1985–86. 'Wittgenstein's Criticism of Russell's Theory of Judgment'. *Russell: Journal of the Bertrand Russell Archives* 5(2): 132–45.
———. 1991. *Russell's Idealist Apprenticeship*. New York: Oxford University Press.
———, ed. 1992. *The Selected Letters of Bertrand Russell*, vol. 1. London: Routledge.
———. 2003. 'Russell's Philosophical Background'. In Nicholas Griffin (ed.), *The Cambridge Companion to Russell*. Cambridge, UK: Cambridge University Press, 84–107.
Hacker, Peter M. S. 1996. *Wittgenstein's Place in Twentieth Century Analytic Philosophy*. Malden, MA: Blackwell.
———. 2013. 'The Linguistic Turn in Analytic Philosophy'. In Michael Beaney (ed.), *The Oxford Handbook of the History of Analytic Philosophy*. Oxford, UK: Oxford University Press.
Hanks, Peter. 2007. 'How Wittgenstein Defeated Russell's Multiple Relation Theory of Judgment'. *Synthese* 154(1): 121–46.
King, John, and Desmond Lee. 1980. *Wittgenstein's Lectures, Cambridge 1930–32*. Oxford, UK: Blackwell.
Landini, Gregory. 1991. 'A New Interpretation of Russell's Multiple Relation Theory'. *History and Philosophy of Logic* 12(1991): 37–69.
———. 1993. 'Reconciling PM's Ramified Type-Theory with the Doctrine of the Unrestricted Variable of *The Principles*'. In A. D. Irvine and G. A. Wedeking (eds), *Russell and Analytic Philosophy*. Toronto, ON: University of Toronto Press, 361–94.
———. 1998. *Russell's Hidden Substitutional Theory*. New York: Oxford University Press.
———. 2007. *Wittgenstein's Apprenticeship with Russell*. New York: Cambridge University Press.
———. 2020. 'Showing in Wittgenstein's ab-notation'. In Newton Da Costa and Shyam Wuppuluri (eds), *Wittgensteinian*. Cham, Switzerland: Springer Nature Switzerland, 193–226.
———. 2021. *Repairing Russell's 1913 Theory of Knowledge*. London, UK: Palgrave-MacMillan.

Lebens, Samuel. 2017. *Bertrand Russell and the Nature of Propositions: A History and Defense of the Multiple Relation Theory of Judgement*. New York: Routledge.
Linsky, Bernard. 1993. 'Why Russell Abandoned Russellian Propositions'. In A. D. Irvine and G. A. Wedeking (eds), *Russell and Analytic Philosophy*. Toronto, ON: University of Toronto Press, 193–209.
MacBride, Fraser. 2007. 'Neutral Relations Revisited'. *Dialectica* 61(1): 25–56.
———. 2013. 'The Russell-Wittgenstein Dispute: A New Perspective.' In Mark Textor (ed.), *Judgement and Truth in Early Analytic Philosophy and Phenomenology*. Basingstoke: Palgrave, 206–41.
Monk, Raymond. 1991. *Ludwig Wittgenstein: The Duty of Genius*. New York: Penguin Books.
———. 1997. *Bertrand Russell: The Spirit of Solitude*. London: Vintage Books.
Moore, George E. 1899. 'The Nature of Judgement'. *Mind* 8(30): 176–93.
Perovic, Katarina. 2017. 'Mapping the Understanding Complex in Russell's *Theory of Knowledge*'. *Russell* 36: 101–27.
Pincock, Christopher. 2008. 'Russell's Last (and Best) Multiple Relation Theory of Judgment'. *Mind* 117(465): 107–40.
Potter, Michael. 2009. *Wittgenstein's Notes on Logic*. Oxford, UK: Oxford University Press.
Ramsey, Frank. 1923. 'Review: *Tractatus Logico-Philosophicus*'. *Mind* 32(128): 465–78.
Ramsey, Frank. 1931. *The Foundations of Mathematics and Other Logical Essays*. London: Routledge & Keegan Paul.
Rorty, Richard, ed. 1967. *The Linguistic Turn: Recent Essays in Philosophical Method*. Chicago, IL: University of Chicago Press.
Schroeder, Severin. 2006. *Wittgenstein: The Way Out of the Fly Bottle*. Cambridge, UK: Polity.
Shosky, John. 1997. 'Russell's Use of Truth Tables'. *Russell: The Journal of the Bertrand Russell Archives* 17(1): 11–26.
Sommerville, Stephen. 1979. *Types, Categories and Significance* (unpublished PhD thesis). McMaster University.
Steinhart, Eric. 2009. *More Precisely: The Math You Need to Do Philosophy*. Peterborough, ON, Canada: Broadview.
Stern, David G., Brian Rogers and Gabriel Citron (eds). 2016. *Wittgenstein Letures, Cambridge 1930-33: From the Notes of G.E. Moore*. Cambridge, UK: Cambridge University Press.
Stevens, Graham. 2003a. 'Re-examining Russell's Paralysis: Ramified Type-Theory and Wittgenstein's Objection to Russell's Theory of Judgment'. *Russell: The Journal of Bertrand Russell Studies* 23(1): 5–26.
———. 2003b. 'Substitution and the Theory of Types'. *Russell: The Journal of Bertrand Russell Studies* 23(2): 161–76.
———. 2004. 'From Russell's Paradox to the Theory of Judgment: Wittgenstein and Russell on the Unity of the Proposition'. *Theoria* 70: 28–60.
———. 2005. *The Russellian Origins of Analytic Philosophy: Bertrand Russell and the Unity of the Proposition*. New York: Routledge.
———. 2018. 'Wittgenstein and Russell'. In Hans-Johann Glock and John Hyman (eds), *A Companion to Wittgenstein*, Blackwell Companions to Philosophy. Malden, MA: Wiley-Blackwell, 92–109.
Stout, Goerge F. 1910–11. 'The Object of Thought and Real Being'. *Proceedings of the Aristotelian Society* 11: 187–205.
———. 1914–15. 'Mr. Russell's Theory of Judgment'. *Proceedings of the Aristotelian Society* 15: 332–52.

Strawson, P. F. 1950. 'On Referring'. *Mind* 59: 320–44.
Weiner, Joan. 1997. 'Frege and the Linguistic Turn'. *Philosophical Topics* 25(2): 265–88.
Williams, Meredith. 1999. *Wittgenstein, Mind & Meaning: Towards a Social Conception of Mind.* London: Routledge.
Wrinch, Dorothy. 1919. 'On the Nature of Judgement'. *Mind* 28(111): 319–29.

INDEX

ab-notation, Wittgenstein's 6, 118, 123–26, 124n3, 128, 149–54, 161–63, 166, 170–72, 189
atomic facts 138
The Autobiography of Bertrand Russell (Russell) 4, 7, 29, 32, 76, 124

being in, prepositional verb 137
being on, prepositional verb 137
The Big Typescript: TS 213 (Wittgenstein) 181
bipolarity 147–54
Blackwell, Kenneth 27–30, 39, 75–76, 102, 114, 119, 131

Cambridge Letters: Correspondence with Russell, Keynes, Moore, Ramsey, and Sraffa (Wittgenstein) 30–32, 67–68, 76, 80, 81, 125–26, 128, 131, 141–42, 148–49, 151–53, 165–66
Carey, Rosalind 2, 5, 114–15, 118, 191
CAT 58–60, 104–9
CI. *See* correspondence interpretation (CI)
classes/relations, substitutional theory of 15–16
colour-exclusion problem 182
commutation 169
contradiction of relativity 3, 8–9, 139
correspondence interpretation (CI) 4, 52, 55–59, 66, 94, 96, 100–106, 109
correspondence problem (CP) 4, 51–52, 54–60, 102–9
CP. *See* correspondence problem (CP)

David, Marian 19–20
diagram of understanding 109–14
dialectic of sciences 7–8

direction problems 33–39
  narrow 3, 21, 33, 35–39, 53–54
  wide 3, 33, 35–40, 52–54

Eames, Elizabeth Ramsden 27–30, 39, 75–76, 102, 114, 119, 131
EI. *See* epistemological interpretation (EI)
elementary proposition 139–44, 147–83
Elkind, Landon 8
epimenides paradox, propositions 15, 46–47
epistemological interpretation (EI) 3–4, 42–44
  MRTJ 42–44
  Stevens critique of 85–90
  direct inspection 42–44
  MRTJ 42–44
  subordinate relation, logical status of 45–46
epistemology 76
equinumerous classes 16
An Essay on the Foundations of Geometry (Russell) 7
expressions 141–43
extensionalism 147–54, 175

facts 138
false propositions, problem of 13–14
Frege, Göttlob 27, 68, 81–82, 142, 166, 184–86
functions, hierarchy of 17–18, 43–44
fundamental thought *(Grundgedanke)* 6, 165–70

Galaugher, Jolen 3, 15
general propositional form 170–78

Giaretta, Pierdaniele 4–5, 119
  relating relation 121–23
  on type* distinctions 4–5, 61–64
Glock, Hans-Johann 6, 184–88
Griffin, Nicholas 2–4, 8, 40, 47, 51, 60, 64, 70, 74–75, 82, 86, 89, 117, 129
Grundgedanke (fundamental thought) 165–70

Hanks, Peter 2, 4
  on judging relation 91–93
  standard reading, critique of 48–50
  unity interpretation 4, 50–51, 54, 91, 93, 191
  Wittgenstein defeated MRTJ, critique on 50–51, 91–93
hierarchy
  of functions 17–18, 43–44
  of orders 17–18, 43–44

ideal language philosophy 6
inference, theory of 156–61
irrelevancy interpretation (IRI) of Wittgenstein's objection 5, 74, 131–32, 191

Jourdain, Philip E. B. 27
judgement 2, 19–26, 54

Kalhat, Javier 6, 184–88

Landini, Gregory 2, 4–5, 8, 17–18, 66, 123
  on type* distinctions 60–62
  on Wittgenstein's critique of MRTJ 64–69, 123–28
Lebens, Samuel 2, 4–5
  on demise of MRTJ 72–74
  on representation concern 69–72, 128–30
  on stoutian evolution of MRTJ 69–72
LI. *See* logical interpretation (LI)
liar paradox, propositions 15
limit ordinal 180
linguistic turn 184
Linsky, Bernard 3, 13
logical forms 24–25, 144–49, 154–56, 161, 165, 170, 178, 187, 191

logical interpretation (LI) 2–5, 32, 75–83, 89, 91, 93–96, 100, 102–3, 106–9, 112–13, 117–32, 170, 191
logical propositions 155
logicism 7, 10, 24–25, 144–49, 154–56, 161, 165, 170, 178, 187, 191

MacBride, Fraser 2, 5, 72–74, 131–32
mathematics 7, 10
  logic 10
  pure 10
matrices of substitution 15–16
Moore, G. E. 8–9, 47, 58, 128, 180
Morrell, Ottoline 27, 29–32, 39, 72–81, 114, 117, 132
MRTJ. *See* multiple relation theory of judgement (MRTJ)
multiple relation theory 2, 19–26
multiple relation theory of judgement (MRTJ), Wittgenstein's critique of 1–6
  correspondence problem (CP) 4, 51–52, 54–60
  demise of 72–74, 130–33
  direction problems for 33–39
  Hanks critique on 50–51
  Landini critique of 64–69
  Lebens, Samuel
    on demise of MRTJ 72–74
    on stoutian evolution of MRTJ 69–72
  multiple relation theory 2, 19–26
  neo-Hegelian origins of 1–2, 7–9
  Pincock's critique
    on Hanks 54
    of SR 51–54
    on unity of judgement 54
  Russellian propositions 2, 9–19
  standard reading
    Hanks's on 39–42
    Pincock's on 51–54
  Stevens critique
    of EI 42–46
    OI of Wittgenstein's objection 46–48
My Philosophical Development (Russell) 7–10, 12, 16–17

narrow direction (ND) problems 3, 21, 33, 35–39, 53–54
neo-Hegelianism 1–2, 7–9
neutral facts interpretation (NFI) 5, 114, 117–19, 191
N-operator notation 126–28, 144, 166, 172, 174, 176, 180
Notebooks 1914–1916 (Wittgenstein) 119, 136, 164
Notes Dictated to Moore in Norway 123, 137
'Notes on Logic' (Wittgenstein) 36, 50–51, 59, 76–78, 85, 93, 100, 104, 106, 110–11, 114, 117–19, 122–25, 131–32, 136–37, 139–42, 145–46, 150–54, 166, 171–72, 193

OI. *See* ontological interpretation (OI)
'On Denoting' (Russell) 65, 105, 161–62, 177–78
'On the Nature of Truth and Falsehood' (Russell) 14, 15, 19
ontological interpretation (OI) 4
   Stevens on 85–90
   of Wittgenstein's objection 46–48
orders, hierarchy of 17–18, 43
Our Knowledge of the External World (Russell) 28, 114

'p_0/a_0' paradox, propositions 15
paradoxes 5, 15–17, 43, 88, 141–44
paralysis, Russell's 75–133
   diagram of understanding 109–14
   Hanks
      on judging relation 91–93
      on Wittgenstein's critique of MRTJ 91–93
   Landini on Wittgenstein's critique of MRTJ 123–28
   logical interpretation 75–82
   MRTJ, demise of 130–33
   Pincock
      on correspondence problem 102–9
      on proposition problem 93–102
   Props 114–19
   representation concern 128–30
   standard reading 82–85
   Stevens on EI and OI 85–90

Theory of Knowledge 130–33
type* distinctions 119–23
PART 57–60, 104, 106–7, 109
Peano postulates 16–17
philosophical grammar 10–11
Philosophical Investigations (Wittgenstein) 183, 187–90, 194
philosophy 76
'The Philosophy of Logical Atomism' (Russell) 92, 96, 98–100, 104–8, 131–32, 192–93
picture theory of propositions 5, 135–41
Pincock, Christopher 2, 4
   correspondence interpretation 4, 52, 55–59, 66, 94, 96, 100–106, 109
   on correspondence problem 102–9
   on Hanks 54
   on proposition problem 93–102
   on standard reading 51–54
   on unity of judgement 54
pluralism 8
Potter, Michael 2
*Principia Mathematica to *56* (Russell and Whitehead) 1, 7, 17, 27, 40–45, 67, 83–84, 86–87, 89, 91–92, 94, 105–6, 119, 127, 139, 147–49, 151–52, 186, 193
Principles of Mathematics (Russel) 7, 9–13, 16–19, 21, 25, 27, 34, 47, 51, 58, 61, 81, 83, 101–2, 127, 148
problem of false propositions 13–14
Problems of Philosophy (Russell) 3, 13–14, 19–20, 22–24, 42, 69, 71, 76–77, 85, 127, 131, 147
propositions, Russellian 2, 9–19, 22, 58
   abandon 13–19
   elementary 139–44, 147–83
   false 13–14
   logical 155
   paradoxes of 15–17
   philosophical grammar 10–11
   picture theory of 5, 135–41
   Pincock on 93–102
   problem 93
   as pure mathematics 10
   real 155
   relating relation 12
   things *vs.* concepts 11

propositions, Russellian (*cont.*)
    type-theory 52, 141–44
    unity of 25, 52
    verbs 11, 137
    vicious circle fallacies 17–18, 44
Props, Russell's 114–19
Prototractatus (Wittgenstein) 169
pure mathematics 10

real propositions 155
relating relation 12
relation 11
'The Relation of Sense Data to Physics' (Russell) 28
relativity, contradiction of 3, 8–9, 139
Russell, Bertrand
    Autobiography 4, 7, 29, 32, 76, 124
    contradiction of relativity 3, 8–9, 139
    corresponding complexes 20–21
    diagram of understanding 109–14
    An Essay on the Foundations of Geometry 7
    My Philosophical Development 7–10, 12, 16–17
    'On Denoting' 65, 105, 161–62, 177–78
    'On the Nature of Truth and Falsehood' 14, 15
    Our Knowledge of the External World 28, 114
    paradoxes 5, 15–17, 43, 88, 141–44
    paralysis 75–133
    'The Philosophy of Logical Atomism' 92, 96, 98–100, 104–8, 131–32, 192–93
    *Principia Mathematica to *56* 1, 7, 17, 27, 40–45, 67, 83–84, 86–87, 89, 91–92, 94, 105–6, 119, 127, 139, 147–49, 151–52, 186, 193
    Principles of Mathematics 7, 9–13, 16–19, 21, 25, 27, 34, 47, 51, 58, 61, 81, 83, 101–2, 127, 148
    Problems of Philosophy 3, 13–14, 19–20, 22–24, 42, 69, 71, 76–77, 85, 127, 131, 147
    propositions 2, 9–19, 22, 58
    Props 114–19
    'The Relation of Sense Data to Physics' 28

Theory of Knowledge: The 1913 Manuscript 1, 3–6, 13–15, 20, 24, 27–43, 51–52, 54–56, 60–62, 64, 66, 68–69, 72–74, 79–86, 92, 94–97, 99–104, 107–14, 119–22, 127–33
    type* distinctions 119–23

Sachverhalten 138
scholarly controversy 33–74
    correspondence problem 54–60
    direction problems 33–39
    Hanks's critique
        of SR 48–50
        on Wittgenstein defeated MRTJ 50–51
    Landini, Gregory
        on type* distinctions 60–62
        on Wittgenstein's critique of MRTJ 64–69
    Lebens, Samuel
        on demise of MRTJ 72–74
        on representation concern 69–72, 128–30
        on stoutian evolution of MRTJ 69–72
    Pincock's critique
        on Hanks 54
        of SR 51–54
        on unity of judgement 54
    standard reading
        Hanks's on 39–42
        Pincock's on 51–54
    Stevens critique
        EI 42–46
        OI of Wittgenstein's objection 46–48
    type* distinctions
        Giaretta on 62–64
        Landini on 60–2
sense-truth regress 6, 161–65
Sommerville, Steven 2–4, 46–47
SR. *See* standard reading (SR)
standard reading (SR) 39–42
    Hanks's critique of 48–50
    Pincock's on 51–54
    Russell's paralysis 82–85

Stevens, Graham 2–4, 17–18
    EI, critique of 85–90
        direct inspection 42–44
        MRTJ 42–44
        subordinate relation, logical status
            of 45–46
        ontological interpretation of
            Wittgenstein's objection
            46–48, 85–90
Stout, G. F. 69–72, 77, 79, 128–30
subordinate relation 21
substitutional theory of classes/
    relations 15–16

Tatsachen 138
tautologies. *See* truth-functions
T/F 58–60, 104, 106–7, 109
theory of inference 156–61
Theory of Knowledge: The 1913 Manuscript
    (Russell) 1, 3–6, 13–15, 20, 24,
    27–43, 51–52, 54–56, 60–62, 64,
    66, 68–69, 72–74, 79–86, 92,
    94–97, 99–104, 107–14,
    119–22, 127–33
Tractarian system 6
Tractatus Logico-Philosophicus (Wittgenstein)
    5–6, 11–12, 50, 59, 67, 69, 76,
    78, 84–85, 90, 104–5, 125–28,
    135–44, 148–53, 156–59, 161,
    163, 165–69, 171–82, 186, 188,
    190, 192–93
truth-functions 6, 87–88, 143–44,
    148–55, 158–59, 162,
    167–82, 189
type* distinctions 4–5, 60–64, 83, 117,
    119–23, 127, 142, 148–49,
    186, 191
    Giaretta on 62–64
    Landini on 60–62
type-theory 52, 141–44

UI. *See* unity interpretation (UI)
understanding, diagram of 109–14
unity interpretation (UI) 4, 50–51, 54, 91,
    93, 191
unity of judgement, Pincock's
    critique on 54

unity of proposition (UP) 25, 51–52, 54,
    93–94, 100–103, 106, 129–30,
    135–36, 140

verb 11, 137
verbal noun 11
vicious circle fallacies 17–18, 44, 143

Whitehead, Alfred North 1
    *Principia Mathematica to *56* 1, 7, 40
    on type hierarchy 44
wide direction (WD) problems 3, 33,
    35–40, 52–54
Wittgenstein, Ludwig 183–94
    ab-notation 6, 118, 123–26, 124n3,
        128, 149–54, 161–63, 166,
        170–72, 189
    The Big Typescript: TS 213 181
    bipolarity 147–54
    at Cambridge 26–27
    *Cambridge Letters: Correspondence with
        Russell, Keynes, Moore, Ramsey, and
        Sraffa* 30–32, 67–68, 76, 80, 81,
        125–26, 128, 131, 141–42,
        148–49, 151–53, 165–66
    chain analogy 138–39
    extensionalism 147–54
    fundamental thought
        (*Grundgedanke*) 165–70
    general propositional form 170–78
    irrelevancy interpretation of objection
        5, 74, 131–32, 191
    logical forms 24–25, 144–49, 154–56,
        161, 165, 170, 178, 187, 191
    N-operator notation 126–28, 144, 166,
        172, 174, 176, 180
    Notebooks 1914–1916 119, 136, 164
    'Notes on Logic' 36, 50–51, 59, 76–78,
        85, 93, 100, 104, 106, 110–11,
        114, 117–19, 122–25, 131–32,
        136–37, 139–42, 145–46,
        150–54, 166, 171–72, 193
    objection, ontological interpretation
        of 46–48, 85–90
    Philosophical Investigations 183, 187–90, 194
    propositions, picture theory of
        5, 135–41

Wittgenstein, Ludwig (*cont.*)
  Prototractatus 169
  Russell's MRTJ, critique of 1–6
    correspondence problem 4, 51–52, 54–60
    demise of 72–74, 130–33
    direction problems for 33–39
    Hanks critique on 50–51
    Landini critique of 64–69
    Lebens on 69–74
    multiple relation theory 2, 19–26
    neo-Hegelian origins of 1–2, 7–9
    Pincock's critique 51–54
    Russellian propositions 2, 9–19
    standard reading 39–42, 51–54
    Stevens critique 42–48
  saying/showing 154–56
  sense-truth regress 161–65
  theory of inference 156–61
  Tractatus Logico-Philosophicus 5–6, 11–12, 50, 59, 67, 69, 76, 78, 84–85, 90, 104–5, 125–28, 135–44, 148–53, 156–59, 161, 163, 165–69, 171–82, 186, 188, 190, 192–93
  transition 178–83
  and type-theory 52, 141–44
Wrinch, Dorothy 70, 129–31

www.ingramcontent.com/pod-product-compliance
Lightning Source LLC
Chambersburg PA
CBHW021141230426
43667CB00005B/210